D1294114

# The Modern Poets

# The Modern Poets

An American-British Anthology edited by
John Malcolm Brinnin and Bill Read,
both of Boston University,
and with photographs by Rollie McKenna

second edition

**McGraw-Hill Book Company**

New York  St. Louis  San Francisco  Düsseldorf
London  Mexico  Panama  Sydney  Toronto

TEXAS STATE TECHNICAL INSTITUTE
ROLLING PLAINS CAMPUS – LIBRARY
SWEETWATER, TEXAS  79556

This book was set in Melior by John C. Meyer & Son, printed on permanent paper by Halliday Lithograph Corporation, and bound by The Maple Press Company. The designer was Betty Binns. The editors were Robert Fry, Cheryl Kupper, and David Dunham. Stuart Levine supervised the production.

## The Modern Poets

Copyright © 1963, 1970 by McGraw-Hill, Inc. All rights reserved. Printed in the United States of America. No part of this publication may be reproduced, stored in a retrieval system, or transmitted, in any form or by any means, electronic, mechanical, photocopying, recording, or otherwise, without the prior written permission of the publisher.

*Library of Congress Catalog Card Number 79-116659*
**ISBN 07-007908-0-07909-9**

**456789-MAMM-76543**
The photographs reproduced herein are used by permission of the copyright holder, Rollie McKenna.

## ACKNOWLEDGMENTS

**Dannie Abse,** "Letter to Alex Comfort" from *Walking Under Water* by Dannie Abse (1952) by permission of The Hutchinson Publishing Group.

**Conrad Aiken,** "Prelude XIV" and "Prelude LVI" from *Preludes* by Conrad Aiken. Copyright © 1930, 1931, 1959, 1966 by Conrad Aiken. Reprinted by permission of Oxford University Press, Inc.

**A. R. Ammons,** "Visit" and "The Wide Land" are reprinted from *A. R. Ammons: Selected Poems.* Copyright © 1968 by Cornell University. Used by permission of Cornell University Press.

**John Ashbery,** "Civilization and Its Discontents" from *Rivers and Mountains* by John Ashbery. Copyright © 1962, 1963, 1964, 1966 by John Ashbery. Reprinted by permission of Holt, Rinehart and Winston, Inc. "Faust," copyright © 1962 by John Ashbery. Reprinted from *The Tennis Court Oath,* by John Ashbery, by permission of Wesleyan University Press.

**W. H. Auden,** excerpt from "Anthem for St. Cecilia's Day," copyright 1945 by W. H. Auden. "As I Walked Out One Evening" and "Musée des Beaux Arts," copyright 1940 and renewed 1968 by W. H. Auden. Reprinted from *Collected Shorter Poems 1927–1957,* by W. H. Auden, by permission of Random House, Inc. and by permission of Faber and Faber Ltd. from *Collected Shorter Poems 1925–1957.*

**George Barker,** "To My Mother" and Part I from "To My Son" by George Barker from *Collected Poems 1930 to 1965,* copyright © 1957, 1962, and 1965 by George Granville Barker. Reprinted by permission of October House Inc. and by permission of Faber and Faber Ltd. from *Collected Poems 1930–1955.*

**Michael Benedikt,** "The European Shoe" and "Some Litanies," copyright © 1967 by Michael Benedikt, by permission of Wesleyan University Press. "Some Litanies" first appeared in *Poetry.*

**John Berryman,** "Winter Landscape" from *The Dispossessed* (1948), John Berryman, published by William Sloane Associates, Inc., copyright by the author. Permission of the author. "Dream Song 14," "Dream Song 62," "Dream Song 76: Henry's Confession," "Dream Song 77" is reprinted with the permission of Farrar, Straus & Giroux, Inc. from *77 Dream Songs* by John Berryman, copyright © 1959, 1962, 1963, 1964 by John Berryman.

**John Betjeman,** "A Subaltern's Love-Song" and "Youth and Age on Beaulieu River, Hants" from *Collected Poems,* John Betjeman, published by Houghton Mifflin Company. Permission of John Murrary (Publishers) Ltd.

**Elizabeth Bishop,** "Letter to New York," "A Cold Spring," "Florida," "The Prodigal" are reprinted with the permission of Farrar, Straus & Giroux, Inc. from *Complete Poems* by Elizabeth Bishop, copyright 1940, 1946, 1947, 1948, 1949, 1951, 1952, 1955 by Elizabeth Bishop.

**Louise Bogan,** "Women" and "Evening in the Sanitarium" are reprinted with the permission of Farrar, Straus & Giroux, Inc. from *Collected Poems* by Louise Bogan, copyright 1954 by Louise Bogan.

**Philip Booth,** "Ego," copyright 1956 by Philip Booth and "First Lesson," copyright © 1957 by Philip Booth from *Letter from a Distant Land* by Philip Booth. "Ego" originally appeared in *The New Yorker.* Reprinted by permission of The Viking Press, Inc.

**John Malcolm Brinnin,** "Hotel Paradiso E Commerciale" and "Nuns at Eve" from *Selected Poems.* Reprinted by permission of the author.

**John Ciardi,** "Elegy Just in Case," © 1945, 1947. John Ciardi. From *Other Skies,* Atlantic Monthly Press-Little Brown. Reprinted by permission of the author.

**Lucille Clifton,** "Miss Rosie," "For de Lawd," and "Good Times," copyright © 1969 by Lucille Clifton. Reprinted from *Good Times,* by Lucille Clifton, by permission of Random House, Inc.

**Tram Combs,** "Ars Poetica About Ultimates," "Aware Aware," and "Just After Noon with Fierce Shears," copyright © 1957 by Tram Combs. Reprinted from *saint thomas poems,* by Tram Combs, by permission of Wesleyan University Press.

**E. E. Cummings,** "nobody loses all the time," copyright, 1940, by E. E. Cummings. "anyone lived in a pretty how town," copyright, 1940, by E. E. Cummings. "somewhere I have never travelled, gladly beyond," copyright, 1931, 1959, by E. E. Cummings. "when serpents bargain for the right to squirm," copyright, 1950, by E. E. Cummings. Reprinted from his volume *Poems 1923–1954* by permission of Harcourt, Brace & World, Inc.

**Peter Davison,** "Lunch at the Coq D'or" from *The City and the Island,* by Peter Davison. Copyright © 1966 by Peter Davison. Reprinted by permission of Atheneum Publishers. This poem originally appeared in *The Reporter.* "The Star Watcher" from *The Breaking of the Day* by Peter Davison. Copyright © 1958, 1959, 1960, 1961, 1963, 1964 by Peter Davison.

**James Dickey,** "For the Nightly Ascent of the Hunter Orion over a Forest Clearing" and "Cherrylog Road," copyright © 1961, 1963 by James Dickey. Reprinted from *Poems 1957–1967,* by James Dickey, by permission of Wesleyan University Press. Originally published in *The New Yorker.*

**Alan Dugan,** "Memorial Service for the Invasion Beach Where the Vacation in the Flesh is Over" and "The

Mirror Perilous" from *Poems* (1961) Alan Dugan, published by Yale University Press, copyright by the author. Permission of the author.

**Richard Eberhart**, "New Hampshire, February" and "The Fury of Aerial Bombardment" from *Collected Poems 1930–1960* by Richard Eberhart. © Richard Eberhart 1960. Reprinted by permission of Oxford University Press, Inc.; and from *Selected Poems*, Richard Eberhart, permission of Chatto & Windus Ltd.

**T. S. Eliot**, "Preludes," "The Love Song of J. Alfred Prufrock," "Portrait of a Lady," and "Journey of the Magi" from *Collected Poems 1909–1962* by T. S. Eliot. Copyright, 1936, by Harcourt, Brace & World, Inc.; copyright, ©, 1963, 1964 by T. S. Eliot. Reprinted by permission of the publisher.; reprinted by permission of Faber and Faber Ltd. from *Collected Poems 1909–1962*.

**D. J. Enright**, "The Laughing Hyena, by Hokusai" and "University Examinations in Egypt" from *The Laughing Hyena*. D. J. Enright. Permission of Routledge & Kegan Paul, Ltd.

**Irving Feldman**, "The Death of Vitellozzo Vitelli" and "The Old Men" from *Works and Days*. Irving Feldman, copyright 1954, © 1957, 1960 by Irving Feldman. Permission of the author.

**Robert Fitzgerald**, "The Imprisoned," "Cobb Would Have Caught It," and "Souls Lake" from *In the Rose of Time*. Copyright 1943 by Robert Fitzgerald. Reprinted by permission of New Directions Publishing Corporation.

**Arthur Freeman**, "The Cell of Himself," copyright by Arthur Freeman. Reprinted from his volume *Estrangements* by permission of Harcourt, Brace & World, Inc.

**Robert Frost**, "Acquainted with the Night," "Stopping by Woods on a Snowy Evening," "The Road Not Taken," "The Runaway," "Provide, Provide," and "The Silken Tent" from *Complete Poems of Robert Frost*. Copyright 1916, 1923, 1928 by Holt, Rinehart and Winston, Inc. Copyright 1936, 1942, 1944, 1951, © 1956 by Robert Frost. Copyright © 1964, 1970 by Lesley Frost Ballantine. Reprinted by permission of Holt, Rinehart and Winston, Inc.

**Jean Garrigue**, "The Mouse" and "The Stranger" are reprinted with the permission of The Macmillan Company from *New and Selected Poems* by Jean Garrigue. Copyright © 1947, 1967 by Jean Garrigue.

**David Gascoyne**, "An Elegy" from *Poems 1937–1942*, David Gascoyne, published by Editions Poetry London. Permission of David Higham Associates, Ltd.

**Allen Ginsberg**, "A Supermarket in California from *Howl and Other Poems* by Allen Ginsberg. Copyright © 1956, 1959 by Allen Ginsberg. "Uptown" from *Planet News* by Allen Ginsberg. Copyright © 1968 by Allen Ginsberg. Reprinted by permission of City Lights Books.

**Robert Graves**, "Flying Crooked," "To Juan at the Winter Solstice," and "In Procession" from *Collected Poems* by Robert Graves. Reprinted by permission of Collins-Knowlton-Wing Inc. and A. P. Watt & Son.

**Thom Gunn**, "Considering the Snail" and "From the Highest Camp" are reprinted from *My Sad Captain* by permission of The University of Chicago Press and Faber and Faber Ltd. © 1961 by Thom Gunn. "On the Move" and "Black Jackets" are reprinted by permission of Faber and Faber Ltd. from *The Sense of Movement*.

**Donald Hall**, "The Sleeping Giant" from *The Alligator Bride Poems New and Selected* by Donald Hall. Copyright © 1955 by Donald Hall. Originally appeared in *The New Yorker* and reprinted by permission of Harper & Row, Publishers. "The Body Politic" is reprinted by permission of the author.

**Robert Hayden**, "Summertime and the Living . . ." by Robert Hayden from *Selected Poems*. Copyright © 1966 by Robert Hayden. © Reprinted by permission of October House Inc.

**Seamus Heaney**, "Digging" and "Twice Shy" from *Death of a Naturalist* by Seamus Heaney. © 1966 by Seamus Heaney. Reprinted by permission of Oxford University Press, Inc.; reprinted by permission of Faber and Faber Ltd. from *Death of a Naturalist*.

**John Heath-Stubbs**, "A Charm Against the Toothache" from *Selected Poems* by John Heath-Stubbs, published by Oxford University Press. "The Lady's Complaint" from *Triumph of the Muse*, published by Oxford University Press. Reprinted by permission of David Higham Associates, Ltd.

**Anthony Hecht**, "Samuel Sewell" is reprinted by permission of the author. "More Light, More Light!" and "Lizards and Snakes" from *The Hard Hours* by Anthony Hecht. Copyright © 1959, 1967 by Anthony E. Hecht. Reprinted by permission of Atheneum Publishers. "More Light, More Light!" appeared originally in the *Hudson Review*.

**Daryl Hine**, "The Survivors" and "Untitled" from *Minutes*, by Daryl Hine. Copyright © 1968 by Daryl Hine. Reprinted by permission of Atheneum Publishers.

**Daniel Hoffman**, "The Seals in Penobscot Bay" from *An Armada of Thirty Whales*, Daniel Hoffman. By permission of the author.

**John Hollander**, "The Lady's Maid Song" and "The Great Bear" from *A Crackling of Thorns* Copyright © 1958 by Yale University Press. Reprinted by permission of Yale University Press.

**Richard Howard**, "Crepuscular," copyright © 1967 by Richard Howard. Reprinted from *The Damages*, by Richard Howard, by permission of Wesleyan University Press. This poem was first published in *Poetry*.

**Barbara Howes**, "Chimera" and "Home Leave," copyright © 1958, 1959 by Barbara Howes. Reprinted from *Light and Dark* by Barbara Howes, by permission of Wesleyan University Press.

**Ted Hughes**, "Hawk Roosting," copyright © 1959 by Ted Hughes and "View of a Pig," copyright © 1960 by Ted Hughes from *Lupercal* by Ted Hughes. By permission of Harper & Row, Publishers; reprinted by permission of Faber and Faber Ltd. from *Lupercal*.

**David Ignatow**, "News Report," copyright 1955 by David Ignatow. "Simultaneously," copyright 1962 by David Ignatow. Reprinted from *Figures of the Human*. "The Bagel," copyright © 1966 by David Ignatow. Reprinted from *Rescue the Dead*, by David Ignatow, by permission of Wesleyan University Press.

**Randall Jarrell**, "Nestus Gurley" and "The Woman at the Washington Zoo" from *The Woman at the Washington Zoo* by Randall Jarrell. Copyright © 1956 by The Virginia Quarterly Review. Copyright © 1960 by Randall Jarrell. Reprinted by permission of Atheneum Publishers. "The Snow Leopard" from *Little Friend, Little Friend* (1945), Randall Jarrell, published by The Dial Press, Inc., copyright by the author. By permission of the author.

740150

**Donald Justice,** "Memo from the Desk of X," copyright 1967 by Donald Justice. "The Tourist from Syracuse," copyright 1965 by Donald Justice. Reprinted from *Night Light*, by Donald Justice, by permission of Wesleyan University Press.

**Bob Kaufman,** "Afterwards, They Shall Dance" and "To My Son Parker, Asleep in the Next Room" from Bob Kaufman, *Solitudes Crowded with Loneliness*. Copyright © 1959, 1965 by Bob Kaufman. Reprinted by permission of New Directions Publishing Corporation.

**X. J. Kennedy,** "Artificer," copyright 1962 by the Yeoman Committee for an Oberlin Quarterly; "Driving Cross-country," copyright © 1969 by X. J. Kennedy from *Growing Into Love*, by X. J. Kennedy. Reprinted by permission of Doubleday & Company, Inc.

**Galway Kinnell,** "First Song," "Duck-Chasing," and "To Christ Our Lord" from *What a Kingdom It Was*. Copyright © 1960 by Galway Kinnell. Reprinted by permission of the publisher, Houghton Mifflin Company.

**Thomas Kinsella,** "The Secret Garden," copyright © 1968 by Thomas Kinsella. "Folk Wisdom," copyright © 1967 by Thomas Kinsella. Reprinted from *Nightwalker and Other Poems*, by Thomas Kinsella, by permission of Alfred A. Knopf, Inc.

**Stanley Kunitz,** "The Science of the Night," copyright 1953 by Stanley Kunitz. "Father and Son," copyright 1958 by Stanley Kunitz. From *Selected Poems 1928–1958* by Stanley Kunitz; by permission of Atlantic-Little, Brown and Co.

**Philip Larkin,** "Poetry of Departures" and "Church Going" are reprinted from *The Less Deceived,* © copyright The Marvell Press, 1955, 1970 by permission of The Marvell Press, Hessle, Yorkshire.

**Denise Levertov,** "Bedtime" and "Psalm Concerning the Castle" from Denise Levertov, *The Sorrow Dance*. Copyright © 1966 by Denise Levertov Goodman. Reprinted by permission of New Directions Publishing Corporation.

**Cecil Day Lewis,** "Departure in the Dark," "Reconciliation," and "The Dead" from *Short Is the Time: Poems 1936–1943* by C. Day Lewis. Copyright by C. Day Lewis. Reprinted by permission of the Harold Matson Company, Inc.; from *Collected Poems 1954*, C. Day Lewis, by permission of Jonathan Cape Ltd.

**Robert Lowell,** "Death from Cancer" and "Mr. Edwards and the Spider" from *Lord Weary's Castle*, copyright, 1944, 1946, by Robert Lowell. Reprinted by permission of Harcourt, Brace & World, Inc. "Ford Madox Ford" is reprinted with permission of Farrar, Straus & Giroux, Inc. from *Life Studies* by Robert Lowell, copyright © 1955 by Robert Lowell. "For the Union Dead" is reprinted with permission of Farrar, Straus & Giroux, Inc. from *For the Union Dead* by Robert Lowell, copyright © 1960 by Robert Lowell.

**Edward Lucie-Smith,** "The Lesson" and "Poet in Winter" from *A Tropical Childhood*, by Edward Lucie-Smith, published by the Oxford University Press.

**Archibald MacLeish,** "You, Andrew Marvell" and "Not Marble Nor the Gilded Monuments" from *Collected Poems 1917–1952*. Copyright 1952 by Archibald MacLeish. Reprinted by permission of the publisher, Houghton Mifflin Company.

**Louis MacNeice,** "The Sunlight on the Garden," "Morning Sun," and "Prayer Before Birth" from *Eighty-five Poems* by Louis MacNeice. © Louis MacNeice 1959. Reprinted by permission of Oxford University Press; reprinted by permission of Faber and Faber Ltd. from *Collected Poems of Louis MacNeice*.

**James Merrill,** "Kite Poem," from *First Poems* by James Merrill, copyright 1950 by James Merrill; "Laboratory Poem," copyright © 1958 by James Merrill. "Voices from the Other World," copyright © 1957, 1958 by James Merrill, from *The Country of a Thousand Years of Peace* by James Merrill. By permission of the author.

**W. S. Merwin,** "Thorn Leaves in March," from *Green With Beasts*, by W. S. Merwin. Published 1956 by Alfred A. Knopf Inc. Reprinted by permission. Also reprinted by permission of David Higham Associates, Ltd. "The Drunk in the Furnace" from *The Drunk in the Furnace*, by W. S. Merwin. Reprinted by permission of Harold Ober Associates Incorporated. Copyright © 1958 by W. S. Merwin. Also reprinted by permission of David Higham Associates, Ltd.

**Christopher Middleton,** "In Some Seer's Cloud Car," reprinted from *Nonsequences: Selfpoems* by Christopher Middleton. By permission of W. W. Norton & Company, Inc. Copyright © 1961, 1962, 1963, 1964, 1965 by Christopher Middleton and by permission of Longman Group Limited, publishers. "Edward Lear in February" from *Torse 3*, copyright, 1962, by Christopher Middleton. Reprinted by permission of Harcourt, Brace & World, Inc. and by permission of Longman Group Limited, publishers.

**Marianne Moore,** "A Carriage from Sweden" is reprinted with permission of The Macmillan Company from *Collected Poems* by Marianne Moore. Copyright 1944 by Marianne Moore. "The Student" and "Four Quartz Crystal Clocks" are also reprinted with permission of The Macmillan Company from *Collected Poems* by Marianne Moore. Copyright 1941 by Marianne Moore, renewed 1969 by Marianne Moore.

**Howard Moss,** "The Gift to Be Simple" (Copyright 1955 Howard Moss) and "Underwood" (Copyright 1954 Howard Moss) first appeared in *The New Yorker* and are reprinted with the permission of the author from *A Swimmer in the Air* by Howard Moss. "Great Spaces" from *Second Nature* by Howard Moss. Copyright © 1968 by Howard Moss. Reprinted by permission of Atheneum Publishers. This poem appeared originally in *Poetry*.

**Howard Nemorov,** "Learning by Doing" from *The Blue Swallows* by Howard Nemerov. Copyright by Howard Nemerov, 1967. "Mousemeal" from *New and Selected Poems*, copyright by the University of Chicago Press, 1960. Reprinted by permission of the Margot Johnson Agency.

**Marge Piercy,** "The Peaceable Kingdom," copyright © 1968 by Marge Piercy. Reprinted from *Breaking Camp*, by Marge Piercy, by permission of Wesleyan University Press.

**Sylvia Plath,** "The Applicant," copyright © 1963 by Ted Hughes and "Daddy," copyright © 1963 by Ted Hughes from *Ariel* by Sylvia Plath. By permission of Harper & Row, Publishers, and Miss Olwyn Hughes.

**Ezra Pound,** "Further Instructions," "Commission," "The Garden," "Portrait d'une Femme," "The River Merchant's Wife: A Letter" from Ezra Pound, *Personae*. Copyright 1926 by Ezra Pound. Reprinted by permission of New Directions Publishing Corporation.

**John Crowe Ransom,** "Survey of Literature" and "Dead

...

Boy," copyright 1927 by Alfred A. Knopf, Inc. and renewed 1955 by John Crowe Ransom. "Captain Carpenter," copyright 1924 by Alfred A. Knopf, Inc. and renewed 1952 by John Crowe Ransom. Reprinted from *Selected Poems*, 3rd Revised Edition by John Crowe Ransom, by permission of the publisher.

**Alastair Reid,** "Pigeons," from *Oddments Inklings Omens Moments* by Alastair Reid. Copyright 1959 by Alastair Reid, by permission of Little, Brown and Co.

**Theodore Roethke,** "I Knew a Woman," copyright 1954 by Theodore Roethke; "Prayer," copyright 1935 by Theodore Roethke; "A Field of Light," copyright 1948 by Tiger's Eye; "Elegy for Jane," copyright 1950 by Theodore Roethke; and "The Waking," copyright 1953 by Theodore Roethke. From *The Collected Poems of Theodore Roethke*. Reprinted by permission of Doubleday & Company.

**Muriel Rukeyser,** "Boy with His Hair Cut Short," copyright; 1938 by Muriel Rukeyser. "Effort at Speech between Two People," copyright; 1935 by Yale University Press, copyright 1960 by Muriel Rukeyser. Permission of Monica McCall, Inc.

**Delmore Schwartz,** "The Ballet of the Fifth Year" *and* "The Heavy Bear Who Goes with Me" from Delmore Schwartz. *Selected Poems: Summer Knowledge.* Copyright 1938 by New Directions. Reprinted by permission of New Directions Publishing Corporation. "Baudelaire," copyright 1954 by Delmore Schwartz from *Summer Knowledge* by Delmore Schwartz. Reprinted by permission of Doubleday & Company, Inc.

**James Scully,** "Midsummer" and "The Glass Blower" from *The Marches* by James Scully. Copyright © 1962 by James Scully. Reprinted by permission of Holt, Rinehart and Winston, Inc.

**Anne Sexton,** "Letter Written on a Ferry Crossing Long Island Sound" and "Her Kind" from *All My Pretty Ones*. Copyright © 1961, 1962 by Anne Sexton. Reprinted by permission of the publisher, Houghton Mifflin Company.

**Karl Shapiro,** "Nostalgia" and "Haircut," copyright 1942 by Karl Jay Shapiro. "Drug Store," copyright 1941 and renewed 1969 by Karl Shapiro. Reprinted from *Selected Poems*, by Karl Shapiro, by permission of Random House, Inc.

**Jon Silkin,** "Death of a Son," copyright © 1954 by John Silkin. Reprinted from *Poems New and Selected*, by John Silkin, by permission of Wesleyan University Press and Chatto and Windus Ltd.

**Louis Simpson,** "Hot Night on Water Street," copyright © 1957 by Louis Simpson. Reprinted from *A Dream of Governors*, by Louis Simpson. "My Father in the Night Commanding No," copyright © 1963 by Louis Simpson. Reprinted from *At the End of the Open Road*, by Louis Simpson. This poem was first published in *The New Yorker*. By permission of Wesleyan University Press.

**L. E. Sissman,** "A Disappearance in West Cedar Street," copyright 1967 by L. E. Sissman and "In and Out: Severance of Connections," copyright 1967 by L. E. Sissman. From *Dying* by L. E. Sissman, by permission of Little, Brown and Co.

**Edith Sitwell,** "Heart and Mind," "Still Falls the Rain," and "Scotch Rhapsody" from *Collected Poems of Edith Sitwell*, copyright © 1949, 1953, 1954 by the author. Permission of Vanguard Press, Inc. and David Higham Associates, Ltd.

**William Jay Smith,** "American Primitive," "Independence Day," and "The Closing of the Rodeo" are reprinted from *New and Selected Poems* by William Jay Smith. Copyright © 1944, 1946, 1947, 1948, 1949, 1950, 1951, 1952, 1953, 1954, 1956, 1957, 1959, 1961, 1962, 1963, 1964, 1965, 1966, 1967, 1970 by William Jay Smith. A Seymour Lawrence Book/Delacorte Press. Used by permission.

**W. D. Snodgrass,** "The Campus on the Hill," copyright © 1958 by W. D. Snodgrass. "April Inventory," copyright © 1957 by W. D. Snodgrass. Reprinted from *Heart's Needle* by W. D. Snodgrass, by permission of Alfred A. Knopf, Inc.

**Stephen Spender,** "The Express," copyright 1934 and renewed 1962 by Stephen Spender. "An Elementary School Classroom" and "Port Bou," copyright 1942 by Stephen Spender. Reprinted from *Collected Poems 1928–1953*, by Stephen Spender, by permission of Random House, Inc. and by permission of Faber and Faber Ltd. from *Collected Poems*.

**George Starbuck,** "Bone Thoughts on a Dry Day" from *Bone Thoughts*. George Starbuck. Permission of the author. "New Strain" from *Bone Thoughts*, copyright © 1960 by George Starbuck. Permission of Yale University Press.

**Wallace Stevens,** "The Poems of Our Climate," "The Sense of the Sleight-of-Hand Man," and "Mrs. Alfred Uruguay," copyright 1942 by Wallace Stevens. "Peter Quince at the Clavier," copyright 1923 and renewed 1951 by Wallace Stevens. Reprinted from *The Collected Poems of Wallace Stevens*, by permission of Alfred A. Knopf, Inc.

**Mark Strand,** "The Tunnel" and "The Last Bus" from *Reasons for Moving* by Mark Strand. Copyright © 1964, 1967 by Mark Strand. Reprinted by permission of Atheneum Publishers. "The Tunnel" appeared originally in the *Partisan Review*; "The Last Bus" in *The New Yorker*.

**May Swenson,** "The Centaur" (Copyright © 1956 May Swenson) is reprinted with permission of Charles Scribner's Sons from *To Mix with Time* by May Swenson.

**Allan Tate,** "Mr. Pope" and "Death of Little Boys" are reprinted with the permission of Charles Scribner's Sons from *Poems* by Allan Tate.

**James Tate,** "The Lost Pilot" from *The Lost Pilot* by James Tate. Copyright © 1967 by Yale University. Reprinted by permission of the publisher, Yale University Press.

**Dylan Thomas,** "The Hunchback in the Park," "A Refusal to Mourn the Death, by Fire, of a Child in London," "Do Not Go Gentle into That Good Night," and "Fern Hill" from Dylan Thomas, *Collected Poems*. Copyright 1939, 1946 by New Directions Publishing Corporation. Copyright 1952 by Dylan Thomas. Reprinted by permission of New Directions Publishing Corporation; from *Collected Poems* by permission of the Trustees of the Dylan Thomas Estate and J. M. Dent & Sons, Ltd., London.

**Charles Tomlinson,** "Las Trampas U. S. A." and "At Barstow" from *American Scenes and Other Poems*, by Charles Tomlinson, published by Oxford University Press.

**Derek Walcott,** "Ruins of a Great House" is reprinted with the permission of Farrar, Straus & Giroux from *Selected Poems* by Derek Walcott, copyright © 1962 by Derek Walcott; from *In a Green Night* by Derek Walcott. Reprinted by permission of Jonathan Cape Ltd.

**Robert Penn Warren,** "Bearded Oaks" and "Pursuit," copyright 1942 by Robert Penn Warren. Reprinted from *Selected Poems: New and Old, 1923–1966*, by Robert Penn Warren, by permission of Random House, Inc.

**Vernon Watkins,** "The Heron" and "The Lady with the Unicorn" from Vernon Watkins, *Selected Poems*. Copyright © Faber and Faber, 1967. All Rights Reserved. Reprinted by permission of New Directions Publishing Corporation; reprinted by permission of Faber and Faber Ltd. from *The Lady with the Unicorn* and *The Death Bell*.

**Theodore Weiss,** "The Last Day and the First" is reprinted with permission of The Macmillan Company from *The Last Day and the First* by Theodore Weiss. Copyright © by Theodore Weiss, 1968.

**David Wevill,** "The Birth of a Shark" from the book *Birth of a Shark* by David Wevill, by permission of The Macmillan Co. Ltd., London, The Macmillan Company of Canada Limited, and St. Martin's Press, Inc.

**Richard Wilbur,** "Digging for China," "Beasts," and "A Baroque Wall-Fountain in the Villa Sciarra" from *Things of This World*, copyright 1956 by Richard Wilbur. "Advice to a Prophet," copyright, 1959, by Robert Lowell. Reprinted from his volume *Advice to a Prophet and Other Poems*. First published in *The New Yorker*. Reprinted by permission of Harcourt, Brace & World, Inc.

**William Carlos Williams,** "Pastoral," "The Lonely Street," "Tract," and "The Bull" from William Carlos Williams, *Collected Earlier Poems*. Copyright 1938 by William Carlos Williams. Reprinted by permission of New Directions Publishing Corporation.

**James Wright,** "A Blessing," copyright © 1961 by James Wright. Reprinted from *The Branch Will Not Break*, by James Wright. This poem was first published in *Poetry*. "Inscription for the Tank," copyright © 1966 by James Wright. Reprinted from *Shall We Gather at the River*. By permission of Wesleyan University Press.

# Preface

**This** collection is weighted on the side of pleasure—the pleasure of first encounter, the pleasure of old acquaintance, the pleasure of poems that speak with the particularly human resonance of a voice enchanted.

Most poets of consequence at times produce work that is dense, tough, and technically adventurous. They also write poems that are at once clear, pithy, and engaging, and which seem to be technically artless. In making selections for this anthology, we have invariably turned to the latter. We wanted to be sure that the poems we chose would be read and enjoyed—that they would overtake their readers, so to speak—before it would occur to anyone that they might also be studied, dismantled, and reassembled.

In the matter of representation we are confident that we have made worthy choices from seven or eight generations of poets who have written vastly different kinds of poetry. Yet, when the name of any one of a hundred unincluded poets is mentioned, we are vulnerable. Twentieth-century poetry in English is so rich and diverse that, instead of a mere ninety-nine poets, we could have included—given the space, the time, the money—one hundred and ninety-nine poets and still have come up with an anthology in which tastes and judgments more or less like ours would be wholly satisfied.

In the matter of youth versus age, or vice versa, we have been oblivious to anything but the sound and shape of a poem, the authority of the created thing. We have tried to forget that fashion and hierarchy exist. In the matter of ratings—as if a poet's quotations earned him a place on a board of stock quotations—we deplore the flashy and calculated boosts of publicity that shift attention from the poem to the poet, just as we deplore the desertion of standards by once independent and sober-minded readers who now seem to spend their lives giddily trying to determine where the action is. And as we witness the shameful, sudden downgrading of great, hard-bought poetic reputations by literary historians on-the-make and weathercock critics ruffled by every new wind, we begin to see a virtue in antidisestablishmentarianism.

Poets whose faces are familiar and whose stanzas are famous appear here alongside poets who have just begun to command attention. In younger poets we have looked for inklings of wit, objectivity, and the rhythms that give formality to feeling. In other words, we have looked for indications that they practice poetry as an art whose demands they would honor and not as a convenient means to self-exploitation or group therapy. The poems included in this anthology are made objects, not effusions but fusions — joinings of passion and skill. These poems incorporate their own music and suggest their own point and counterpoint. Poems as ephemera to be sung by the laureates of the electric guitar have their place, but that place is not in this anthology. Paul Simon of Simon & Garfunkel makes the distinction for us: "The lyrics of pop songs are so banal that if you show a spark of intelligence they call you a poet. And if you say you're not a poet then people think you're putting yourself down. But the people who call you a poet are people who never read poetry. Like poetry was something defined by Bob Dylan. They never read, say, Wallace Stevens. That's poetry."

Instead of the customary notes we have supplied informal commentaries and brief biographies. The photographic portraits by Rollie McKenna should have documentary interest in themselves. Determined to avoid the sort of well-meaning apparatus which is designed to initiate and instruct but which, too often, only alienates and befuddles, we have otherwise allowed the poems to speak for themselves. Where we have provided commentary, our aim has been merely to set a perspective, identify an allusion, turn a key that may help to make a first reading a comparatively full and easy one. Commentary cannot account for the ultimate values of any poem. By supplying points of information and by suggesting interpretations, we can perhaps provide the basis on which these values may be discovered.

John Malcolm Brinnin
Bill Read

# Contents

# The Modern Poets

# Dannie Abse

*Dannie Abse, born September, 1923, in Wales, lives in*
*Golders Green, London, with his wife and two children.*
*His early life as a member of a socially conscious Jewish*
*family in Wales is recorded in his autobiographical novel*
*Ash on a Young Man's Sleeve. Like his father, he is a*
*physician and during World War II served with the*
*Medical Corps of the Royal Air Force. He was one of*
*the founders of a mid-fifties movement in poetry whose*
*members were known as "mavericks" and whom critics*
*tended to categorize as "neo-Georgian."*

## Letter to Alex Comfort

Alex, perhaps a colour of which neither of us had dreamt
may appear in the test-tube with God knows what admonition.
Ehrlich certainly was one who broke down the mental doors,
yet only after his six hundred and sixth attempt.

Koch also, painfully and with true German thoroughness
eliminated the impossible, and proved that too many of us
are dying from the same disease. Yet was his green dream,
like yours, fired to burn away an ancient distress.

Still I, myself, don't like Germans, but prefer the unkempt
voyagers, who, like butterflies drunk with suns,

**Dannie Abse   1**

can only totter crookedly in the dazed air
to reach charmingly their destination, as if by accident.

That Greek one then is my hero, who watched the bath water
rise above his navel and rushed out naked, 'I found it,
I found it' into the street in all his shining, and forgot
that others would only stare at his genitals. What laughter!

Or Newton, leaning in Woolsthorpe against the garden wall
forgot his indigestion and all such trivialities,
but gaped up at heaven in just surprise, and with
true gravity, witnessed the vertical apple fall.

O what a marvellous observation! Who would have reckoned
that such a pedestrian miracle could alter history,
that henceforward everyone must fall, whatever
their rank, at thirty-two feet per second, per second?

You too, I know, have waited for doors to fly open and played
with your cold chemicals and written long letters
to the Press; listened to the truth afraid and dug deep
into the wriggling earth for a rainbow, with an honest spade.

But nothing rises. Neither spectres, nor oil, nor love.
And the old professor must think you mad, Alex, as you rehearse
poems in the laboratory like vows, and curse those clever scientists
who dissect away the wings and the haggard heart from the dove.

---

**Letter to Alex Comfort:** *The person to whom this poem is
addressed is, like the author, both a physician and a poet.
Ehrlich was the German scientist who discovered salvarsan
after 606 experiments; Koch was another German, who
devised a method of staining bacteria with aniline dyes,
leading to his discovery of the bacterial causes of many
infectious diseases; "that Greek" is Archimedes, whose cry,
translated back to its original, was "Eureka!"*

**Dannie Abse** 2

# Conrad Aiken

*Conrad Aiken, born August 5, 1889, in Savannah, Georgia,
has recently returned with his wife to live in his native
city after having for many years lived variously in the
village of Brewster on Cape Cod, an apartment in New
York City, and several houses in Rye, on the Sussex
coast of England. He went to Harvard as a member of
the famous class of 1911, which included T. S. Eliot,
Heywood Broun, Robert Benchley, and Walter Lippmann,
and has subsequently published scores of works
including novels, short stories, plays, criticism, and the
autobiography Ushant, in which he recounts the story of
his equal but divided loyalty to his own culture and that
of England. He was Consultant in Poetry at the Library of
Congress for two years but has otherwise declined public
positions and avoided public appearances.*

## Prelude xiv

—You went to the verge, you say, and come back safely?
Some have not been so fortunate,—some have fallen.
Children go lightly there, from crag to crag,
And coign to coign,—where even the goat is wary,—
And make a sport of it. . . . They fling down pebbles,
Following, with eyes undizzied, the long curve,
The long slow outward curve, into the abyss,
As far as eye can follow; and they themselves

Turn back, unworried, to the here and now. . . .
But you have been there, too?—

    —I saw at length
The space-defying pine, that on the last
Outjutting rock has cramped its powerful roots.
There stood I too: under that tree I stood:
My hand against its resinous bark: my face
Turned out and downward to the fourfold kingdom.
The wind roared from all quarters. The waterfall
Came down, it seemed, from Heaven. The mighty sound
Of pouring elements,—earth, air, and water,—
The cry of eagles, chatter of falling stones,—
These were the frightful language of that place.
I understood it ill, but understood.—

—You understood it? Tell me, then, its meaning.
It was an all, a nothing, or a something?
Chaos, or divine love, or emptiness?
Water and earth and air and the sun's fire?
Or else, a question, simply?—

    —Water and fire were there,
And air and earth; there too was emptiness;
All, and nothing, and something too, and love.
But these poor words, these squeaks of ours, in which
We strive to mimic, with strained throats and tongues,
The spawning and outrageous elements—
Alas, how paltry are they! For I saw—

—What did you see?

    —I saw myself and God.
I saw the ruin in which godhead lives:
Shapeless and vast: the strewn wreck of the world:
Sadness unplumbed: misery without bound.
Wailing I heard, but also I heard joy.
Wreckage I saw, but also I saw flowers.

**Conrad Aiken**  *6*

Hatred I saw, but also I saw love. . . .
And thus, I saw myself.

　　　—And this alone?

—And this alone awaits you, when you dare
To that sheer verge where horror hangs, and tremble
Against the falling rock; and, looking down,
Search the dark kingdom. It is to self you come,—
And that is God. It is the seed of seeds:
Seed for disastrous and immortal worlds.

It is the answer that no question asked.


**Prelude lvi**

Rimbaud and Verlaine, precious pair of poets,
Genius in both (but what is genius?) playing
Chess on a marble table at an inn
With chestnut blossom falling in blond beer
And on their hair and between knight and bishop—
Sunlight squared between them on the chess-board
Cirrus in heaven, and a squeal of music
Blown from the leathern door of Ste. Sulpice—

Discussing, between moves, iamb and spondee
Anacoluthon and the open vowel
God the great peacock with his angel peacocks
And his dependent peacocks the bright stars:
Disputing too of fate as Plato loved it,
Or Sophocles, who hated and admired,
Or Socrates, who loved and was amused:

Verlaine puts down his pawn upon a leaf
And closes his long eyes, which are dishonest,
And says 'Rimbaud, there is one thing to do:

**Conrad Aiken**　7

We must take rhetoric, and wring its neck! . . . '
Rimbaud considers gravely, moves his Queen;
And then removes himself to Timbuctoo.

And Verlaine dead,—with all his jades and mauves;
And Rimbaud dead in Marseilles with a vision,
His leg cut off, as once before his heart;
And all reported by a later lackey,
Whose virtue is his tardiness in time.

Let us describe the evening as it is:—
The stars disposed in heaven as they are:
Verlaine and Shakspere rotting, where they rot,
Rimbaud remembered, and too soon forgot;

Order in all things, logic in the dark;
Arrangement in the atom and the spark;
Time in the heart and sequence in the brain—

Such as destroyed Rimbaud and fooled Verlaine.
And let us then take godhead by the neck—

And strangle it, and with it, rhetoric.

**Conrad Aiken** *8*

# A. R. Ammons

*A. R. Ammons, born February 18, 1926, in Whiteville,*
*North Carolina, lives with his wife and small son in*
*Ithaca, New York, where he teaches at Cornell. He*
*attended Wake Forest College and the University of*
*California, then was a businessman before turning to an*
*academic career. Ingeniously simple yet charged with*
*sophistication, his work shows a broad concern with*
*qualities of the American landscape and with phases of*
*American experience.*

## Visit

    It is not far to my place:
you can come smallboat,
pausing under shade in the eddies
   or going ashore
       to rest, regard the leaves

    or talk with birds and
shore weeds: hire a full-grown man not
late in years to oar you
   and choose a canoe-like thin ship;
      (a dumb man is better and no

    costlier; he will attract
the reflections and silences under leaves:)

travel light: a single book, some twine:
    the river is muscled at rapids with trout
        and a laurel limb

    will make a suitable spit: if you
leave in the forenoon, you will arrive
with plenty of light
    the afternoon of the third day: I will
        come down to the landing

    (tell your man to look for it,
the dumb have clear sight and are free of
visions) to greet you with some made
    wine and a special verse:
        or you can come by shore:

    choose the right: there the rocks
cascade less frequently, the grade more gradual:
treat yourself gently: the ascent thins both
    mind and blood and you must
        keep still a dense reserve

    of silence we can poise against
conversation: there is little news:
I found last month a root with shape and
    have heard a new sound among
        the insects: come.

## The wide land

Having split up the chaparral
blasting my sight
the wind said
        You know I'm
            the result of
forces beyond my control

I don't hold it against you
I said
It's all right I understand

Those pressure bowls and cones
the wind said
are giants in their continental gaits
I know I said I know
they're blind giants
Actually the wind said I'm
        if anything beneficial
            resolving extremes
filling up lows with highs
No I said you don't have
to explain
It's just the way things are

Blind in the wide land I
turned and risked my feet
to loose stones and sudden

alterations of height

# John Ashbery

*John Ashbery, born July 28, 1927, in Rochester, New York,
lives in New York City. After he had completed his
formal education at Harvard and Columbia, he lived
from 1955 to 1965 in Paris where his work as a critic of
modern art led to his present position as an executive
editor of* Art News. *His poetry reflects an intimate
knowledge of forms of twentieth-century graphic
expression, and is sometimes explicable only with
reference to certain inventions of modern painters. Since
the death in 1967 of his close friend Frank O'Hara, he is
the most important member of a group of painterly poets
who have become known as "The New York School."*

## Civilization and its discontents

A people chained to aurora
I alone disarming you

Millions of facts of distributed light

Helping myself with some big boxes
Up the steps, then turning to no neighborhood;
The child's psalm, slightly sung
In the hall rushing into the small room.
Such fire! leading away from destruction.
Somewhere in outer ether I glimpsed you

Coming at me, the solo barrier did it this time,
Guessing us staying, true to be at the blue mark
Of the threshold. Tired of planning it again and again,
The cool boy distant, and the soaked-up
Afterthought, like so much rain, or roof.

The miracle took you in beside him.
Leaves rushed the window, there was clear water and the
    sound of a lock.
Now I never see you much any more.
The summers are much colder than they used to be
In that other time, when you and I were young.
I miss the human truth of your smile,
The halfhearted gaze of your palms,
And all things together, but there is no comic reign
Only the facts you put to me. You must not, then,
Be very surprised if I am alone: it is all for you,
The night, and the stars, and the way we used to be.

There is no longer any use in harping on
The incredible principle of daylong silence, the dark sunlight
As only the grass is beginning to know it,
The wreath of the north pole,
Festoons for the late return, the shy pensioners
Agasp on the lamplit air. What is agreeable
Is to hold your hand. The gravel
Underfoot. The time is for coming close. Useless
Verbs shooting the other words far away.

I had already swallowed the poison
And could only gaze into the distance at my life
Like a saint's with each day distinct.
No heaviness in the upland pastures. Nothing
In the forest. Only life under the huge trees
Like a coat that has grown too big, moving far away,
Cutting swamps for men like lapdogs, holding its own,
Performing once again, for you and for me.

**John Ashbery   14**

**Faust**

If only the phantom would stop reappearing!
Business, if you wanted to know, was punk at the opera.
The heroine no longer appeared in *Faust*.
The crowds strolled sadly away. The phantom
Watched them from the roof, not guessing the hungers
That must be stirred before disappointment can begin.

One day as morning was about to begin
A man in brown with a white shirt reappearing
At the bottom of his yellow vest, was talking hungers
With the silver-haired director of the opera.
On the green-carpeted floor no phantom
Appeared, except yellow squares of sunlight, like those in *Faust*.

That night as the musicians for *Faust*
Were about to go on strike, lest darkness begin
In the corridors, and through them the phantom
Glide unobstructed, the vision reappearing
Of blonde Marguerite practicing a new opera
At her window awoke terrible new hungers

In the already starving tenor. But hungers
Are just another topic, like the new Faust
Drifting through the tunnels of the opera
(In search of lost old age? For they begin
To notice a twinkle in his eye. It is cold daylight reappearing
At the window behind him, itself a phantom

Window, painted by the phantom
Scene painters, sick of not getting paid, of hungers
For a scene below of tiny, reappearing
Dancers, with a sandbag falling like a note in *Faust*
Through purple air. And the spectators begin
To understand the bleeding tenor star of the opera.)

**John Ashbery**  *16*

That night the opera
Was crowded to the rafters. The phantom
Took twenty-nine curtain calls. "Begin!
Begin!" In the wings the tenor hungers
For the heroine's convulsive kiss, and Faust
Moves forward, no longer young, reappearing

And reappearing for the last time. The opera
*Faust* would no longer need its phantom.
On the bare, sunlit stage the hungers could begin.

---

**Civilization and its discontents:** *The title of this poem, first used by Sigmund Freud for a work dealing with cultural analysis, is here applied to a meditation on loss. Like many modern paintings and musical compositions, the poem is nonsequential and deliberately nonlogical. Instead of conventional order, drama, argument, it provides a "field of action" in which words and ideas are seriously at play.*

**Faust:** *This poem is a sestina: the same set of six end-words is used in each of the six six-line stanzas, and all these are then incorporated into the final three-line stanza. Dealing with the ubiquitous figure of the medieval Faust, the poem makes extensive reference to Gounod's musical work and to the famous old Lon Chaney movie* The Phantom of the Opera.

**John Ashbery** *17*

# W. H. Auden

W. H. Auden, born February 21, 1907, in York, England,
lives in New York City and in Kirchstetten, Austria. He
was educated at Oxford, where he began to publish the
poems that were to set the tone and climate for what
later became known as the "Auden generation" of poets.
After a short period of participation in the Spanish Civil
War as a civilian on the Loyalist side, and marriage to
Erika, the daughter of Thomas Mann, he came to the
United States in 1939 and, a few years later, became an
American citizen. He has taught for short periods at the
University of Michigan, Swarthmore, Smith, and at the
New School for Social Research, in New York City,
where his course in Shakespeare drew such crowds of
students that a secretary was moved to remark, "You'd
think Shakespeare was giving a course in Auden."
Besides many volumes of poetry, volumes of essays, and
two travel books, Letters from Iceland and Journey to a
War, on which he collaborated with Louis MacNeice and
the novelist Christopher Isherwood, respectively, he has
collaborated with Isherwood on three plays and with
Chester Kallman on the librettos of two operas.

## Anthem for St. Cecilia's Day

In a garden shady this holy lady
With reverent cadence and subtle psalm,
Like a black swan as death came on
Poured forth her song in perfect calm:
And by ocean's margin this innocent virgin
Constructed an organ to enlarge her prayer,
And notes tremendous from her great engine
Thundered out on the Roman air.

Blonde Aphrodite rose up excited,
Moved to delight by the melody,
White as an orchid she rode quite naked
In an oyster shell on top of the sea;
At sounds so entrancing the angels dancing
Came out of their trance into time again,
And around the wicked in Hell's abysses
The huge flame flickered and eased their pain.

*Blessed Cecilia, appear in visions*
*To all musicians, appear and inspire:*
*Translated Daughter, come down and startle*
*Composing mortals with immortal fire.*


## Musée des Beaux Arts

About suffering they were never wrong,
The Old Masters: how well they understood
Its human position; how it takes place
While someone else is eating or opening a window or just walking
    dully along;
How, when the aged are reverently, passionately waiting
For the miraculous birth, there always must be
Children who did not specially want it to happen, skating
On a pond at the edge of the wood:

They never forgot
That even the dreadful martyrdom must run its course
Anyhow in a corner, some untidy spot
Where the dogs go on with their doggy life, and the torturer's horse
Scratches its innocent behind on a tree.

In Breughel's *Icarus,* for instance: how everything turns away
Quite leisurely from the disaster; the ploughman may
Have heard the splash, the forsaken cry,
But for him it was not an important failure; the sun shone
As it had to on the white legs disappearing into the green
Water; and the expensive delicate ship that must have seen
Something amazing, a boy falling out of the sky,
Had somewhere to get to and sailed calmly on.


## As I walked out one evening

As I walked out one evening,
    Walking down Bristol Street,
The crowds upon the pavement
    Were fields of harvest wheat.

And down by the brimming river
    I heard a lover sing
Under an arch of the railway:
    "Love has no ending.

I'll love you, dear, I'll love you
    Till China and Africa meet,
And the river jumps over the mountain
    And the salmon sing in the street.

I'll love you till the ocean
    Is folded and hung up to dry,
And the seven stars go squawking
    Like geese about the sky.

**W. H. Auden**  *21*

The years shall run like rabbits,
   For in my arms I hold
The Flower of the Ages,
   And the first love of the world."

But all the clocks in the city
   Began to whirr and chime:
"O let not Time deceive you,
   You cannot conquer Time.

In the burrows of the Nightmare
   Where Justice naked is,
Time watches from the shadow
   And coughs when you would kiss.

In headaches and in worry
   Vaguely life leaks away,
And Time will have his fancy
   Tomorrow or today.

Into many a green valley
   Drifts the appalling snow;
Time breaks the threaded dances
   And the diver's brilliant bow.

O plunge your hands in water,
   Plunge them in up to the wrist;
Stare, stare in the basin
   And wonder what you've missed.

The glacier knocks in the cupboard,
   The desert sighs in the bed,
And the crack in the tea-cup opens
   A lane to the land of the dead.

Where the beggars raffle the banknotes
   And the Giant is enchanting to Jack,

**W. H. Auden  22**

And the Lily-white Boy is a Roarer,
    And Jill goes down on her back.

O look, look in the mirror,
    O look in your distress;
Life remains a blessing
    Although you cannot bless.

O stand, stand at the window
    As the tears scald and start;
You shall love your crooked neighbor
    With your crooked heart."

It was late, late in the evening,
    The lovers they were gone;
The clocks had ceased their chiming,
    And the deep river ran on.

---

**Anthem for St. Cecilia's Day:** *St. Cecilia, who lived in second- or third-century Rome, is the virgin martyr who came to be regarded as the patroness of music. In literature and art she is usually represented at the organ. The vision of Aphrodite (Venus), goddess of love, invoked here, recalls Botticelli's painting* The Birth of Venus.

**Musée des Beaux Arts:** *The title of this poem is the name of a museum in Brussels where Breughel's painting* The Fall of Icarus *is permanently housed. The commentary in the poem is general until line 14. After that, all of the references are specifically concerned with this painting.*

**W. H. Auden** *23*

# George Barker

*George Barker, born February 26, 1913, in Loughton, Essex, lives on a farm in Haslemere, Surrey, with his wife and children. He attended no university, his sketchy formal education having been undertaken in short periods of study at the Marlborough Road School, in Chelsea, and the Regent Street Polytechnic. When he left school at the age of fourteen, he tried his hand at many jobs and was at one time a designer of wallpaper and at another a garage mechanic. Having made an impressive early reputation as a poet, he was appointed visiting professor of English literature at the Imperial Tohoku University in Japan in 1939, after which he came to the United States, remaining for four years before returning to England and ground service with the Royal Air Force.* He has published three novels: Alanna Autumnal; Janus; The Dead Seagull.

**To my mother**

Most near, most dear, most loved and most far,
Under the window where I often found her
Sitting as huge as Asia, seismic with laughter,
Gin and chicken helpless in her Irish hand,
Irresistible as Rabelais, but most tender for
The lame dogs and hurt birds that surround her,—

She is a procession no one can follow after
But be like a little dog following a brass band.

She will not glance up at the bomber, or condescend
To drop her gin and scuttle to a cellar,
But lean on the mahogany table like a mountain
Whom only faith can move, and so I send
O all my faith, and all my love to tell her
That she will move from mourning into morning.


*from* **To my son**

PART I

My darkling child the stars have obeyed
In your deliverance and laid
You cold on the doorstep of a house
Where few are happy and times get worse.
I will not gild your nativity
With a desirable lie, nor pity
The birth that invests me with a second
Heart on which I had not reckoned:
No less than I do you will drink
Cold comfort at a loveless brink,
And when the wheel of mischance grazes
You as you play I shall know pauses
Of the skipping heart. Let the day, bending
A bright hand about you, attend you
Into the fatherless night when we
Are each of us alone and at sea
Without a North Star—but may
The night seem safer the next day.
The best of all is not to be born,
But how can we tell this to the morning
That, as we groan, comes up over the hill
Of our midnight grief? I see you, still,

**George Barker**   *26*

An unbroken daybreak in my darkest
Heart, destined to illuminate the stark
Day of necessity in proper season.
Why were you born? I love. This is the reason.
But do not ask me why or whom—
Does it much matter what prefix doom
Wears to her name? She and I
Shall always meet when all wishes
Under a dazzle of unpropitious
But irresistible ascendencies
Clasp each other because they freeze.
I saw her face. Saw fate had taught her
That she was an elected daughter
And in obedience to the pull
Of that which knows it is beautiful
I moved towards her in the cold
And fell into a moon. The golden
Undergrowth of her sex enmeshed
The dying fugitive it refreshed
For henceforward daily dying.
Sucking blood a Venus, sighing,
Toys her prey back into life:
He rules her with the sexual knife
That kills him. But all this
Comes later, my dear son, and is
Knowledge of a kind that seems
Too bitter for the simple schemes
Of a world in which the killer
Neither hates nor loves the killed.
Your bed is a kingdom where
Tears pacify the dogs of despair
And the cold sheets, getting warm,
Protect you all night long from harm.
My bed is made. I lie on love
Like dynamos. The rub and shove
Turn generations on their way.
We weep as we embrace and die.

When the normal day begins
We, rising, step out of our sins
Not even smiling. The monsters settle
Back into their sleeping metal.
My dear son, you rode down on
The spinal throes of a mastodon
One quiet night in May. I bare
That hour because I do not dare
Let flesh grow over it. Your own
Heartburst, one day, like a cyst,
Will fester so, if you desist
From speech. The tongue is a bird
Where the worm, in the heart interred,
Can be caught by no other. Let him, ringing
Lark of the bloodiest field, bring
The overworn heart relief. I write
These lines in a train on a night
You sleep away in Ireland. Do not stir.
I would not have my unpleasanter
Thoughts disturb you. It is late.
The moon stares down, dispassionate
As the world stares up at her.
All things are lost in genera.
The train crawls on. The coast creeps near.
The rain has started. And the year
Is almost ended. I have been
Too long away from my domain:
Too much pursued my own will o'
The whips against a stranger pillow,
Too many seas of wounds sailed over
To think that destinations cover
The running sore of separation.
I, like the train, must learn my station
And stop a while there. Let me hide
My restlessness at your bedside,
Where, my dear son, you keep
Four better guardians of your sleep.

**To my mother:** *In the first sense, this sonnet is a completely personal poem; in a second, the poet's portrait of his mother is a statement in which the endurance and resurgent vitality of civilians during the bombing of London are regarded as monumental virtues.*

# Michael Benedikt

*Michael Benedikt, born May 26, 1937, in New York City,
now makes his home there with his wife. An editorial
associate on the magazine Art News, he has taught at
Bennington and Sarah Lawrence, and he is also an
authority on experimental forms of contemporary drama
in French, German, Spanish, as well as in English. His
poetry shows influences from surrealist painting, from the
Theatre of the Absurd, and from those works of Gertrude
Stein in which logical sequence is disregarded in favor
of playful distributions of content and order.*

## The European shoe

The European Shoe is constructed of grass and reed, bound up and
    wound around so that it may slip easily over the wearer's head.

In case you are an aircraft pilot, you must take care that the
    European Shoe does not creep off your foot, and begin to
    make its way carefully along the fuselage.

The European Shoe pressed against the fugitive's nose, preventing it
    from imminent departure.

The European Shoe spends summers in delightful ways. A lady feels
    its subtle and unexpected pressure the length of her decolletage.
    (It winters in pain.)

That time I lent you my European Shoe you departed with a look of
    grandeur, and in total disrepair.

The European Shoe knocks on the door of the carefree farmerette.
    "The harvest has been gathered in, ha, ha," it says, moving
    shyly forth along the edge of the couch.

I pointed to the European Shoe. I ate the European Shoe. I married
    the European Shoe.

Tears fall from the eye of the European Shoe as it waves goodbye to us
    from the back balcony of the speeding train.

It helps an old lady, extremely crippled and arthritic, move
    an enormous cornerstone. It invents a watch, which, when wound
    up tightly, flies completely to pieces.

It was a simple and dignified ceremony, distinguished for its gales
    of uncontrollable laughter, in which I married the European Shoe.

If it rains, the European Shoe becomes very heavy. I failed to cross
    the river, where thousands of European shoes lay capsized.

And so we lived alone, we two, the envy of our neighborhoods, the
    delight of our lively hordes of children.

I saw a flightful of graceful swallows heading to distant, half-
    forgotten islands over the distant seas; and in the midst of that
    annually questing company, I saw the European Shoe.

It never harmed anyone, and yet it never helped anyone.

Gaily it sets out into the depths of my profoundest closet, to do battle
    with the dusts of summer.

**Michael Benedikt**   *32*

## Some litanies

1

Was the arrangement made between the two couples legal?

No.

Did they spread the word around?

No.

Have you visited the two couples lately? Did you have an
    interesting time? Was it illegal?

No.

What was the decoration like?

It was furnished in Swedish "modern." Strings were hanging
    down in the living room. A bird flew in the window once
    and out again.

Will you ever marry?

No.

Have you ever been married?

I don't remember.

Do you love your husband?

Yes.

2

May I please have this dance?

No.

**Michael Benedikt**   *33*

May I please have that dance?

No.

Aren't you going to wear anything to the dance?

Yes.

Are you a good dancer?

Yes.

Do you know how to dance?

No.

May I in that case have your company during the dance
    they decide to play exactly at midnight, whatever it is?
    I have fallen in love with your eyes, lips, hands and hair.

No.

3

During the lapse of several years, during which I spent
    most of my time in Barcelona, was the magazine published?

Yes.

During the lapse of several years, during which I spent
    most of my time in Barcelona, was the magazine published?

No.

Aren't you absolutely sure?

No.

Aren't you absolutely sure?

**Michael Benedikt**  *34*

Yes.

Will you ever come to Barcelona with me?

No. I am afraid to leave behind the business affairs
       of the magazine, of which I am general manager.

Are you really that conscientious?

No.

4

Would you care to deal him the death-dealing blow?

No.

Would you care to pay him a little visit?

No.

Would you care to improve his laundry service by
      making persistent inquiries?

No.

Are you really his legal guardian?

No.

Would you care to hand him this large can of
      fortified beeswax?

No.

Do you have a favorite hobby?

Yes. Devoting myself entirely to that boy.

**Michael Benedikt**  *35*

# John Berryman

*John Berryman, born October 25, 1914, in McAlester,
Oklahoma, lives in Minneapolis, where he teaches in the
English department of the University of Minnesota.
Educated at Columbia and at Clare College, Cambridge, he
has taught for short periods at many American universities,
including Wayne, Princeton, and Brown. He is the author
of a critical biography of Stephen Crane. Long before the
appearance of his famous Dream Songs sequence, he
published one of the few highly regarded long poems
recently written in America, Homage to Mistress
Bradstreet.*

## Winter landscape

The three men coming down the winter hill
In brown, with tall poles and a pack of hounds
At heel, through the arrangement of the trees,
Past the five figures at the burning straw,
Returning cold and silent to their town,

Returning to the drifted snow, the rink
Lively with children, to the older men,
The long companions they can never reach,
The blue light, men with ladders, by the church
The sledge and shadow in the twilit street,

Are not aware that in the sandy time
To come, the evil waste of history
Outstretched, they will be seen upon the brow
Of that same hill: when all their company
Will have been irrecoverably lost,

These men, this particular three in brown
Witnessed by birds will keep the scene and say
By their configuration with the trees,
The small bridge, the red houses and the fire,
What place, what time, what morning occasion

Sent them into the wood, a pack of hounds
At heel and the tall poles upon their shoulders,
Thence to return as now we see them and
Ankle-deep in snow down the winter hill
Descend, while three birds watch and the fourth flies.


## Dream song 14

Life, friends, is boring. We must not say so.
After all, the sky flashes, the great sea yearns,
we ourselves flash and yearn,
and moreover my mother told me as a boy
(repeatingly) 'Ever to confess you're bored
means you have no

Inner Resources.' I conclude now I have no
inner resources, because I am heavy bored.
Peoples bore me,
literature bores me, especially great literature,
Henry bores me, with his plights & gripes
as bad as achilles,

who loves people and valiant art, which bores me.
And the tranquil hills, & gin, look like a drag

**John Berryman**   *38*

and somehow a dog
has taken itself & its tail considerably away
into mountains or sea or sky, leaving
behind: me, wag.


## Dream song 62

That dark brown rabbit, lightness in his ears
& underneath, gladdened our afternoon
munching a crab-'.
That rabbit was a fraud, like a black bull
*prudent* I admired in Zaragoza, who
certainly was brave as a demon

but would not charge, being willing not to die.
The rabbit's case, a little different,
consisted in alert
& wily looks down the lawn, where nobody was,
with prickt ears, while rapt but chatting on the porch
we sat in view nearby.

Then went he mildly by, and around behind
my cabin, and when I followed, there he just sat.
Only at last
he turned down around, passing my wife at four feet
and hopped the whole lawn and made thro' the hedge for the big house.
—Mr Bones, we all brutes & fools.


## Dream song 76: Henry's confession

Nothin very bad happen to me lately.
How you explain that?—I explain that, Mr Bones,
terms o' your bafflin odd sobriety.
Sober as man can get, no girls, no telephones,

what could happen bad to Mr Bones?
—*If* life is a handkerchief sandwich,

in a modesty of death I join my father
who dared so long agone leave me.
A bullet on a concrete stoop
close by a smothering southern sea
spreadeagled on an island, by my knee.
—You is from hunger, Mr Bones,

I offers you this handkerchief, now set
your left foot by my right foot,
shoulder to shoulder, all that jazz,
arm in arm, by the beautiful sea,
hum a little, Mr Bones.
—I saw nobody coming, so I went instead.


**Dream song 77**

Seedy Henry rose up shy in de world
& shaved & swung his barbells, duded Henry up
and p.a.'d poor thousands of persons on topics of grand
moment to Henry, ah to those less & none.
Wif a book of his in either hand
he is stript down to move on.

—Come away, Mr Bones.

—Henry is tired of the winter,
& haircuts, & a squeamish comfy     ruin-prone proud national
   mind,     & Spring (in the city so called).
Henry likes Fall.
Hé would be prepared to líve in a world of Fáll
for ever, impenitent Henry.
But the snows and summers grieve & dream;

**John Berryman**   *40*

thése fierce & airy occupations, and love,
raved away so many of Henry's years
it is a wonder that, with in each hand
one of his own mad books and all,
ancient fires for eyes, his head full
& his heart full, he's making ready to move on.

---

**Winter landscape:** *The pictorial subject of this poem is the
painting Hunters in the Snow, by Breughel. Every image in
the poem is a transcription of its counterpart in the painting.*

**Dream song 14:** *Of the celebrated long poem from which
these segments are taken, the author has written: "The
poem . . . whatever its wide cast of characters, is essentially
about an imaginary character (not the poet, not me) named
Henry, a white American in early middle age sometimes in
blackface, who has suffered an irreversible loss and talks
about himself sometimes in the first person, sometimes in the
third, sometimes even in the second; he has a friend, never
named, who addresses him as Mr Bones and variants thereof."*

# John Betjeman

*John Betjeman, born 1906 in England, lives in the*
*Smithfield market district of London and in Wantage,*
*Berkshire. He is married and has a son and a daughter.*
*Educated at Marlborough and at Oxford, he was British*
*Press Attaché in Dublin from 1941 to 1943 and, in 1944,*
*held a post in the British Admiralty. Although he has for*
*many years written poems and is well known as an expert*
*on architecture, particularly Victorian, his wide fame in*
*England did not arrive until the publication of his*
*Collected Poems, which became one of the best selling*
*volumes of verse since Byron. In recent years he has*
*gained a wide popular reputation through appearances on*
*British television and was knighted by the Queen in 1969.*
*Sir John is pictured here dressed in clothes that once*
*belonged to Henry James.*

## A subaltern's love-song

Miss J. Hunter Dunn, Miss J. Hunter Dunn,
Furnish'd and burnish'd by Aldershot sun,
What strenuous singles we played after tea,
We in the tournament—you against me!

Love-thirty, love-forty, oh! weakness of joy,
The speed of a swallow, the grace of a boy,

With carefullest carelessness, gaily you won,
I am weak from your loveliness, Joan Hunter Dunn.

Miss Joan Hunter Dunn, Miss Joan Hunter Dunn,
How mad I am, sad I am, glad that you won.
The warm-handled racket is back in its press,
But my shock-headed victor, she loves me no less.

Her father's euonymus shines as we walk,
And swing past the summer-house, buried in talk,
And cool the verandah that welcomes us in
To the six-o'clock news and a lime-juice and gin.

The scent of the conifers, sound of the bath,
The view from my bedroom of moss-dappled path,
As I struggle with double-end evening tie,
For we dance at the Golf Club, my victor and I.

On the floor of her bedroom lie blazer and shorts
And the cream-coloured walls are be-trophied with sports,
And westering, questioning settles the sun
On your low-leaded window, Miss Joan Hunter Dunn.

The Hillman is waiting, the light's in the hall,
The pictures of Egypt are bright on the wall,
My sweet, I am standing beside the oak stair
And there on the landing's the light on your hair.

By roads "not adopted", by woodlanded ways,
She drove to the club in the late summer haze,
Into nine-o'clock Camberly, heavy with bells
And mushroomy, pine-woody, evergreen smells.

Miss Joan Hunter Dunn, Miss Joan Hunter Dunn,
I can hear from the car-park the dance has begun.
Oh! full Surrey twilight! importunate band!
Oh! strongly adorable tennis-girl's hand!

**John Betjeman**  44

Around us are Rovers and Austins afar,
Above us, the intimate roof of the car,
And here on my right is the girl of my choice,
With the tilt of her nose and the chime of her voice,

And the scent of her wrap, and the words never said,
And the ominous, ominous dancing ahead.
We sat in the car-park till twenty to one
And now I'm engaged to Miss Joan Hunter Dunn.

## Youth and age on Beaulieu River, Hants

Early sun on Beaulieu water
    Lights the undersides of oaks,
Clumps of leaves it floods and blanches,
All transparent glow the branches
    Which the double sunlight soaks;
  To her craft on Beaulieu water
  Clemency the General's daughter
    Pulls across with even strokes.

Schoolboy-sure she is this morning;
    Soon her sharpie's rigg'd and free.
Cool beneath a garden awning
    Mrs. Fairclough, sipping tea
And raising large long-distance glasses
As the little sharpie passes,
    Sighs our sailor girl to see:

Tulip figure, so appealing,
    Oval face, so serious-eyed,
Tree-roots pass'd and muddy beaches.
On to huge and lake-like reaches,
    Soft and sun-warm, see her glide—
  Slacks the slim young limbs revealing,

**John Betjeman**  45

Sun-brown arm the tiller feeling—
    With the wind and with the tide.

Evening light will bring the water,
    Day-long sun will burst the bud,
Clemency, the General's daughter,
    Will return upon the flood.
But the older woman only
Knows the ebb-tide leaves her lonely
    With the shining fields of mud.

# Elizabeth Bishop

*Elizabeth Bishop, born February 8, 1911, in Worcester,*
*Massachusetts, makes her home part of the time in San*
*Francisco and part of the time in Ouro Preto, Minas*
*Gerais, Brazil. As a child she lived for a number of years*
*in Nova Scotia and later spent much of her time in*
*Key West. Educated at Vassar College, she has published*
*a number of highly acclaimed short stories and a*
*translation from the Portuguese,* Diary of Helena
Morley. *Of her poems Robert Lowell has said, "When we*
*read her, we enter the classical serenity of a new*
*country."*

## Letter to N. Y.

In your next letter I wish you'd say
where you are going and what you are doing;
how are the plays, and after the plays
what other pleasures you're pursuing:

taking cabs in the middle of the night,
driving as if to save your soul
where the road goes round and round the park
and the meter glares like a moral owl,

and the trees look so queer and green
standing alone in big black caves

and suddenly you're in a different place
where everything seems to happen in waves,

and most of the jokes you just can't catch,
like dirty words rubbed off a slate,
and the songs are loud but somehow dim
and it gets so terribly late,

and coming out of the brownstone house
to the gray sidewalk, the watered street,
one side of the buildings rises with the sun
like a glistening field of wheat.

—Wheat, not oats, dear. I'm afraid
if it's wheat it's none of your sowing,
nevertheless I'd like to know
what you are doing and where you are going.


## A cold spring

*for Janey Dewey. Maryland*

*Nothing is so beautiful as spring.*
                HOPKINS

A cold spring:
the violet was flawed on the lawn.
For two weeks or more the trees hesitated;
the little leaves waited,
carefully indicating their characteristics.
Finally a grave green dust
settled over your big and aimless hills.
One day, in a chill white blast of sunshine,
on the side of one a calf was born.
The mother stopped lowing
and took a long time eating the after-birth,
a wretched flag,

**Elizabeth Bishop** *49*

but the calf got up promptly
and seemed inclined to feel gay.

The next day
was much warmer.
Greenish-white dogwood infiltrated the wood,
each petal burned, apparently, by a cigarette-butt;
and the blurred redbud stood
beside it, motionless, but almost more
like movement than any placeable color.
Four deer practised leaping over your fences.
The infant oak-leaves swung through the sober oak.
Song-sparrows were wound up for the summer,
and in the maple the complementary cardinal
cracked a whip, and the sleeper awoke,
stretching miles of green limbs from the south.
In his cap the lilacs whitened,
then one day they fell like snow.

Now, in the evening,
a new moon comes.
The hills grow softer. Tufts of long grass show
where each cow-flop lies.
The bull-frogs are sounding,
slack strings plucked by heavy thumbs.
Beneath the light, against your white front door,
the smallest moths, like Chinese fans,
flatten themselves, silver and silver-gilt
over pale yellow, orange, or gray.
Now, from the thick grass, the fireflies
begin to rise:
up, then down, then up again:
lit on the ascending flight,
drifting simultaneously to the same height,
—exactly like the bubbles in champagne.
—Later on they rise much higher.
And your shadowy pastures will be able to offer
these particular glowing tributes
every evening now throughout the summer.

**Elizabeth Bishop**  *50*

## Florida

The state with the prettiest name,
the state that floats in brackish water,
held together by mangrove roots
that bear while living oysters in clusters,
and when dead strew white swamps with skeletons,
dotted as if bombarded, with green hummocks
like ancient cannon-balls sprouting grass.
The state full of long S-shaped birds, blue and white,
and unseen hysterical birds who rush up the scale
every time in a tantrum.
Tanagers embarrassed by their flashiness,
and pelicans whose delight it is to clown;
who coast for fun on the strong tidal currents
in and out among the mangrove islands
and stand on the sand-bars drying their damp gold wings
on sun-lit evenings.
Enormous turtles, helpless and mild,
die and leave their barnacled shells on the beaches,
and their large white skulls with round eye-sockets
twice the size of a man's.
The palm trees clatter in the stiff breeze
like the bills of the pelicans. The tropical rain comes down
to freshen the tide-looped strings of fading shells:
Job's Tear, the Chinese Alphabet, the scarce Junonia,
parti-colored pectins and Ladies' Ears,
arranged as on a gray rag of rotted calico,
the buried Indian Princess's skirt;
with these the monotonous, endless, sagging coast-line
is delicately ornamented.
Thirty or more buzzards are drifting down, down, down,
over something they have spotted in the swamp,
in circles like stirred up flakes of sediment
sinking through water.
Smoke from woods-fires filters fine blue solvents.
On stumps and dead trees the charring is like black velvet.
The mosquitoes

**Elizabeth Bishop**  *51*

go hunting to the tune of their ferocious obbligatos.
After dark, the fire-flies map the heavens in the marsh
until the moon rises.
Cold white, not bright, the moonlight is coarse-meshed,
and the careless, corrupt state is all black specks
too far apart, and ugly whites; the poorest
post-card of itself.
After dark, the pools seem to have slipped away.
The alligator, who has five distinct calls:
friendliness, love, mating, war, and a warning,
whimpers and speaks in the throat
of the Indian Princess.


**The prodigal**

The brown enormous odor he lived by
was too close, with its breathing and thick hair,
for him to judge. The floor was rotten; the sty
was plastered halfway up with glass-smooth dung.
Light-lashed, self-righteous, above moving snouts,
the pigs' eyes followed him, a cheerful stare—
even to the sow that always ate her young—
till, sickening, he leaned to scratch her head.
But sometimes mornings after drinking bouts
(he hid the pints behind a two-by-four),
the sunrise glazed the barnyard mud with red;
the burning puddles seemed to reassure.
And then he thought he almost might endure
his exile yet another year or more.

But evenings the first star came to warn.
The farmer whom he worked for came at dark
to shut the cows and horses in the barn
beneath their overhanging clouds of hay,
with pitchforks, faint forked lightnings, catching light,
safe and companionable as in the Ark.

**Elizabeth Bishop**  *52*

The pigs stuck out their little feet and snored.
The lantern—like the sun, going away—
laid on the mud a pacing aureole.
Carrying a bucket along a slimy board,
he felt the bats' uncertain staggering flight,
his shuddering insights, beyond his control,
touching him. But it took him a long time
finally to make his mind up to go home.

# Louise Bogan

*Louise Bogan, born August 11, 1897, in Livermore Falls,
Maine, lives in New York City. She attended Boston
Girls' Latin School and Boston University and then was
married and, within a few years, widowed with one
daughter. Her second husband was the poet Raymond
Holden, from whom she was divorced in 1937. For more
than twenty years she has been poetry critic for* The New
Yorker. *She was Consultant in Poetry at the Library of
Congress in 1945 and 1946; in 1954 her* Collected Poems
*was awarded the Bollingen Prize.*

## Women

Women have no wilderness in them,
They are provident instead,
Content in the tight hot cell of their hearts
To eat dusty bread.

They do not see cattle cropping red winter grass,
They do not hear
Snow water going down under culverts
Shallow and clear.

They wait, when they should turn to journeys,
They stiffen, when they should bend.
They use against themselves that benevolence
To which no man is friend.

**Louise Bogan**   55

They cannot think of so many crops to a field
Or of clean wood cleft by an axe.
Their love is an eager meaninglessness
Too tense, or too lax.

They hear in every whisper that speaks to them
A shout and a cry.
As like as not, when they take life over their door-sills
They should let it go by.


## Evening in the sanitarium

The free evening fades, outside the windows fastened
    with decorative iron grilles.
The lamps are lighted; the shades drawn; the nurses
    are watching a little.
It is the hour of the complicated knitting on the safe
    bone needles; of the games of anagrams and bridge;
The deadly game of chess; the book held up like a mask.

The period of the wildest weeping, the fiercest delusion, is over.
The women rest their tired half-healed hearts; they are
    almost well.
Some of them will stay almost well always: the blunt-faced
    woman whose thinking dissolved
Under academic discipline; the manic-depressive girl
Now leveling off; one paranoiac afflicted with jealousy,
Another with persecution. Some alleviation has been
    possible.

O fortunate bride, who never again will become elated
    after childbirth!
O lucky older wife, who has been cured of feeling
    unwanted!
To the suburban railway station you will return, return,
To meet forever Jim home on the 5:35.

**Louise Bogan** *56*

You will be again as normal and selfish and heartless as
    anybody else.

There is life left: the piano says it with its octave smile.
The soft carpets pad the thump and splinter of the suicide
    to be.
Everything will be splendid: the grandmother will not
    drink habitually.
The fruit salad will bloom on the plate like a bouquet
And the garden produce the blue-ribbon aquilegia.
The cats will be glad; the fathers feel justified; the
    mothers relieved.
The sons and husbands will no longer need to pay the bills.
Childhoods will be put away, the obscene nightmare abated.

At the ends of the corridors the baths are running.
Mrs. C. again feels the shadow of the obsessive idea.
Miss R. looks at the mantel-piece, which must mean something.

---

**Evening in the sanitarium:** *This poem was originally
published with the subtitle "Imitated from Auden" and
parodies the latter's tendency, particularly in his early poems,
to make sociological observations in clinical terms and to
view the world as an enormous hospital in which everyone
is a patient.*

# Philip Booth

*Philip Booth, born 1925 in Hanover, New Hampshire,*
*lives with his wife and three daughters in Syracuse,*
*New York, and in a summer home on the shore of*
*Penobscot Bay, in Maine. He was educated at Dartmouth,*
*where he won a varsity letter as a member of the skiing*
*team, and in World War II served as a pilot in the*
*Air Force. He has taught at Bowdoin, Dartmouth,*
*Wellesley, and Syracuse where he is now professor of*
*English and poet-in-residence.*

## Ego

When I was on Night Line,
flying my hands to park
a big-bird B-29,
I used to command the dark:
four engines were mine

to jazz; I was ground-crew,
an unfledged pfc,
but when I waved planes through
that flight line in Tennessee,
my yonder was wild blue.

Warming up, I was hot
on the throttle, logging an hour
of combat, I was the pilot
who rogered the tower.
I used to take off a lot.

With a flat-hat for furlough
and tin wings to sleep on,
I fueled my high-octane ego:
I buzzed, I landed my jeep on
the ramp, I flew low.

When a cross-country hop
let down, I was the big deal
who signaled big wheels to stop.
That's how I used to feel.
I used to get all revved up.

## First lesson

Lie back, daughter, let your head
be tipped back in the cup of my hand.
Gently, and I will hold you. Spread
your arms wide, lie out on the stream
and look high at the gulls. A dead-
man's float is face down. You will dive
and swim soon enough where this tidewater
ebbs to the sea. Daughter, believe
me, when you tire on the long thrash
to your island, lie up, and survive.
As you float now, where I held you
and let go, remember when fear
cramps your heart what I told you:
lie gently and wide to the light-year
stars, lie back, and the sea will hold you.

# John Malcolm Brinnin

*John Malcolm Brinnin, born September 13, 1916, in
Halifax, Nova Scotia, lives in Cambridge and in Duxbury,
Massachusetts. He was educated at the University of
Michigan and at Harvard, taught at Vassar College and
the University of Connecticut, served as director of the
Poetry Center of the YM-YWHA in New York City from
1950 to 1956, and now teaches at Boston University.
Besides poetry, his books include the memoir* Dylan
Thomas in America *and the biography* The Third Rose:
Gertrude Stein and Her World.

## Hotel Paradiso e Commerciale

Another hill town:
another dry Cinzano in the sun.
I couldn't sleep in that enormous echo—
silence and water music, sickly street lamps
neither on nor off—a night
of islands and forgotten languages.

Yet morning, marvellously frank, comes up
with bells, with loaves, with letters
distributed like gifts. I watch a fat priest
spouting grape seeds, a family weeping
in the fumes of a departing bus.

This place is nowhere
but on the map. Wheels spin the sun,
with a white clatter shutters are shut to,
umbrellas bloom in striped and sudden groves.
The day's away, impossibly the same,
and only minutes are at all important—
if women by a wall,
a lean dog, and a cheerful humpback
selling gum and ball-points
are important. My glass is empty.
It is Wednesday. It is not going to rain.

Observation
without speculation. How soon
the eye craves what it cannot see,
goes limpid, glazed, unanswerable,
lights on a pigeon walking in a circle,
hangs on a random shadow,
would rather sleep.

How old am I?
What's missing here? What do these people
feed on that won't feed on them? This town
needs scrolls, celestial delegations,
a swoon of virgins, apostles in apple green,
a landscape riding on a holy shoulder.

The morning stays.
As though I kept an old appointment,
I start by the cats' corridors (*Banco di Roma*,
wineshops, gorgeous butcheries)
toward some mild angel of annunciation—
upstairs, most likely, badly lit,
speaking in rivets on a band of gold.

Praise God, this town keeps one
unheard-of masterpiece to justify
a million ordinary mornings
and pardon this one.

**John Malcolm Brinnin** *62*

# Nuns at eve

On St. Martin's evening green
Imaginary diamond, between
The vestry buttress and the convent wall,
Solemn as sea-birds in a sanctuary,
Under the statue of the Virgin they play baseball.
They are all named Mary,
Sister Mary, Mary Anthony or Mary Rose,
And when the softball flies
In the shadow of the cross
The little chaplet of the Virgin's hands
Contains their soft excitements like a house.

A flying habit traces
The unprecedented rounding of the bases
By Sister Mary Agatha, who thanks God
For the easy triple and turns her eyes toward home;
As *Mary, Mother, help me* echoes in her head,
Mild cries from the proud team
Encourage her, and the obliging sun,
Dazzling the pitcher's box
With a last celestial light upon
The gold-spiked halo of the Virgin in her niche,
Leads Sister Mary John to a wild pitch.

Prayer wins the game.
As Sister Mary Agatha comes sailing home
Through infield dusk, like birds fan-wise
In the vague cloisters of slow-rising mist,
Winners and losers gather in to praise
The fleetness of a bride of Christ.
Flushed and humble, Agatha collects the bats
And balls, while at her belt
Catcher's and pitcher's mitts
—Brute fingers, toes and gross lopsided heads—
Fumble the ropes of her long swinging beads.

# John Ciardi

*John Ciardi, born June 24, 1916, in Boston, lives with his wife and two children in Metuchen, New Jersey. He was educated at Bates College, Tufts College, and the University of Michigan and has taught at the University of Kansas City, Harvard, and Rutgers. During World War II he served in the Air Corps, flying many missions in the Pacific as an aerial gunner. He is an editor of the Saturday Review and a leading, sometimes controversial, spokesman for the dissemination and acceptance of the modern idiom in poetry.*

## Elegy just in case

Here lie Ciardi's pearly bones
In their ripe organic mess.
Jungle blown, his chromosomes
Breed to a new address.

Was it bullets or a wind
Or a rip-cord fouled on Chance?
Artifacts the natives find
Decorate them when they dance.

Here lies the sgt.'s mortal wreck
Lily spiked and termite kissed,

Spiders pendant from his neck
And a beetle on his wrist.

Bring the tic and southern flies
Where the land crabs run unmourning
Through a night of jungle skies
To a climeless morning.

And bring the chalked eraser here
Fresh from rubbing out his name.
Burn the crew-board for a bier.
(Also Colonel what's-his-name.)

Let no dice be stored and still.
Let no poker deck be torn.
But pour the smuggled rye until
The barracks threshold is outworn.

File the papers, pack the clothes,
Send the coded word through air—
"We regret and no one knows
Where the sgt. goes from here."

"Missing as of inst. oblige,
Deepest sorrow and remain—"
Shall I grin at persiflage?
Could I have my skin again

Would I choose a business form
Stilted mute as a giraffe,
Or a pinstripe unicorn
On a cashier's epitaph?

Darling, darling, just in case
Rivets fail or engines burn,
I forget the time and place
But your flesh was sweet to learn.

**John Ciardi**  *67*

Swift and single as a shark
I have seen you churn my sleep;
Now if beetles hunt my dark
What will beetles find to keep?

Fractured meat and open bone—
Nothing single or surprised.
Fragments of a written stone,
Undeciphered but surmised.

# Lucille Clifton

*Lucille Clifton, born June 27, 1936, in Depew, New York,
studied at Howard University for two years and more
briefly at New York State Teachers College at Fredonia.
Married, with six children, she lives in Baltimore,
Maryland. She has written two children's books and is
currently working on a long piece of nonfiction.*

## Miss Rosie

When I watch you
wrapped up like garbage
sitting, surrounded by the smell
of too old potato peels
or
when I watch you
in your old man's shoes
with the little toe cut out
sitting, waiting for your mind
like next week's grocery
I say
when I watch you
you wet brown bag of a woman
who used to be the best looking gal in Georgia
used to be called the Georgia Rose
I stand up
through your destruction
I stand up

## For deLawd

people say they have a hard time
understanding how I
go on about my business
playing my Ray Charles
hollering at the kids—
seem like my Afro
cut off in some old image
would show I got a long memory
and I come from a line
of black and going on women
who got used to making it through murdered sons
and who grief kept on pushing
who fried chicken
ironed
swept off the back steps
who grief kept
for their still alive sons
for their sons coming
for their sons gone
just pushing


## Good times

My Daddy has paid the rent
and the insurance man is gone
and the lights is back on
and my uncle Brud has hit
for one dollar straight
and they is good times
good times
good times

My Mama has made bread
and Grampaw has come

**Lucille Clifton** *71*

and everybody is drunk
and dancing in the kitchen
and singing in the kitchen
oh these is good times
good times
good times

oh children think about the
good times

# Tram Combs

*Tram Combs, born September 25, 1924, in Riverview,*
*Alabama, lives in St. Thomas, Virgin Islands, where he*
*is an antiquarian bookseller specializing in the literature*
*and history of the Caribbean and Latin America. He*
*studied physics at the University of California,*
*meteorology at the University of Chicago, and did*
*postgraduate work in electronic engineering at Harvard*
*and MIT. Before moving to St. Thomas in 1951, he lived*
*in San Francisco, where he was associated with many of*
*the writers who came into prominence with the Beat*
*Generation.*

## Ars poetica about ultimates

when    you    first    rub    up    against    God's    own    skin
He    turns    out    to    be    rougher    than    Christ's    men    most
   expect,
like    a    wood-rat,    -rasp    or    ravenous
connoisseur    with    tender    grapes       a    rough    trade!
yet    this    seduction    and    adoration
of    Him    we    must    get    done,    dangerous
though    it    go;       poetry's    ways're
strewn    with    the    early—de • railed,    • ridden,    • filed    who
heard    its    sirens;    and    rose    to    go
singing,    but    couldn't    make    it,    hammered
and    strove    but    with    beats    unsuccessful

to get on to come on with
the real jazz and sea     for one's
self, to reach      follow•, fellow•, father•
ship with Him!


**Aware aware**

that corner of earth
where I beat to death
some dozen of those oozing creatures
that feed on the garden's rottings
haunts me
they, too, sentient, Buddha—like, felt
and I hurt them

perhaps, though, it's the fresh un•life there
I sense that troubles me;
certainly my pangs to them were brief

cast here pyramidal we fleshes compete
for space, to feed     each on others     greens ——
our grace co-existence with mutual aid there-toward
    (in dry summers Thoreau would
    water the wood-land orchids.)
and he's most graceful in the butchery
who's most aware
all's done there.
    in these matters in space     of our meetings
    we 'rive to acts below the mind's potential
        visions.

animal cannibal creature born we strive to rise
by our mind's unsettling
lifts and ecstasies,
struggles
        we re•vere to this

         actuality   we
find   ourselves   apart   in,   unable   to   understand,
but   lift   from   our   closes   competing
         wolf,   ant,   mouse;
         and   flesh—eaters   will   eat   flesh  ——
thus   to   this   race
         in   these   our   circuits   temporary




**Just after noon with fierce shears**

just   after   noon   with   fierce   shears
I   set   to   at   the   hibiscus   trees,
hacking   away   their   under   branches,
for   a   tunnel   to   study   the   mornings   in.

then   at   the   banked—up   flower—beds  ——
withered   iris   out,   down   with   vines   dry   for   ten
         years  ——
sparing   with   care   the   life—lines   of   the   daisies  ——
         African,   orange  ——
that   plunge   like   comets   from   the   spindling   palm.

what   a   litter   on   the   slates'   dark—green!
rust   cans,   decay—gray'd   paper,   hunks   of   red   brick,
         wilting   leaves  ——
I   lean   against   the   wall   and   all's   silent.
and   keeping   the   silence   the   lizards   come  ——   one
         two   three

I   see   now,   six,   a   dozen   they   crawl
on   the   rotted   wood   chunks,   run   along   walls;
one   springs   to   a   vine   and   flows   down   it,   another
peers   'round   a   sphere   of   pink   lace.

the   bared   and   dying   all-ways   of   their   world

**Tram Combs**   *76*

they    stare    at,    walk    over.
once    in    a    life
such    wonder.

# E. E. Cummings

E. E. Cummings was born October 14, 1894, in Cambridge,
Massachusetts, and, until his death in September, 1962,
lived with his wife, the photographer and former fashion
model Marion Morehouse, in Greenwich Village, New
York City, and in Silver Lake, New Hampshire. He was
educated at Harvard and in World War I served with the
Norton Harjes Ambulance Corps in France, where,
through an error on the part of a military censor, he was
imprisoned in a detention camp for three months, an
experience recorded in his famous book The Enormous
Room. Some of his works beside poetry include the play
Him; the unorthodox journal of a trip through the Soviet
Union, Eimi; and the published text of talks delivered
when he was the Charles Eliot Norton lecturer at Harvard
in 1952, i: six nonlectures. Eccentricity of language,
punctuation, and typography is the hallmark of his
poetry, and in his "nonlectures" he reasserted his lifelong
position as an iconoclast, an individualist, an enemy of
systems and restriction and regimentation.


## nobody loses all the time

nobody loses all the time

i had an uncle named
Sol who was a born failure and

nearly everybody said he should have gone
into vaudeville perhaps because my Uncle Sol could
sing McCann He Was A Diver on Xmas Eve like Hell Itself which
may or may not account for the fact that my Uncle

Sol indulged in that possibly most inexcusable
of all to use a highfalootin phrase
luxuries that is or to
wit farming and be
it needlessly
added

my Uncle Sol's farm
failed because the chickens
ate the vegetables so
my Uncle Sol had a
chicken farm till the
skunks ate the chickens when

my Uncle Sol
had a skunk farm but
the skunks caught cold and
died and so
my Uncle Sol imitated the
skunks in a subtle manner

or by drowning himself in the watertank
but somebody who'd given my Uncle Sol a Victor
Victrola and records while he lived presented to
him upon the auspicious occasion of his decease a
scrumptious not to mention splendiferous funeral with
tall boys in black gloves and flowers and everything and

i remember we all cried like the Missouri
when my Uncle Sol's coffin lurched because

somebody pressed a button
(and down went
my Uncle
Sol

and started a worm farm)




**anyone lived in a pretty how town**

anyone lived in a pretty how town
(with up so floating many bells down)
spring summer autumn winter
he sang his didn't he danced his did.

Women and men(both little and small)
cared for anyone not at all
they sowed their isn't they reaped their same
sun moon stars rain

children guessed(but only a few
and down they forgot as up they grew
autumn winter spring summer)
that noone loved him more by more

when by now and tree by leaf
she laughed his joy she cried his grief
bird by snow and stir by still
anyone's any was all to her

someones married their everyones
laughed their cryings and did their dance
(sleep wake hope and then)they
said their nevers they slept their dream

stars rain sun moon
(and only the snow can begin to explain
how children are apt to forget to remember
with up so floating many bells down)
one day anyone died i guess
(and noone stooped to kiss his face)
busy folk buried them side by side
little by little and was by was

all by all and deep by deep
and more by more they dream their sleep
noone and anyone earth by april
wish by spirit and if by yes.

Women and men (both dong and ding)
summer autumn winter spring
reaped their sowing and went their came
sun moon stars rain


**somewhere i have never travelled, gladly beyond**

somewhere i have never travelled,gladly beyond
any experience,your eyes have their silence:
in your most frail gesture are things which enclose me,
or which i cannot touch because they are too near

your slightest look easily will unclose me
though i have closed myself as fingers,
you open always petal by petal myself as Spring opens
(touching skilfully,mysteriously) her first rose

or if your wish be to close me,i and
my life will shut very beautifully,suddenly,

as when the heart of this flower imagines
the snow carefully everywhere descending;

nothing which we are to perceive in this world equals
the power of your intense fragility:whose texture
compels me with the colour of its countries,
rendering death and forever with each breathing
(i do not know what it is about you that closes
and opens;only something in me understands
the voice of your eyes is deeper than all roses)
nobody,not even the rain,has such small hands


## when serpents bargain for the right to squirm

when serpents bargain for the right to squirm
and the sun strikes to gain a living wage—
when thorns regard their roses with alarm
and rainbows are insured against old age

when every thrush may sing no new moon in
if all screech-owls have not okayed his voice
—and any wave signs on the dotted line
or else an ocean is compelled to close

when the oak begs permission of the birch
to make an acorn—valleys accuse their
mountains of having altitude—and march
denounces april as a saboteur

then we'll believe in that incredible
unanimal mankind(and not until)

---

**anyone lived in a pretty how town:** *This poem, written in
the sort of rhythm children naturally fall into when they are
playing games or skipping rope, tells a very old and very*

*simple story: two little people, "anyone" and "noone," meet,*
*fall in love, marry, and die. These greatest of human events*
*take place against the wheeling movements of the seasons*
*and the stars, to which they are intimately related in life but*
*completely anonymous in time.*

# Peter Davison

*Peter Davison, born June 27, 1928, in New York City, lives in Cambridge, Massachusetts, with his wife and two children. A son of the English poet, Edward Davison, he was educated at Harvard College and Cambridge University, served for a time as a page in the United States Senate, and then as a sergeant in the Army. He is director of the Atlantic Monthly Press in Boston.*

## Lunch at the Coq D'or

The place is called the Golden Cock. Napkins
Stand up like trumpets under every chin.
Each noon at table tycoons crow
And flap their wings around each other's shoulders.
Crumbling bread, I wade at the edge of whiskey
Waiting for my man to embody himself
Until in time he shadows the head waiter
And plumps his bottom in the other chair.
Once he is seated with his alibis
We order drinks, we talk. His voice is rich.
Letters I had written him all winter
Had washed my mind of him, till Purdy,
Warm of heart and hearty of handshake,
Had shrunk into a signature, a stamp.
The fine print vanishes. I see him plain.
I know my man. Purdy's a hard-nosed man.

Another round for us. It's good to work
With such a man. "Purdy," I hear myself,
"It's good to work with you." I raise
My arm, feathery in the dim light, and extend
Until the end of it brushes his padded shoulder.
"Purdy, how are you? How you doodle do?"


## The star watcher

*For R. F.*

Stars had the look of dogs to him sometimes,
Sometimes of bears and more than once of flowers,
But stars were never strange to him because
Of where they stood. We knew him jealous
And in his younger days a little sly
About his place among the poesies;
Yet when his eyes showed envy or delight
They rested upon knowledge, not on distance.
All that he saw, up close or farther off,
Was capable of being understood,
Though not by him perhaps. He had enough
Of science in him to be optimistic,
Enough of tragedy to know the worst,
Enough of wit to keep on listening,
Or watching, when it came to stars. He knew,
Across the distance that their light might travel,
That nothing matters to the stars but matter,
Yet that their watchers have to learn the difference
Between the facts of knowledge and of love,
Or of love's opposite, which might be hate.
Therefore he taught, and, like the best of teachers,
Often annoyed the students at his feet,
Whether they learned too much or not enough,
Whether or not they understood him wrong.
Two was his pleasure, and the balance held

In love, in conversation, or in verse.
With knuckles like burled hemlock roots, his hands
Had, in his age, smooth palms as white as milk;
And, through the massy cloudbanks of his brows,
His eyes burned shrewdly as emerging stars.

# James Dickey

*James Dickey, born February 2, 1923, in Atlanta, Georgia,
attended Vanderbilt University and served as a fighter
pilot in World War II and in the Korean War. For a
number of years he followed an executive career in the
field of advertising, but eventually turned all of his
attention to writing and to teaching at Reed College, the
University of Wisconsin, and elsewhere. Ingeniously
dramatic, Dickey's work has brought him to the forefront
of American poetry with a swiftness almost without
precedent.*

## For the nightly ascent of the hunter Orion over a forest clearing

Now secretness dies of the open.
Yet all around, all over, night
Things are waking fast,
Waking with all their power.
Who can arise

From his dilating shadow
When one foot is longing to tiptoe
And the other to take the live
Stand of a tree that belongs here?
As the owl's gaze

Most slowly begins to create
Its sight from the death of the sun,

As the mouse feels the whole wood turn
The gold of the owl's new eyes,
And the fox moves

Out of the ground where he sleeps,
No man can stand upright
And drag his body forth
Through an open space in the foliage
Unless he rises

As does the hunter Orion,
Thinking to cross a blue hollow
Through the dangers of twilight,
Feeling that he must run
And that he will

Take root forever and stand,
Does both at once, and neither,
Grows blind, and then sees everything,
Steps and becomes a man
Of stars instead,

Who from invisibility
Has come, arranged in the light
Of himself, revealed tremendously
In his fabulous, rigid, eternal
Unlooked-for role.


## Cherrylog Road

Off Highway 106
At Cherrylog Road I entered
The '34 Ford without wheels,
Smothered in kudzu,
With a seat pulled out to run
Corn whiskey down from the hills,

And then from the other side
Crept into an Essex
With a rumble seat of red leather
And then out again, aboard
A blue Chevrolet, releasing
The rust from its other color,

Reared up on three building blocks.
None had the same body heat;
I changed with them inward, toward
The weedy heart of the junkyard,
For I knew that Doris Holbrook
Would escape from her father at noon

And would come from the farm
To seek parts owned by the sun
Among the abandoned chassis,
Sitting in each in turn
As I did, leaning forward
As in a wild stock-car race

In the parking lot of the dead.
Time after time, I climbed in
And out the other side, like
An envoy or movie star
Met at the station by crickets.
A radiator cap raised its head,

Become a real toad or a kingsnake
As I neared the hub of the yard,
Passing through many states,
Many lives, to reach
Some grandmother's long Pierce-Arrow
Sending platters of blindness forth

From its nickel hubcaps
And spilling its tender upholstery
On sleepy roaches,

The glass panel in between
Lady and colored driver
Not all the way broken out,

The back-seat phone
Still on its hook.
I got in as though to exclaim,
"Let us go to the orphan asylum,
John; I have some old toys
For children who say their prayers."

I popped with sweat as I thought
I heard Doris Holbrook scrape
Like a mouse in the southern-state sun
That was eating the paint in blisters
From a hundred car tops and hoods.
She was tapping like code,

Loosening the screws,
Carrying off headlights,
Sparkplugs, bumpers,
Cracked mirrors and gear-knobs,
Getting ready, already,
To go back with something to show

Other than her lips' new trembling
I would hold to me soon, soon,
Where I sat in the ripped back seat
Talking over the interphone,
Praying for Doris Holbrook
To come from her father's farm

And to get back there
With no trace of me on her face
To be seen by her red-haired father
Who would change, in the squalling barn,
Her back's pale skin with a strop,
Then lay for me

**James Dickey** 92

In a bootlegger's roasting car
With a string-triggered 12-gauge shotgun
To blast the breath from the air.
Not cut by the jagged windshields,
Through the acres of wrecks she came
With a wrench in her hand,

Through dust where the blacksnake dies
Of boredom, and the beetle knows
The compost has no more life.
Someone outside would have seen
The oldest car's door inexplicably
Close from within:

I held her and held her and held her,
Convoyed at terrific speed
By the stalled, dreaming traffic around us,
So the blacksnake, stiff
With inaction, curved back
Into life, and hunted the mouse

With deadly overexcitement,
The beetles reclaimed their field
As we clung, glued together,
With the hooks of the seat springs
Working through to catch us red-handed
Amidst the gray breathless batting

That burst from the seat at our backs.
We left by separate doors
Into the changed, other bodies
Of cars, she down Cherrylog Road
And I to my motorcycle
Parked like the soul of the junkyard

Restored, a bicycle fleshed
With power, and tore off

Up Highway 106, continually
Drunk on the wind in my mouth,
Wringing the handlebar for speed,
Wild to be wreckage forever.

# Alan Dugan

*Alan Dugan, born February 12, 1923, in Brooklyn,
New York, is a graduate of Mexico City College and has
taught at Connecticut College for Women, Sarah
Lawrence, and the University of North Carolina at
Greensboro ("all girls' schools," he says, "an interesting
fate, and enjoyable.") His first book, published in 1961,
was given the Yale Series of Younger Poets Award, the
National Book Award, and the Pulitzer Prize. His
Collected Poems were published in 1969.*

## Memorial service for the invasion beach
## where the vacation in the flesh is over

I see that there it is on the beach. It is
ahead of me and I walk toward it: its
following vultures and contemptible dogs
are with it, and I walk toward it. If,
in the approach to it, I turn my back
to it, then I walk backwards: I
approach it as a limit. Even if I fall
to hands and knees, I crawl to it.
Backwards or forwards I approach it.

There is the land on one hand, rising, and
the ocean on the other, falling away;
what the sky does, I can not look to see,
but it's around, as ever, all around.

The courteous vultures move away in groups
like functionaries. The dogs circle and stare
like working police. One wants a heel
and gets it. I approach it, concentrating so
on not approaching it, going so far away
that when I get there I am sideways like
the crab, too limited by carapace to say:

"Oh here I am arrived, all; yours today."
No: kneeling and facing away, I will
fall over backwards in intensity of life
and lie convulsed, downed struggling,
sideways even, and should a vulture ask
an eye as its aperitif, I grant it,
glad for the moment wrestling by a horse
whose belly has been hollowed from the rear,
who's eyeless. The wild dog trapped in its ribs
grins as it eats its way to freedom. Not
conquered outwardly, and after rising once,
I fall away inside, and see the sky around
rush out away into the vulture's craw
and barely can not hear them calling, "Here's one."

## The mirror perilous

I guess there is a garden named
"Garden of Love." If so, I'm in it:
I am the guesser in the garden.
There is a notice by the central pond
that reads: "Property of Narcissus.
Trespass at your own risk,"
so I went there. That is where,
having won but disdained a lady,
he fell for his own face and died,
rightly, "not having followed through,"
as the sentence read, read by the lady:

**Alan Dugan**   *97*

Oh you could hear her crying all about
the wilderness and wickedness of law.
I looked in that famous mirror perilous
and it wasn't much: my own face,
beautiful, and at the bottom,
bone, a rusty knife, two beads,
and something else I cannot name.
I drank my own lips on the dare
but could not drink the lips away.
The water was heavy, cool, and clear,
but did not quench. A lady laughed
behind my back; I learned the worst:
I could take it or leave it, go or stay,
and went back to the office drunk,
possessed of an echo but not a fate.

# Richard Eberhart

*Richard Eberhart, born April 5, 1904, in Austin,*
*Minnesota, lives with his wife and two children in*
*Hanover, New Hampshire, where he is professor of*
*English at Dartmouth College. He studied at the*
*University of Minnesota for two years, graduated from*
*Dartmouth, and then continued his education at*
*Cambridge, where he was a student of I. A. Richards,*
*and later at Harvard. In 1930 he spent a year as tutor to*
*the son of King Prajadhipok of Siam. He has taught at*
*St. Mark's School and, for short periods, at a number of*
*American universities, including Washington, Connecticut,*
*and Princeton. During World War II he served in the*
*Navy and was a lieutenant commander at the time of his*
*discharge. From 1959 to 1961 he was Consultant in Poetry*
*at the Library of Congress.*

## New Hampshire, February

Nature had made them hide in crevices,
Two wasps so cold they looked like bark.
Why I do not know, but I took them
And I put them
In a metal pan, both day and dark.

Like God touching his finger to Adam
I felt, and thought of Michaelangelo,

For whenever I breathed on them,
The slightest breath,
They leaped, and preened as if to go.

My breath controlled them always quite.
More sensitive than electric sparks
They came into life
Or they withdrew to ice,
While I watched, suspending remarks.

Then one in a blind career got out,
And fell to the kitchen floor. I
Crushed him with my cold ski boot,
By accident. The other
Had not the wit to try or die.

And so the other is still my pet.
The moral of this is plain.
But I will shirk it.
You will not like it. And
God does not live to explain.


**The fury of aerial bombardment**

You would think the fury of aerial bombardment
Would rouse God to relent; the infinite spaces
Are still silent. He looks on shock-pried faces.
History, even, does not know what is meant.

You would feel that after so many centuries
God would give man to repent; yet he can kill
As Cain could, but with multitudinous will,
No farther advanced than in his ancient furies.

Was man made stupid to see his own stupidity?
Is God by definition indifferent, beyond us all?

**Richard Eberhart**  *101*

TEXAS STATE TECHNICAL INSTITUTE
ROLLING PLAINS CAMPUS – LIBRARY
SWEETWATER, TEXAS  79556

Is the eternal truth man's fighting soul
Wherein the Beast ravens in his own avidity?

Of Van Wettering I speak, and Averill,
Names on a list, whose faces I do not recall
But they are gone to early death, who late in school
Distinguished the belt feed lever from the belt holding pawl.

# T. S. Eliot

T. S. Eliot, born September 26, 1888, in St. Louis,
Missouri, died in 1965 in London where he lived with his
second wife and served as a director of a publishing house.
Educated at Milton Academy, Harvard, the Sorbonne,
and Merton College, Oxford, he made his home in
England after World War I and became a British subject
in 1927. His eminence as a poet was internationally
recognized and as a critic he was a leading arbiter of
taste in literature. The range of his work encompassed
both epic poetry—The Waste Land—and doggerel verse—
Old Possum's Book of Practical Cats—and he was the
only modern poet to have achieved wide public success
in the field of poetic drama, notably with The Cocktail
Party and Murder in the Cathedral. He made frequent
trips to the United States, on each of which he gave a
limited number of public readings. At an appearance at
the University of Minnesota he drew more people to hear
him, it was noted, than any poet since Sophocles. He was
awarded the Nobel Prize in 1948.

## Preludes

I

The winter evening settles down
With smell of steaks in passageways.
Six o'clock.
The burnt-out ends of smoky days.

And now a gusty shower wraps
The grimy scraps
Of withered leaves about your feet
And newspapers from vacant lots;
The showers beat
On broken blinds and chimney-pots,
And at the corner of the street
A lonely cab-horse steams and stamps.
And then the lighting of the lamps.

II

The morning comes to consciousness
Of faint stale smells of beer
From the sawdust-trampled street
With all its muddy feet that press
To early coffee-stands.
With the other masquerades
That time resumes,
One thinks of all the hands
That are raising dingy shades
In a thousand furnished rooms.

III

You tossed a blanket from the bed,
You lay upon your back, and waited;
You dozed, and watched the night revealing
The thousand sordid images
Of which your soul was constituted;
They flickered against the ceiling.
And when all the world came back
And the light crept up between the shutters
And you heard the sparrows in the gutters,
You had such a vision of the street
As the street hardly understands;
Sitting along the bed's edge, where
You curled the papers from your hair,
Or clasped the yellow soles of feet
In the palms of both soiled hands.

**T. S. Eliot**  *105*

IV

His soul stretched tight across the skies
That fade behind a city block,
Or trampled by insistent feet
At four and five and six o'clock;
And short square fingers stuffing pipes,
And evening newspapers, and eyes
Assured of certain certainties,
The conscience of a blackened street
Impatient to assume the world.

I am moved by fancies that are curled
Around these images, and cling:
The notion of some infinitely gentle
Infinitely suffering thing.

Wipe your hand across your mouth, and laugh;
The worlds revolve like ancient women
Gathering fuel in vacant lots.


## The love song of J. Alfred Prufrock

*S'io credesse che mia risposta fosse*
*A persona che mai tornasse al mondo,*
*Questa fiamma staria senza piu scosse.*
*Ma perciocche giammai di questo fondo*
*Non torno vivo alcun, s'i'odo il vero,*
*Senza tema d'infamia ti rispondo.*

Let us go then, you and I,
When the evening is spread out against the sky
Like a patient etherised upon a table;
Let us go, through certain half-deserted streets,
The muttering retreats
Of restless nights in one-night cheap hotels
And sawdust restaurants with oyster-shells:
Streets that follow like a tedious argument

**T. S. Eliot**   *106*

Of insidious intent
To lead you to an overwhelming question . . .
Oh, do not ask, "What is it?"
Let us go and make our visit.

In the room the women come and go
Talking of Michelangelo.

The yellow fog that rubs its back upon the window-panes,
The yellow smoke that rubs its muzzle on the window-panes
Licked its tongue into the corners of the evening,
Lingered upon the pools that stand in drains,
Let fall upon its back the soot that falls from chimneys,
Slipped by the terrace, made a sudden leap,
And seeing that it was a soft October night,
Curled once about the house, and fell asleep.

And indeed there will be time
For the yellow smoke that slides along the street,
Rubbing its back upon the window-panes;
There will be time, there will be time
To prepare a face to meet the faces that you meet;
There will be time to murder and create,
And time for all the works and days of hands
That lift and drop a question on your plate;
Time for you and time for me,
And time yet for a hundred indecisions,
And for a hundred visions and revisions,
Before the taking of a toast and tea.

In the room the women come and go
Talking of Michelangelo.

And indeed there will be time
To wonder, "Do I dare?" and, "Do I dare?"
Time to turn back and descend the stair,
With a bald spot in the middle of my hair—
[They will say: "How his hair is growing thin!"]

**T. S. Eliot** *107*

My morning coat, my collar mounting firmly to the chin,
My necktie rich and modest, but asserted by a simple pin—
[They will say: "But how his arms and legs are thin!"]
Do I dare
Disturb the universe?
In a minute there is time
For decisions and revisions which a minute will reverse.

For I have known them all already, known them all:—
Have known the evenings, mornings, afternoons,
I have measured out my life with coffee spoons;
I know the voices dying with a dying fall
Beneath the music from a farther room.
        So how should I presume?

And I have known the eyes already, known them all—
The eyes that fix you in a formulated phrase,
And when I am formulated, sprawling on a pin,
When I am pinned and wriggling on the wall,
Then how should I begin
To spit out all the butt-ends of my days and ways?
        And how should I presume?

And I have known the arms already, known them all—
Arms that are braceleted and white and bare
[But in the lamplight, downed with light brown hair!]
Is it perfume from a dress
That makes me so digress?
Arms that lie along a table, or wrap about a shawl.
        And should I then presume?
        And how should I begin?

                    .   .   .   .   .

Shall I say, I have gone at dusk through narrow streets
And watched the smoke that rises from the pipes
Of lonely men in shirt-sleeves, leaning out of windows? . . .

**T. S. Eliot**  *108*

I should have been a pair of ragged claws
Scuttling across the floors of silent seas.

. . . . .

And the afternoon, the evening, sleeps so peacefully!
Smoothed by long fingers,
Asleep . . . tired . . . or it malingers,
Stretched on the floor, here beside you and me.
Should I, after tea and cakes and ices,
Have the strength to force the moment to its crisis?
But though I have wept and fasted, wept and prayed,
Though I have seen my head [grown slightly bald] brought in upon
    a platter,
I am no prophet—and here's no great matter;
I have seen the moment of my greatness flicker,
And I have seen the eternal Footman hold my coat, and snicker,
And in short, I was afraid.

    And would it have been worth it, after all,
After the cups, the marmalade, the tea,
Among the porcelain, among some talk of you and me,
Would it have been worth while,
To have bitten off the matter with a smile,
To have squeezed the universe into a ball
To roll it toward some overwhelming question,
To say: "I am Lazarus, come from the dead,
Come back to tell you all, I shall tell you all"—
If one, settling a pillow by her head,
        Should say: "That is not what I meant at all.
        That is not it, at all."

    And would it have been worth it, after all,
Would it have been worth while,
After the sunsets and the dooryards and the sprinkled streets,
After the novels, after the teacups, after the skirts that trail along
    the floor—

And this, and so much more?—
It is impossible to say just what I mean!
But as if a magic lantern threw the nerves in patterns on a screen:
Would it have been worth while
If one, settling a pillow or throwing off a shawl,
And turning toward the window, should say:
    "That is not it at all,
    That is not what I meant, at all."


      .  .  .  .  .


No! I am not Prince Hamlet, nor was meant to be;
Am an attendant lord, one that will do
To swell a progress, start a scene or two,
Advise the prince; no doubt, an easy tool,
Deferential, glad to be of use,
Politic, cautious, and meticulous;
Full of high sentence, but a bit obtuse;
At times, indeed, almost ridiculous—
Almost, at times, the Fool.

    I grow old . . . I grow old . . .
I shall wear the bottoms of my trousers rolled.

    Shall I part my hair behind? Do I dare to eat a peach?
I shall wear white flannel trousers, and walk upon the beach.
I have heard the mermaids singing, each to each.

    I do not think that they will sing to me.

    I have seen them riding seaward on the waves
Combing the white hair of the waves blown back
When the wind blows the water white and black.

    We have lingered in the chambers of the sea
By sea-girls wreathed with seaweed red and brown
Till human voices wake us, and we drown.

**T. S. Eliot**   *110*

# Portrait of a lady

*Thou hast committed—*
*Fornication: but that was in another country,*
*And besides, the wench is dead.*
THE JEW OF MALTA

I

Among the smoke and fog of a December afternoon
You have the scene arrange itself—as it will seem to do—
With "I have saved this afternoon for you";
And four wax candles in the darkened room,
Four rings of light upon the ceiling overhead,
An atmosphere of Juliet's tomb
Prepared for all the things to be said, or left unsaid.
We have been, let us say, to hear the latest Pole
Transmit the Preludes, through his hair and fingertips.
"So intimate, this Chopin, that I think his soul
Should be resurrected only among friends
Some two or three, who will not touch the bloom
That is rubbed and questioned in the concert room."
—And so the conversation slips
Among velleities and carefully caught regrets
Through attenuated tones of violins
Mingled with remote cornets
And begins.
"You do not know how much they mean to me, my friends,
And how, how rare and strange it is, to find
In a life composed so much, so much of odds and ends,
[For indeed I do not love it . . . you knew? you are not blind!
How keen you are!]
To find a friend who has these qualities,
Who has, and gives
Those qualities upon which friendship lives.
How much it means that I say this to you—
Without these friendships—life, what *cauchemar!*"

Among the windings of the violins
And the ariettes

**T. S. Eliot** *111*

Of cracked cornets
Inside my brain a dull tom-tom begins
Absurdly hammering a prelude of its own,
Capricious monotone
That is at least one definite "false note."
—Let us take the air, in a tobacco trance,
Admire the monuments,
Discuss the late events,
Correct our watches by the public clocks.
Then sit for half an hour and drink our bocks.

## II

Now that lilacs are in bloom
She has a bowl of lilacs in her room
And twists one in her fingers while she talks.
"Ah, my friend, you do not know, you do not know
What life is, you who hold it in your hands";
(Slowly twisting the lilac stalks)
"You let it flow from you, you let it flow,
And youth is cruel, and has no remorse
And smiles at situations which it cannot see."
I smile, of course,
And go on drinking tea.
"Yet with these April sunsets, that somehow recall
My buried life, and Paris in the Spring,
I feel immeasurably at peace, and find the world
To be wonderful and youthful, after all."

The voice returns like the insistent out-of-tune
Of a broken violin on an August afternoon:
"I am always sure that you understand
My feelings, always sure that you feel,
Sure that across the gulf you reach your hand.

You are invulnerable, you have no Achilles' heel.
You will go on, and when you have prevailed
You can say: at this point many a one has failed.
But what have I, but what have I, my friend,

To give you, what can you receive from me?
Only the friendship and the sympathy
Of one about to reach her journey's end.

I shall sit here, serving tea to friends. . . ."

I take my hat: how can I make a cowardly amends
For what she has said to me?
You will see me any morning in the park
Reading the comics and the sporting page.
Particularly I remark
An English countess goes upon the stage.
A Greek was murdered at a Polish dance,
Another bank defaulter has confessed.
I keep my countenance,
I remain self-possessed
Except when a street piano, mechanical and tired
Reiterates some worn-out common song
With the smell of hyacinths across the garden
Recalling things that other people have desired.
Are these ideas right or wrong?

III

The October night comes down; returning as before
Except for a slight sensation of being ill at ease
I mount the stairs and turn the handle of the door
And feel as if I had mounted on my hands and knees.
"And so you are going abroad; and when do you return?
But that's a useless question.
You hardly know when you are coming back,
You will find so much to learn."
My smile falls heavily among the bric-à-brac.

"Perhaps you can write to me."
My self-possession flares up for a second;
This is as I had reckoned.
"I had been wondering frequently of late
(But our beginnings never know our ends!)

**T. S. Eliot**  *113*

Why we have not developed into friends."
I feel like one who smiles, and turning shall remark
Suddenly, his expression in a glass.
My self-possession gutters; we are really in the dark.

   "For everybody said so, all our friends,
They all were sure our feelings would relate
So closely! I myself can hardly understand.
We must leave it now to fate.
You will write, at any rate.
Perhaps it is not too late.
I shall sit here, serving tea to friends."

   And I must borrow every changing shape
To find expression . . . dance, dance
Like a dancing bear,
Cry like a parrot, chatter like an ape.
Let us take the air, in a tobacco trance—

   Well! and what if she should die some afternoon,
Afternoon grey and smoky, evening yellow and rose;
Should die and leave me sitting pen in hand
With the smoke coming down above the housetops;
Doubtful, for a while
Not knowing what to feel or if I understand
Or whether wise or foolish, tardy or too soon . . .
Would she not have the advantage, after all?
This music is successful with a "dying fall"
Now that we talk of dying—
And should I have the right to smile?


**Journey of the Magi**

'A cold coming we had of it,
Just the worst time of the year
For a journey, and such a long journey:
The ways deep and the weather sharp,

The very dead of winter.'
And the camels galled, sore-footed, refractory,
Lying down in the melting snow.
There were times we regretted
The summer palaces on slopes, the terraces,
And the silken girls bringing sherbet.
Then the camel men cursing and grumbling
And running away, and wanting their liquor and women,
And the night-fires going out, and the lack of shelters.
And the cities hostile and the towns unfriendly
And the villages dirty and charging high prices:
A hard time we had of it.
At the end we preferred to travel all night,
Sleeping in snatches,
With the voices singing in our ears, saying
That this was all folly.

Then at dawn we came down to a temperate valley,
Wet, below the snow line, smelling of vegetation;
With a running stream and a water-mill beating the darkness,
And three trees on the low sky,
And an old white horse galloped away in the meadow.
Then we came to a tavern with vine-leaves over the lintel,
Six hands at an open door dicing for pieces of silver,
And feet kicking the empty wine-skins.
But there was no information, and so we continued
And arrived at evening, not a moment too soon
Finding the place; it was (you may say) satisfactory.

All this was a long time ago, I remember,
And I would do it again, but set down
This set down
This: were we led all that way for
Birth or Death? There was a Birth, certainly,
We had evidence and no doubt. I had seen birth and death,
But had thought they were different; this Birth was
Hard and bitter agony for us, like Death, our death.
We returned to our places, these Kingdoms,

But no longer at ease here, in the old dispensation,
With an alien people clutching their gods.
I should be glad of another death.

---

**The love song of J. Alfred Prufrock:** *The epigraph to this
poem may be translated thus: "If I thought that my reply
would be to one who would ever return to the world, this
flame would stay without further movement; but since none
has ever returned alive from this depth, if what I hear is true,
I answer you without fear of infamy" (Dante, Inferno, XXVII,
61–66). These are the words spoken to Dante by Guido da
Montelfeltro, who is shut up in his flame as punishment for
having been a false counselor. He tells of his evil doings
because he thinks that Dante, like himself, is doomed never
to return to earth.*

*The speaker of this dramatic monologue is an acutely
sensitive and self-conscious man who feels out of place in
the only society he knows. He details the triviality of his
existence, sees himself in various dramatic attitudes, all of
which he realizes are absurd, and finally invokes a fantasy
world of beauty and simplicity—a world from which he is
kept by the intrusions of reality.*

**Portrait of a lady:** *As in the case of many likenesses made by
painters, this portrait tells more about the artist than it does
about the subject. The young man who is involved in an
ambiguous relationship with an older woman at first feels
superior to her and her obvious romantic pretensions.
However, as he continues to see her through the course of a
year, his attitude toward her undergoes a change: she may
be foolish and hopelessly romantic, but his own character is
not sufficiently resolved to allow him to maintain the
smugness that marked their earlier encounters. As the
epigraph suggests, he would like to feel that this episode is
over and done with; but uncertainty plagues him. He has
done a kind of violence to a woman and begins to suspect
that his unresolved emotions are as damaging to himself as
they have been to her.*

**Journey of the Magi:** *Long after the event, one of the three
wise men who journeyed to the place of Christ's birth here
recalls his long trek from the East and meditates upon the
meaning of that experience.*

**T. S. Eliot** *116*

# D. J. Enright

*D. J. Enright, born March 11, 1920, in Leamington,*
*Warwickshire, lives with his wife and daughter in*
*Singapore, where he teaches at the University of Malaya.*
*He was educated at Leamington College and Downing*
*College, Cambridge, and then took teaching assignments*
*in England, Egypt, Japan, Germany, and Thailand before*
*assuming his present post. His acerbity as a commentator*
*on modern letters is demonstrated in a collection of his*
*critical writings entitled* Conspirators and Poets.

## The laughing hyena, by Hokusai

For him, it seems, everything was molten. Court-ladies flow in gentle
    streams,
Or, gathering lotus, strain sideways from their curving boat,
A donkey prances, or a kite dances in the sky, or soars like sacrificial
    smoke.
All is flux: waters fall and leap, and bridges leap and fall.
Even his Tortoise undulates, and his Spring Hat is lively as a pool
    of fish.
All he ever saw was sea: a sea of marble splinters—
Long bright fingers claw across his pages, fjords and islands and
    shatter trees—

And the Laughing Hyena, cavalier of evil, as volcanic as the rest:
Elegant in a flowered gown, a face like a bomb-burst,

Featured with fangs and built about a rigid laugh,
Ever moving, like a pond's surface where a corpse has sunk.

Between the raised talons of the right hand rests an object—
At rest, like a pale island in a savage sea—a child's head,
Immobile, authentic, torn and bloody—
The point of repose in the picture, the point of movement in us.

Terrible enough, this demon. Yet it is present and perfect,
Firm as its horns, curling among its thick and handsome hair.
I find it an honest visitant, even consoling, after all
Those sententious phantoms, choked with rage and uncertainty,
Who grimace from contemporary pages. It, at least,
Knows exactly why it laughs.


## University examinations in Egypt

The air is thick with nerves and smoke: pens tremble in sweating hands:
Domestic police flit in and out, with smelling salts and aspirin:
And servants, grave-faced but dirty, pace the aisles,
With coffee, Players and Coca-Cola.

Was it like this in my day, at my place? Memory boggles
Between the aggressive fly and curious ant—but did I really
Pause in my painful flight to light a cigarette or swallow drugs?

The nervous eye, patrolling these hot unhappy victims,
Flinches at the symptoms of a year's hard teaching—
'Falstaff indulged in drinking and sexcess', and then,
'Doolittle was a dusty man' and 'Dr. Jonson edited the Yellow Book.'

Culture and aspirin: the urgent diploma, the straining brain—all in
   the evening fall
To tric-trac in the café, to Hollywood in the picture-house:
Behind, like tourist posters, the glamour of laws and committees,
Wars for freedom, cheap textbooks, national aspirations—

**D. J. Enright**  *119*

And, farther still and very faint, the foreign ghost of happy Shakespeare,
Keats who really loved things, Akhenaton who adored the Sun,
And Goethe who never thought of Thought.

---

**University examinations in Egypt:** *Players are British
cigarettes; Akhenaton was a king of ancient Egypt who
believed that the sun was god and god alone and attempted
to found a new religion based on his belief.*

**D. J. Enright**  *120*

# Irving Feldman

*Irving Feldman, born September 22, 1928, in Coney Island, New York, lives with his wife and young son in Buffalo where he is professor of English at the State University of New York. Educated at the City College of New York and at Columbia University, he began writing with the encouragement of the critic Lionel Trilling. Subsequently he taught for a number of years at the University of Puerto Rico, in Rio Piedras and in Mayaguez, where he met his wife, and then spent two years in France on a Fulbright Fellowship.*

## The death of Vitellozzo Vitelli

Vitelli rides west toward Fano, the morning sun
Has spread his shadow before him, his head is cast
Upon the road beyond the horse, and now in vain

He works his spurs and whip. For all his speed, his past
Like a heavy wind has thrown his death far before
Him, and not till midday shall he fill the waste

Of light he has made with the goldness of his spur
And the greenness of his cape. Then shall he stand
At last by the bridge at Fano and know no more

His way than the farmer at noon who looks from his land
To his heart and knows not where next to turn his plow;
Or lovers who have stayed abed and reach a hand

And yet have turned away, even as they do so,
To move their legs and sigh, wearied of their embrace
—Yet nothing else seems worth their while. His road shall go

Before him, having broken itself in two ways:
One goes to Borgia in Fano, and one toward Rome.
But his shadow hurries from his feet to his face.

## The old men

Ho! Persephone brings flowers, to them
New styles in spring. In seven glittering
Greys, under round grey hats of straw
—Lo! to the fifing sun's tune
The old men come on, stride, march,
Drill, straight as the ties of lovers!
(And their bones have drawn together
In gentle communities of joints,
Like weary soldiers dreaming head to head.)

Hup, they go, ho! in grey jackets,
Grey shoes, sleek as boys, smiling,
Striding on, the gay granite legions,
Persephone's grooms, all together, raise
Chins, link arms, step out, hiking, marching,
Down down into the earth!

---

**The death of Vitellozzo Vitelli:** *Vitellozzo Vitelli, a nobleman who was murdered by Cesare Borgia in 1502, is here presented in circumstances that reflect the whimsical, or predetermined, course of the fate of any man.*

**Irving Feldman   122**

# Robert Fitzgerald

*Robert Fitzgerald, born October 12, 1910, in Geneva, New York, lives with his wife and large family in Cambridge, Massachusetts, where he is Boylston Professor of Rhetoric at Harvard, and in Italy where he has kept a second home for many years. He once worked as a reporter for the New York Herald Tribune and was later a leading writer in several departments of Time. During World War II he was on the staff of the Commander in Chief, Pacific Ocean Areas, first at Pearl Harbor and later at Guam. His reputation is based not only on his own original work but on his widely praised and frequently performed translations, in collaboration with Dudley Fitts, of the Greek playwrights.*

## The imprisoned

I

The newsvendor with his hut and crutch
And black palm polished by pennies
Chinked me swiftly my worn-out silver;
Then I went underground.
    Many went down there,
Down blowing passages and dimness where
Rocketing cars were sucked out of sound in the tunnel.

A train came and expired, opening slots to us
All alacritous moving in voiceless numbers,
Haunch to haunch, elbow to hard elbow.

One would sleep, gaping and sagged in a corner,
One might wish for a seat by the girl yonder;
Each a-sway with his useless heavy headpiece.

II

Tenements: "islands" in the ancient city.
Neither under the old law nor the new
Could any insulation make them gentle.

Here I retired, here I did lay me down—

Beyond the washing lines reeled in at evening,
Beyond the roofpots and the lightless skylights,
The elevated grated round a curve
To pick up pitch diminishing toward silence—
And took my ease amid that hardihood:
The virago at her sill obscenely screeching
Or the lutanist plucking away at "My Lady Greensleeves."

III

The down beat, off beat, beat.
A hopped up drummer's perfect
Tocking periodicity and abandon.

Cush a cush cush a cush. Whang.
Diddle di daddle di yup yup
Whisper to me daddy. On the
Down, the down beat, beat.

The spot's on blondie, see her croon,
See that remarkable subtle pelvic
Universal joint softly rolling.
Honey take it sweet and slow,
Honey, take your time.
Roll those eyes and send, baby, send.

And swing it. O cats
Express your joys and savoir faire

**Robert Fitzgerald**   *126*

You hot lick connoisseurs: shake
A laig like New Orleans. Or

Rumba. O you Arthur Murray, O you Murray boys
With your snappy steward jackets keeping young,
Steer and sway, you accomplished dancers.
Won't you come over to my table.
Meet Rosemary. This is Rosemary.

IV

The manhole disks were prone shields of morning
Where the sun greeted the avenue.
O lumbering conveyances! O yellow
Gliding of cabs, thousand-footed dimpling stir!
The fresh net placed on the fair hair!

The steel shutters removed at Tiffany's
And the doorman pulling his beige gloves on;

The elevator boy holding down his yawn
And the cool engineer with his briefcase;

The sun striking over the void city room
And the first hasteners through the concourse;

The riveter walking out on the flaking plank
And the welder donning his goggles;

The steel drawer sliding from the office file
And the receptionist fixing her lipline;

The towsled showgirl a-drool on the pillow
And the schoolyard filling with cries;

The roominghouse suicide at peace by the gasjet
And the nun smiling across the ward—

Against the shine of windows, visual
Madness of intersecting multitudes,
Their speech torn to bits in the torrent.

## Cobb would have caught it

In sunburnt parks where Sundays lie,
Or the wide wastes beyond the cities,
Teams in grey deploy through sunlight.

Talk it up, boys, a little practice.

Coming in stubby and fast, the baseman
Gathers a grounder in fat green grass,
Picks it stinging and clipped as wit
Into the leather: a swinging step
Wings it deadeye down to first.
Smack. Oh, attaboy, attyoldboy.

Catcher reverses his cap, pulls down
Sweaty casque, and squats in the dust:
Pitcher rubs new ball on his pants,
Chewing, puts a jet behind him;
Nods past batter, taking his time.
Batter settles, tugs at his cap:
A spinning ball: step and swing to it,
Caught like a cheek before it ducks
By shivery hickory: socko, baby:
Cleats dig into dust. Outfielder,
On his way, looking over shoulder,
Makes it a triple. A long peg home.

Innings and afternoons. Fly lost in sunset.
Throwing arm gone bad. There's your old ball game.
Cool reek of the field. Reek of companions.


## Souls lake

The evergreen shadow and the pale magnolia
Stripping slowly to the air of May
Stood still in the night of the honey trees.

**Robert Fitzgerald**  *128*

At rest above a star pool with my friends,
Beside that grove most fit for elegies,
I made my phrase to out-enchant the night.

The epithalamion, the hush were due,
For I had fasted and gone blind to see
What night might be beyond our passages;
Those stars so chevalier in fearful heaven
Could not but lay their steel aside and come
With a grave glitter into my low room.

Vague though the population of the earth
Lay stretched and dry below the cypresses,
It was not round-about but in my night,
Bone of my bone, as an old man would say;
And all its stone weighed my mortality;
The pool would be my body and my eyes,

The air my garment and material
Whereof that wateriness and mirror lived—
The colorable, meek and limpid world.
Though I had sworn my element alien
To the pure mind of night, the cold princes,
Behold them there, and both worlds were the same.

The heart's planet seemed not so lonely then,
Seeing what kin it found in that reclining.
And ah, though sweet the catch of your chorales,
I heard no singing there among my friends;
But still were the great waves, the lions shining,
And infinite still the discourse of the night.

---

**Cobb would have caught it:** *The baseball immortal, Ty Cobb,
died in 1961. In a kind of poetic shorthand, the poem
attempts to catch the speech and rhythm of the national
pastime without any sort of imposed comment.*

# Arthur Freeman

*Arthur Freeman, born 1938, in Cambridge, Massachusetts,
lives in his native town and teaches English at Boston
University. He was educated at Harvard, where he
received his B.A. and Ph.D., and was a member of the
Society of Fellows. A distinguished scholar as well as a
poet, he pursues an avocation as a dealer in antiquarian
books and writes much of his poetry in places as far
afield as Malta and Persia.*

## The cell of himself

*"Fermons nos coeurs à double tour"*

In the middle of the night in the next room
a man who is no friend of mine cries out,
struggling with sleep; it is a nightmare.
It is not my nightmare. We share nothing
but the awareness of each other through one wall,
the groan of a drain, an occasional involuntary
outcry, and no more. We want no more.
We could be happier with less.

And there are others like us, billeted
all over the impartial city
in similar honeycombs at the same rates,
keeping apart for the particular reason
that no reason binds us, silhouettes

of habit, ghosts of motion. Nothing remains
of what is laudable in each but noise
to alien ears which value absence best.

And ultimately more who have cast off
proximity like mooring, and float free
of the contiguities we suffer by.
Wax in a window may consume itself
for them, but they are admirably gone,
past echo and sight; and if the piled
horizon whitens them no unbroached shores,
sea will suffice, and they will bear with sea.

And I would have it no way else: no smile
extracted on the stair, no hesitant
exchange, no names. Drains are enough.
The intimacy each man may cultivate
with his own cloudy mirror does for me,
and when that image grates on the dry sight,
let me acquaint myself with anyone
but this, whose dreamt fright arrogates my sleep.

Now it is four, my clock walks heavily.
I hear him settling, reassured, to rest,
with a clear mind and a diminished pulse.
But I lie now wide-eyed in the grey light
continuing his dream like a disease
my mind made welcome when his cast it out.
My cry caught in my throat, while the thin walls
thicken like distance, I am most alone.

# Robert Frost

Robert Frost, born March 26, 1874, in San Francisco,
died in Boston, January 29, 1963. In the last decades of
his life he made his home in Cambridge, Massachusetts,
during the winter, and on his farm in Ripton, Vermont,
during the summer. He attended Dartmouth and Harvard
but took degrees from neither. After an early and
unsuccessful career of farming and intermittent school
teaching, he went with his wife and young family to
England in 1912, and there his first book, A Boy's Will,
was published. He returned in 1915, his reputation as a
poet already established. Honored by more awards and
greater public favor than that granted to any other
American poet, he lectured and read his poems for many
years throughout the United States. On March 24, 1950,
the United States Senate unanimously adopted a resolution
honoring him. His poems, according to the citation,
"have helped to guide American thought with humor,
and wisdom, setting forth to our minds a reliable
representation of ourselves and of all men. . . ." In 1958
he went to England to receive honorary degrees from
both Oxford and Cambridge. In 1961 he read his poem
"The Gift Outright" as part of the ceremonies attending
the inauguration of President John F. Kennedy.

## Acquainted with the night

I have been one acquainted with the night.
I have walked out in rain—and back in rain.
I have outwalked the furthest city light.

I have looked down the saddest city lane.
I have passed by the watchman on his beat
And dropped my eyes, unwilling to explain.

I have stood still and stopped the sound of feet
When far away an interrupted cry
Came over houses from another street,

But not to call me back or say good-bye;
And further still at an unearthly height,
One luminary clock against the sky

Proclaimed the time was neither wrong nor right.
I have been one acquainted with the night.


## Stopping by woods on a snowy evening

Whose woods these are I think I know.
His house is in the village though;
He will not see me stopping here
To watch his woods fill up with snow.

My little horse must think it queer
To stop without a farmhouse near
Between the woods and frozen lake
The darkest evening of the year.

He gives his harness bells a shake
To ask if there is some mistake.

**Robert Frost**  *135*

The only other sound's the sweep
Of easy wind and downy flake.

The woods are lovely, dark and deep.
But I have promises to keep,
And miles to go before I sleep,
And miles to go before I sleep.

**The road not taken**

Two roads diverged in a yellow wood,
And sorry I could not travel both
And be one traveler, long I stood
And looked down one as far as I could
To where it bent in the undergrowth;

Then took the other, as just as fair,
And having perhaps the better claim,
Because it was grassy and wanted wear;
Though as for that the passing there
Had worn them really about the same,

And both that morning equally lay
In leaves no step had trodden black.
Oh, I kept the first for another day!
Yet knowing how way leads on to way,
I doubted if I should ever come back.

I shall be telling this with a sigh
Somewhere ages and ages hence:
Two roads diverged in a wood, and I—
I took the one less traveled by,
And that has made all the difference.

**Robert Frost**   *136*

## The runaway

Once when the snow of the year was beginning to fall,
We stopped by a mountain pasture to say, 'Whose colt?'
A little Morgan had one forefoot on the wall,
The other curled at his breast. He dipped his head
And snorted at us. And then he had to bolt.
We heard the miniature thunder where he fled,
And we saw him, or thought we saw him, dim and grey,
Like a shadow against the curtain of falling flakes.
'I think the little fellow's afraid of the snow.
He isn't winter-broken. It isn't play
With the little fellow at all. He's running away.
I doubt if even his mother could tell him, "Sakes,
It's only weather." He'd think she didn't know!
Where is his mother? He can't be out alone.'
And now he comes again with clatter of stone,
And mounts the wall again with whited eyes
And all his tail that isn't hair up straight.
He shudders his coat as if to throw off flies.
'Whoever it is that leaves him out so late,
When other creatures have gone to stall and bin,
Ought to be told to come and take him in.'


## Provide, provide

The witch that came (the withered hag)
To wash the steps with pail and rag,
Was once the beauty Abishag,

The picture pride of Hollywood.
Too many fall from great and good
For you to doubt the likelihood.


**Robert Frost** *137*

Die early and avoid the fate.
Or if predestined to die late,
Make up your mind to die in state.

Make the whole stock exchange your own!
If need be occupy a throne,
Where nobody can call you crone.

Some have relied on what they knew;
Others on being simply true.
What worked for them might work for you.

No memory of having starred
Atones for later disregard,
Or keeps the end from being hard.

Better to go down dignified
With boughten friendship at your side
Than none at all. Provide, provide!


**The silken tent**

She is as in a field a silken tent
At midday when a sunny summer breeze
Has dried the dew and all its ropes relent,
So that in guys it gently sways at ease,
And its supporting central cedar pole,
That is its pinnacle to heavenward
And signifies the sureness of the soul,
Seems to owe naught to any single cord,
But strictly held by none, is loosely bound
By countless silken ties of love and thought
To everything on earth the compass round,
And only by one's going slightly taut
In the capriciousness of summer air
Is of the slightest bondage made aware.

**Robert Frost**  *138*

**The silken tent:** *A tribute to the poet's wife, this poem, a sonnet, is remarkable, not only for the fact that the spiritual qualities of a woman are metaphorically seen in relation to the physical properties of a pitched tent on a summer's day, but for the technical mastery by which a fourteen-line poem is presented as one sentence.*

# Jean Garrigue

*Jean Garrigue, born December 8, 1914, in Evansville,*
*Indiana, lives in Greenwich Village, New York City.*
*She graduated from the University of Chicago and during*
*World War II edited a publication sheet for the USO.*
*She then went to the University of Iowa to begin a*
*teaching career that eventually included residence at*
*Queens College, Bard College, and the University of*
*Connecticut.*

## The mouse

When the mouse died at night
He was all overgrown with delight,
His whiskers thick as a wood
From exploring the Polar cupboard
And his eyes still agape
From risky accomplishment.
No honor or drum was his bait.
The more glorious, he
Who with no shame for time
Then boldly died,
Three weeks a rich spell
Of sound and pure smell
And all his long leisure
For meat of short measure

(An ant could carry it.)
Praise him who sweetens
On a small hate.


## The stranger

Now upon this piteous year
I sit in Denmark beside the quai
And nothing that the fishers say
Or the children carrying boats
Can recall me from that place
Where sense and wish departed me
Whose very shores take on
The whiteness of anon.
For I beheld a stranger there
Who moved ahead of me
So tensile and so dancer made
That like a thief I followed her
Though my heart was so alive
I thought myself the equal beauty.
But when at last a turning came
Like the branching of a river
And I saw if she walked on
She would be gone forever,
Fear, then, so wounded me
As fell upon my ear
The voice a blind man dreams
And broke on me the smile
I dreamed as deaf men hear,
I stood there like a spy,
My tongue and eyelids taken
In such necessity.
Now upon this piteous year
The rains of Autumn fall.
Where may she be?
I suffered her to disappear

Who hunger in the prison of my fear.
That lean and brown, that stride,
That cold and melting pride,
For whom the river like a clear,
Melodic line and the distant carrousel
Where lovers on their beasts of play
Rose and fell, that wayfare where the swan adorned
With every wave and eddy
The honor of his sexual beauty,
Create her out of sorrow
That, never perishing,
Is a stately thing.

# David Gascoyne

*David Gascoyne, born October, 1916, in Harrow,*
*Middlesex, England, lives in London. He was educated*
*at Salisbury Cathedral Choir School and Regent Street*
*Polytechnic. He lived for a number of years in France,*
*where he wrote a book about surrealism, a movement*
*which deeply influenced an important phase of his*
*poetic career. In 1952 he spent several months in the*
*United States.*

## An elegy

*R.R. 1916–41*

Friend, whose unnatural early death
In this year's cold, chaotic Spring
Is like a clumsy wound that will not heal:
What can I say to you, now that your ears
Are stoppered-up with distant soil?
Perhaps to speak at all is false; more true
Simply to sit at times alone and dumb
And with most pure intensity of thought
And concentrated inmost feeling, reach
Towards your shadow on the years' crumbling wall.

I'll say not any word in praise or blame
Of what you ended with the mere turn of a tap;
Nor to explain, deplore nor yet exploit

The latent pathos of your living years—
Hurried, confused and unfulfilled—
That were the shiftless years of both our youths
Spent in the monstrous mountain-shadow of
*Catastrophe* that chilled you to the bone:
The certain imminence of which always pursued
You from your heritage of fields and sun . . .

I see your face in hostile sunlight, eyes
Wrinkled against its glare, behind the glass
Of a car's windscreen, while you seek to lose
Your self in swift devouring of white roads
Unwinding across Europe or America;
Taciturn at the wheel, wrapped in a blaze
Of restlessness that no fresh scene can quench;
In cities of brief sojourn that you pass
Through in your quest for respite, heavy drink
Alone enabling you to bear each hotel night.

Sex, Art and Politics: those poor
Expedients! You tried them each in turn,
With the wry inward smile of one resigned
To join in every complicated game
Adults affect to play. Yet girls you found
So prone to sentiment's corruptions; and the joy
Of sensual satisfaction seemed so brief, and left
Only new need. It proved hard to remain
Convinced of the Word's efficacity; or even quite
Certain of World-Salvation through "the Party Line" . . .

Cased in the careful armour that you wore
Of wit and nonchalance, through which
Few quizzed the concealed countenance of fear,
You waited daily for the sky to fall;
At moments wholly panic-stricken by
A sense of stifling in your brittle shell;
Seeing the world's damnation week by week

**David Gascoyne   146**

The conflagration broke out with a roar,
And from those flames you fled through whirling smoke,

To end at last in bankrupt exile in
That sordid city, scene of *Ulysses*; and there,
While War sowed all the lands with violent graves,
You finally succumbed to a black, wild
Incomprehensibility of fate that none could share . . .
Yet even in your obscure death I see
The secret candour of that lonely child
Who, lost in the storm-shaken castle-park,
Astride his crippled mastiff's back was borne
Slowly away into the utmost dark.

# Allen Ginsberg

*Allen Ginsberg, born June 3, 1926, in Newark, New Jersey,*
*is the son of the poet Louis Ginsberg. During his years*
*as a student at Columbia College, he developed a delicate*
*lyrical style reminiscent of certain seventeenth-century*
*English poets. Soon afterwards he turned to the broad,*
*loose, dithyrambic modes of expression that have become*
*his hallmark. He has been identified with the Beat*
*Generation and its poetic and political movements in San*
*Francisco and New York. In his travels around the world*
*Ginsberg has become a kind of minister plenipotentiary*
*to disenchanted segments of the younger generation.*
*In 1965 a vast gathering of Czechoslovakian students*
*named him "King of May."*

## A supermarket in California

What thoughts I have of you tonight, Walt Whitman, for
I walked down the sidestreets under the trees with a headache
self-conscious looking at the full moon.

In my hungry fatigue, and shopping for images, I went
into the neon fruit supermarket, dreaming of your enumerations!

What peaches and what penumbras! Whole families shopping
at night! Aisles full of husbands! Wives in the avocados,
babies in the tomatoes!—and you, Garcia Lorca, what were you
doing down by the watermelons?

I saw you, Walt Whitman, childless, lonely old grubber, poking among the meats in the refrigerator and eyeing the grocery boys.

I heard you asking questions of each: Who killed the pork chops? What price bananas? Are you my Angel?

I wandered in and out of the brilliant stacks of cans following you, and followed in my imagination by the store detective.

We strode down the open corridors together in our solitary fancy tasting artichokes, possessing every frozen delicacy, and never passing the cashier.

Where are we going, Walt Whitman? The doors close in an hour. Which way does your beard point tonight?

(I touch your book and dream of our odyssey in the supermarket and feel absurd.)

Will we walk all night through solitary streets? The trees add shade to shade, lights out in the houses, we'll both be lonely.

Will we stroll dreaming of the lost America of love past blue automobiles in driveways, home to our silent cottage?

Ah, dear father, graybeard, lonely old courage-teacher, what America did you have when Charon quit poling his ferry and you got out on a smoking bank and stood watching the boat disappear on the black waters of Lethe?

## Uptown

Yellow-lit Budweiser signs over oaken bars,
"I've seen everything"—the bartender handing me change of $10,
I stared at him amiably eyes thru an obvious Adamic beard—
with Montana musicians homeless in Manhattan, teen age
curly hair themselves—we sat at the antique booth & gossiped,
Madame Grady's literary salon a curious value in New York—
"If I had my way, I'd cut off your hair and send you to Vietnam"—

**Allen Ginsberg** *150*

"Bless you then" I replied to a hatted thin citizen hurrying to
   the barroom door
upon wet dark Amsterdam Avenue decades later—
"And if I couldn't do that I'd cut your throat" he snarled farewell,
and "Bless you sir" I added as he went to his fate in the rain,
   dapper Irishman.

# Robert Graves

Robert Graves, born July 24, 1895, in London, lives in
Spain on the island of Majorca. His early career was
identified with that of the "trench poets" of World War I,
during which, as a member of the Royal Welch Fusiliers,
he saw much action and was wounded. He later studied
at Oxford and taught for a year at the University of
Cairo. He is one of the most prolific of contemporary
authors, famous for his historical novels as well as for
his critical essays, translations, and mythological studies,
notably The White Goddess. In recent years he has made
several visits to the United States to read his poems;
in 1961 he was elected professor of poetry at Oxford,
a position in which he succeeded W. H. Auden.

## Flying crooked

The butterfly, a cabbage-white,
(His honest idiocy of flight)
Will never now, it is too late,
Master the art of flying straight,
Yet has—who knows so well as I?—
A just sense of how not to fly:
He lurches here and here by guess
And God and hope and hopelessness.
Even the aerobatic swift
Has not his flying-crooked gift.

## To Juan at the winter solstice

There is one story and one story only
That will prove worth your telling,
Whether as learned bard or gifted child;
To it all lines or lesser gauds belong
That startle with their shining
Such common stories as they stray into.

Is it of trees you tell, their months and virtues,
Or strange beasts that beset you,
Of birds that croak at you the Triple will?
Or of the Zodiac and how slow it turns
Below the Boreal Crown,
Prison of all true kings that ever reigned?

Water to water, ark again to ark,
From woman back to woman:
So each new victim treads unfalteringly
The never altered circuit of his fate,
Bringing twelve peers as witness
Both to his starry rise and starry fall.

Or is it of the Virgin's silver beauty,
All fish below the thighs?
She in her left hand bears a leafy quince;
When, with her right she crooks a finger smiling,
How may the King hold back?
Royally then he barters life for love.

Or of the undying snake from chaos hatched,
Whose coils contain the ocean,
Into whose chops with naked sword he springs,
Then in black water, tangled by the reeds,
Battles three days and nights,
To be spewed up beside her scalloped shore?

**Robert Graves**   *154*

Much snow is falling, winds roar hollowly,
The owl hoots from the elder,
Fear in your heart cries to the loving-cup:
Sorrow to sorrow as the sparks fly upward.
The log groans and confesses
There is one story and one story only.

Dwell on her graciousness, dwell on her smiling,
Do not forget what flowers
The great boar trampled down in ivy time.
Her brow was creamy as the crested wave,
Her sea-blue eyes were wild
But nothing promised that is not performed.


**In procession**

Often, half-way to sleep,
Not yet sunken deep—
The sudden moment on me comes
From a mountain shagged and steep,
With terrible roll of dream drums,
Reverberations, cymbals, horns replying.
When with standards flying,
Horsemen in clouds behind,
The coloured pomps unwind,
The Carnival wagons
With their saints and their dragons
On the scroll of my teeming mind:
The Creation and Flood
With our Saviour's Blood
And fat Silenus' flagons,
And every rare beast
From the South and East,
Both greatest and least,
On and on,

**Robert Graves**  *155*

In endless, different procession.
I stand at the top rungs
Of a ladder reared in the air,
And I rail in strange tongues,
So the crowds murmur and stare;
Then volleys again the blare
Of horns, and summer flowers
Fly scattering in showers,
And the sun leaps in the sky,
While the drums thumping by
Proclaim me . . . .
      Oh, then, when I wake,
Could I courage take
To renew my speech,
Could I stretch and reach
The flowers and the ripe fruit
Laid out at the ladder's foot,
Could I rip a silken shred
From the banner tossed ahead,
Could I call a double-flam
From the drums, could the goat
Horned with gold, could the ram
With a flank like a barn-door,
The dwarf, the blackamoor,
Could Jonah and the Whale
And the Holy Grail,
The Ape with his platter
Going clitter-clatter,
The Nymphs and the Satyr,
And every marvellous matter
Come before me here,
Standing near and clear—
Could I make it so that you
Might wonder at them too!
—Glories of land and sea,
Of Heaven glittering free,
Castles hugely built in Spain,
Glories of Cockaigne,

**Robert Graves**  *156*

Of that spicy kingdom, Cand,
Of the Delectable Land,
Of the Land of Crooked Stiles.
Of the Fortunate Isles,
Of the more than three-score miles
That to Babylon lead
(A pretty city indeed
Built on a four-square plan),
Of the Land of the Gold Man
Whose eager horses whinny
In their cribs of gold,
Of the Land of Whipperginny,
Of the land where none grows old . . . .
But cowardly I tell,
Rather, of the Town of Hell—
A huddle of dirty woes
And houses in fading rows
Straggled through space:
Hell has no market-place,
Nor point where four ways meet,
Nor principal street,
Nor barracks, nor Town Hall,
Nor shops at all,
Nor rest for weary feet,
Nor theatre, square, or park,
Nor lights after dark,
Nor churches, nor inns,
Nor convenience for sins—
Neither ends nor begins,
Rambling, limitless, hated well,
This Town of Hell
Where between sleep and sleep I dwell.

---

**To Juan at the winter solstice:** *Robert Grave's seventh child,*
*Juan, was born on December 21, 1945. The fact that the winter*
*solstice falls on this date and that it is also the traditional*

birthday of many figures of divinty such as the Greek
Apollo, Dionysus, Zeus, Hermes, the Syrian Tammuz, the
Egyptian Horus, the Welsh Merlin and Llew Llaw, etc.,
leads the poet to address his son as one in a great
succession of heroes. His fate, like theirs, he suggests,
will be a retelling of "one story and one story only": the
Moon Goddess will appear to him in her different characters
at different seasons of the year, i.e., at different years of his
life span, as mother, lover, and widow. The Boreal Crown
is Corona Borealis, which was the purgatory where many
such heroes went after death. The "log" in the fifth stanza
is the yule log, traditionally burned at the end of the year.
The "great boar" is the beast that kills heroes at the fall
of the year. Understand your fate, the poet says to his
infant son, accept it, and live it.

# Thom Gunn

*Thom Gunn, born August 29, 1929, in Gravesend, England,
now lives in San Francisco. Educated at Cambridge, he
moved permanently to the United States in 1954, first
as a student of Yvor Winters at Stanford and later as a
teacher at the University of California at Berkeley and
other colleges. Much of his work shows how a British
sensibility, engaged with some of the notorious aspects
of the current American scene, can produce durable
poems rather than sensationalist ephemera.*

## On the move

'Man, you gotta Go.'

The blue jay scuffling in the bushes follows
Some hidden purpose, and the gust of birds
That spurts across the field, the wheeling swallows,
Have nested in the trees and undergrowth.
Seeking their instinct, or their poise, or both,
One moves with an uncertain violence
Under the dust thrown by a baffled sense
Or the dull thunder of approximate words.

On motorcycles, up the road, they come:
Small, black, as flies hanging in heat, the Boys,
Until the distance throws them forth, their hum
Bulges to thunder held by calf and thigh.

In goggles, donned impersonality,
In gleaming jackets trophied with the dust,
They strap in doubt—by hiding it, robust—
And almost hear a meaning in their noise.

Exact conclusion of their hardiness
Has no shape yet, but from known whereabouts
They ride, direction where the tires press.
They scare a flight of birds across the field:
Much that is natural, to the will must yield.
Men manufacture both machine and soul,
And use what they imperfectly control
To dare a future from the taken routes.

It is a part solution, after all.
One is not necessarily discord
On earth; or damned because, half animal,
One lacks direct instinct, because one wakes
Afloat on movement that divides and breaks.
One joins the movement in a valueless world,
Choosing it, till, both hurler and the hurled,
One moves as well, always toward, toward.

A minute holds them, who have come to go:
The self-defined, astride the created will
They burst away; the towns they travel through
Are home for neither bird nor holiness,
For birds and saints complete their purposes.
At worst, one is in motion; and at best,
Reaching no absolute, in which to rest,
One is always nearer by not keeping still.

## Black jackets

In the silence that prolongs the span
Rawly of music when the record ends,
　　The red-haired boy who drove a van
In weekday overalls but, like his friends,

　　Wore cycle boots and jacket here
To suit the Sunday hangout he was in,
　　Heard, as he stretched back from his beer,
Leather creak softly round his neck and chin.

　　Before him, on a coal-black sleeve
Remote exertion had lined, scratched, and burned
　　Insignia that could not revive
The heroic fall or climb where they were earned.

　　On the other drinkers bent together,
Concocting selves for their impervious kit,
　　He saw it as no more than leather
Which, taut across the shoulders grown to it,

　　Sent through the dimness of a bar
As sudden and anonymous hints of light
　　As those that shipping give, that are
Now flickers in the Bay, now lost in night.

　　He stretched out like a cat, and rolled
The bitterish taste of beer upon his tongue,
　　And listened to a joke being told:
The present was the things he stayed among.

　　If it was only loss he wore,
He wore it to assert, with fierce devotion,
　　Complicity and nothing more.
He recollected his initiation,

**Thom Gunn** *162*

And one especially of the rites.
For on his shoulders they had put tattoos:
      The group's name on the left, The Knights,
And on the right the slogan Born To Lose.


## From the highest camp

Nothing in this bright region melts or shifts.
The local names are concepts: the Ravine,
Pemmican Ridge, North Col, Death Camp, they mean
The streetless rise, the dazzling abstract drifts,

To which particular names adhere by chance,
From custom lightly, not from character.
We stand on a white terrace and confer;
This is the last camp of experience.

What is that sudden yelp upon the air?
And whose are these cold droppings? whose malformed
Purposeless tracks about the slope? We know.
The abominable endures, existing where
Nothing else can: it is—unfed, unwarmed—
Born of rejection, of the boundless snow.


## Considering the snail

The snail pushes through a green
night, for the grass is heavy
with water and meets over
the bright path he makes, where rain
has darkened the earth's dark. He
moves in a wood of desire,

pale antlers barely stirring
as he hunts. I cannot tell
what power is at work, drenched there
with purpose, knowing nothing.
What is a snail's fury? All
I think is that if later

I parted the blades above
the tunnel and saw the thin
trail of broken white across
litter, I would never have
imagined the slow passion
to that deliberate progress.

# Donald Hall

*Donald Hall, born September 20, 1928, in New Haven,
Connecticut, lives in Ann Arbor where he teaches in the
English department of the University of Michigan. He
was educated at Harvard and Oxford, where his poem
"Exile" was awarded the Newdigate Prize. With Robert
Pack and Louis Simpson, he was editor of the anthology
The New Poets of England and America, and he has
published autobiographical prose as well as a study
of the sculptor Henry Moore.*

## The sleeping giant

*(A hill, so named, in Hamden, Connecticut)*

The whole day long, under the walking sun
That poised an eye on me from its high floor,
Holding my toy beside the clapboard house
I looked for him, the summer I was four.

I was afraid the waking arm would break
From the loose earth and rub against his eyes
A fist of trees, and the whole country tremble
In the exultant labor of his rise;

Then he with giant steps in the small streets
Would stagger, cutting off the sky, to seize

The roofs from house and home because we had
Covered his shape with dirt and planted trees;

And then kneel down and rip with fingernails
A trench to pour the enemy Atlantic
Into our basin, and the water rush,
With the streets full and all the voices frantic.

That was the summer I expected him.
Later the high and watchful sun instead
Walked low behind the house, and school began,
And winter pulled a sheet over his head.


## The body politic

I shot my friend to save my country's life,
And when the happy bullet struck him dead,
I was saluted by the drum and fife
Corps of a high school, while the traitor bled.

I never thought until I pulled the trigger
But that I did the difficult and good.
I thought republics stood for something bigger,
For the mind of man, as Plato said they stood.

So when I heard the duty they assigned,
Shooting my friend seemed only sanity;
To keep disorder from the state of mind
Was mental rectitude, it seemed to me.

The audience dispersed. I felt depressed.
I went to where my orders issued from,
But the right number on the street was just
A rickety old house, vacant and dumb.

**Donald Hall**  *167*

I tried to find the true address, but where?
Nobody told me what I really wanted;
Just secretaries sent me here and there
To other secretaries. I was daunted.

Poor Fred. His presence will be greatly missed
By children and by cronies by the score.
The State (I learn too late) does not exist;
Man lives by love, and not by metaphor.

# Robert Hayden

*Robert Hayden, born 1918 in Detroit, studied at the
University of Michigan, then moved with his wife and
daughter to Nashville where for many years he was on
the faculty of Fisk University. In 1969 he returned to his
alma mater as professor of English. As an anthologist
he has demonstrated the continuity of black poetry in
America and introduced new talents whose concerns are
as strongly aesthetic as they are political.*

## "Summertime and the living . . ."

Nobody planted roses, he recalls,
but sunflowers gangled there sometimes,
tough-stalked and bold
and like the vivid children there unplanned.
There circus-poster horses curveted
in trees of heaven
above the quarrels and shattered glass,
and he was bareback rider of them all.

No roses there in summer—
oh, never roses except when people died—
and no vacations for his elders,
so harshened after each unrelenting day
that they were shouting-angry.

But summer was, they said, the poor folks' time
of year. And he remembers
how they would sit on broken steps amid

The fevered tossings of the dusk, the dark,
wafting hearsay with funeral-parlor fans
or making evening solemn by
their quietness. Feels their Mosaic eyes
upon him, though the florist roses
that only sorrow could afford
long since have bidden them Godspeed.

Oh, summer summer summertime—

Then grim street preachers shook
their tambourines and Bibles in the face
of tolerant wickedness;
then Elks parades and big splendiferous
Jack Johnson in his diamond limousine
set the ghetto burgeoning
with fantasies
of Ethiopia spreading her gorgeous wings.

---

**"Summertime and the living . . .":** *Here the title somewhat
ironically echoes part of the opening line—"Summertime and
the livin' is easy"—of a song from the George Gershwin-
Dubose Heyward folk-opera* Porgy and Bess. *Jack Johnson
was the black heavyweight boxer from Galveston, Texas,
who held the world championship from 1908 to 1915.*

**Robert Hayden** *170*

# Seamus Heaney

*Seamus Heaney, born 1941 on a farm in Northern Ireland,*
*lives in Belfast with his wife and two sons. Besides*
*poetry, he contributes criticism to a number of British*
*journals. His first book,* Death of a Naturalist, *according*
*to one critic, registers "the soil-reek of Ireland, the*
*colourful violence of his childhood on a farm in Derry."*

## Digging

Between my finger and my thumb
The squat pen rests; snug as a gun.

Under my window, a clean rasping sound
When the spade sinks into gravelly ground:
My father, digging. I look down

Till his straining rump among the flowerbeds
Bends low, comes up twenty years away
Stooping in rhythm through potato drills
Where he was digging.

The coarse boot nestled on the lug, the shaft
Against the inside knee was levered firmly.
He rooted out tall tops, buried the bright edge deep
To scatter new potatoes that we picked
Loving their cool hardness in our hands.

By God, the old man could handle a spade.
Just like his old man.

My grandfather cut more turf in a day
Than any other man on Toner's bog.
Once I carried him milk in a bottle
Corked sloppily with paper. He straightened up
To drink it, then fell to right away

Nicking and slicing neatly, heaving sods
Over his shoulder, going down and down
For the good turf. Digging.

The cold smell of potato mould, the squelch and slap
Of soggy peat, the curt cuts of an edge
Through living roots awaken in my head.
But I've no spade to follow men like them.

Between my finger and my thumb
The squat pen rests.
I'll dig with it.


**Twice shy**

Her scarf *à la* Bardot,
In suede flats for the walk,
She came with me one evening
For air and friendly talk.
We crossed the quiet river,
Took the embankment walk.

Traffic holding its breath,
Sky a tense diaphragm:
Dusk hung like a backcloth
That shook where a swan swam,

**Seamus Heaney**  *174*

Tremulous as a hawk
Hanging deadly, calm.

A vacuum of need
Collapsed each hunting heart
But tremulously we held
As hawk and prey apart,
Preserved classic decorum,
Deployed our talk with art.

Our juvenilia
Had taught us both to wait,
Not to publish feeling
And regret it all too late—
Mushroom loves already
Had puffed and burst in hate.

So, chary and excited
As a thrush linked on a hawk,
We thrilled to the March twilight
With nervous childish talk:
Still waters running deep
Along the embankment walk.

**Seamus Heaney**  *175*

# John Heath-Stubbs

*John Heath-Stubbs was born July 9, 1918, in London,
where he now lives. He was educated at schools in
Sussex and the Isle of Wight until he was sixteen, when
failing eyesight caused him to be put under private tutors.
After an operation when he was eighteen, he was sent
for a year to the Worcester College for the Blind and then
entered Oxford, where he took a "first class" in English
language and literature. In 1952 he was appointed poet-
in-residence at the University of Leeds and later taught
at the University of Cairo. He has written one volume
of criticism,* The Darkling Plain.

### A charm against the tooth-ache

Venerable Mother Tooth-ache
Climb down from the white battlements,
Stop twisting in your yellow fingers
The fourfold rope of nerves;
And tomorrow I will give you a tot of whiskey
To hold in your cupped hands,
A garland of anise-flowers,
And three cloves like nails.

And tell the attendant gnomes
It is time to knock off now,
To shoulder their little pick-axes,

Their cold-chisels and drills.
And you may mount by a silver ladder
Into the sky, to grind
In the cracked polished mortar
Of the hollow moon.

By the lapse of warm waters,
And the poppies nodding like red coals,
The paths on the granite mountains,
And the plantation of my dreams.

## The lady's complaint

I speak of that lady I heard last night,
    Maudlin over her gin and water,
In a sloppy bar with a fulvous light
    And an air that was smeared with smoke and laughter:
    How youth decamps and cold age comes after,
In fifty years she had found it true—
    She sighed for the damage that time had brought her:
'Oh, after death there's a judgement due.

'What once was as sleek as a seal's pelt,
    My shapeless body has fallen from grace;
My soul and my shoes are worn down to the welt,
    And no cosmetic can mask my face,
    As under talcum and oxide you trace
How the bones stick out, and the ghost peeps through—
    A wanderer, I, in Wraith-bone Place,
And after death there's a judgement due.

'My roundabout horses have cantered away,
    The gilded and garrulous seasons are flown;
What echo is left of the rag-time bray
    Of the tenor sax and the susaphone?
    But I was frightened to sleep alone

**John Heath-Stubbs** *178*

(As now I must do, as now I must do)
    And a chittering bat-voice pipes "Atone,
For after death there's a judgement due."

'Green apples I bit when I was green,
    My teeth are on edge at the maggotty core;
Life is inclement, obscure, obscene;
    Nothing's amusing—not any more;
    But love's abrasions have left me sore—
To hairy Harry and half-mast Hugh
    I gave the love I was starving for,
And after death there's a judgement due.

'Potenate, swirling in stark cold air
    The corn from the husks—I offer to you
My terror-struck and incredulous prayer,
    For after death there's a judgement due.'

# Anthony Hecht

*Anthony Hecht, born January 16, 1923, in New York City,*
*teaches at the University of Rochester. He was educated*
*at Kenyon College and Columbia University, then taught*
*for many years at Bard College and at Smith. His book*
*The Hard Hours was awarded the Pulitzer Prize for 1968,*
*and he spent the following year at the American*
*Academy in Rome.*

## Samuel Sewall

Samuel Sewall, in a world of wigs,
Flouted opinion in his personal hair;
For foppery he gave not any figs,
But in his right and honor took the air.

Thus in his naked style, though well attired,
He went forth in the city, or paid court
To Madam Winthrop, whom he much admired,
Most godly, but yet liberal with the port.

And all the town admired for two full years
His excellent address, his gifts of fruit,
Her gracious ways and delicate white ears,
And held the course of nature absolute.

But yet she bade him suffer a peruke,
"That One be not distinguished from the All";
Delivered of herself this stern rebuke
Framed in the resonant language of St. Paul.

"Madam," he answered her, "I have a Friend
Furnishes me with hair out of His strength,
And He requires only I attend
Unto His charity and to its length."

And all the town was witness to his trust:
On Monday he walked out with the Widow Gibbs,
A pious lady of charm and notable bust,
Whose heart beat tolerably beneath her ribs.

On Saturday he wrote proposing marriage,
And closed, imploring that she be not cruel,
"Your favorable answer will oblige,
Madam, your humble servant, Samuel Sewall."

## "More light! More light!"

*for Heinrich Blücher and Hannah Arendt*

Composed in the Tower before his execution
These moving verses, and being brought at that time
Painfully to the stake, submitted, declaring thus:
"I implore my God to witness that I have made no crime."

Nor was he forsaken of courage, but the death was horrible,
The sack of gunpowder failing to ignite.
His legs were blistered sticks on which the black sap
Bubbled and burst as he howled for the Kindly Light.

And that was but one, and by no means one of the worst;
Permitted at least his pitiful dignity;

**Anthony Hecht**   *182*

And such as were by made prayers in the name of Christ,
That shall judge all men, for his soul's tranquillity.

We move now to outside a German wood.
Three men are there commanded to dig a hole
In which the two Jews are ordered to lie down
And be buried alive by the third, who is a Pole.

Not light from the shrine at Weimar beyond the hill
Nor light from heaven appeared. But he did refuse.
A Lüger settled back deeply in its glove.
He was ordered to change places with the Jews.

Much casual death had drained away their souls.
The thick dirt mounted toward the quivering chin.
When only the head was exposed the order came
To dig him out again and to get back in.

No light, no light in the blue Polish eye.
When he finished a riding boot packed down the earth.
The Lüger hovered lightly in its glove.
He was shot in the belly and in three hours bled to death.

No prayers or incense rose up in those hours
Which grew to be years, and every day came mute
Ghosts from the ovens, sifting through crisp air,
And settled upon his eyes in a black soot.


**Lizards and snakes**

On the summer road that ran by our front porch
   Lizards and snakes came out to sun.
It was hot as a stove out there, enough to scorch
   A buzzard's foot. Still, it was fun
To lie in the dust and spy on them. Near but remote,
   They snoozed in the carriage ruts, a smile

In the set of the jaw, a fierce pulse in the throat
Working away like Jack Doyle's after he'd run the mile.

Aunt Martha had an unfair prejudice
 Against them (as well as being cold
Toward bats.) She was pretty inflexible in this,
 Being a spinster and all, and old.
So we used to slip them into her knitting box.
 In the evening she'd bring in things to mend
And a nice surprise would slide out from under the socks.
It broadened her life, as Joe said. Joe was my friend.

But we never did it again after the day
 Of the big wind when you could hear the trees
Creak like rockingchairs. She was looking away
 Off, and kept saying, "Sweet Jesus, please
Don't let him near me. He's as like as twins.
 He can crack us like lice with his fingernail.
I can see him plain as a pikestaff. Look how he grins
And swinges the scaly horror of his folded tail."

---

**Samuel Sewall:** *Samuel Sewall (1652–1750) was a leading
jurist in Puritan times in Massachusetts. Having once been
a minister, he gave up the cloth for a public career and
became one of the judges responsible for the conviction of
nineteen persons in the famous Salem witchcraft trials.
In this poem, Anthony Hecht is concerned, not with Sewall
as a public man, but solely with the humanly engaging
aspects of the courtship of a man of exemplary, and
sometimes frightening, rectitude.*

**More light! More light!:** *The title of this poem is what are
reputed to be Goethe's last words. The martyr in the first
two stanzas is no actual person, and, according to the author,
"the details are conflated from several executions, including
Latimer and Ridley whose deaths at the stake are described
by Foxe in Acts and Monuments. But neither of them wrote
poems just before their deaths, as others did." The scene is
the concentration camp Buchenwald to which prisoners*

*were marched from the railroad station in Weimar, the home
of that representative of German Enlightenment, Goethe.
The incident involving the Jews and the Pole was an actual
event reported by a man who survived an imprisonment of
five years in Buchenwald.*

**Lizards and snakes:** *The last line of this poem comes from
Milton's "On the Morning of Christ's Nativity." The woman
who quite easily incorporates it into her observation is
"supposed to be a certain kind of devout, Puritan mid-
westerner to whom the Bible and Milton are almost equally
sacred texts, and who has most of both by heart."*

# Daryl Hine

*Daryl Hine, born February 24, 1936, in Burnaby, British Columbia, now lives in Chicago where he is editor of* Poetry: A Magazine of Verse. *He attended McGill University, lived for several years in France, then took a Ph.D. in comparative literature at the University of Chicago. He has published a novel,* The Prince of Darkness and Co., *and a travel book,* Polish Subtitles.

## The survivors

Nowadays the mess is everywhere
And getting worse. Earth after all
Is a battlefield. Through the static
We used to call the music of the spheres

Someone, a survivor, sends this message:
"When it happened I was reading Homer.
Sing—will nobody sing?—the wrath,
Rats and tanks and radioactive rain."

That was before rationing was enforced
On words, of course. Particles went first,
Then substantives. Now only verbs abide
The law, and the odd anarchistic scrawl

How above the crumbling horizon
Brightly shine our neighbours, Venus, Mars.

## Untitled

Here is another poem in a picture:

at the end of the gallery, so you will see them as
you enter, Christ Crucified, the Virgin and Saint
John, attributed to a famous Flemish master.

The attribution of guilt is universal.

There is something distinctly fishy about these figures.
Literally. Streamlined and coldblooded. As weightless
as a fish might feel in water. The man of sorrows not
nailed to his cross but pinned there. Almost as if he
had no body. Nobody to suffer and depend on. No body
to depend on wood and iron and to suffer. Which heresy
pretended he did not? Nonetheless he suffers obviously,
enthroned on his gibbet, naked and erect as if he held it up.

His mother, fainting in the arms of the disciple Jesus
loved, will never in the conceivable future fall to
earth. And this in spite of the gingerly way he holds
her as he leans slightly forward on tiptoe, his fingers
parted and outstretched as if to seize the air. His
tentative, mimic gesture of support. He does not grasp
at anything. There is no strain or effort apparent
anywhere in the composition.

She sinks down as if onto a chair, stricken by grief,
sustained in theory by love. Her hands are clasped,
her eyes are almost closed. And beneath the smooth
expressive drapery one has to infer the insubstantial
flesh. Goodness! one exclaims, What painting, a
craft in the radical sense pretentious, to suggest
what is equivocally there.

Each wears the appropriate expression like an honorary
degree: he an anthropomorphic mask of pity, she

**Daryl Hine**  *188*

negligently the distinction of her tears. Only the
saviour of their world wears nothing except a difficult
crown of thorns which hurts.

The cause of their distress is unconcerned. They
do not look upon him as their redeemer as yet, but
as a son and dear friend whose eccentricities have
got him into trouble. One can forgive too many and
love too much.

The birth and banquet of love look equally far away
and insignificant from here; the resurrection is also
inconceivable. Only the ignominious and painful
moment of death has any meaning now, a meaning
without a future or a past.

The background is conventional, a wall too high to
see over, too smooth to climb, draped here and there
with a red linen cloth, its folds still visible.

Beyond the wall there is a gold leaf sky.

Remember that everything is possible,
The picture, the poem and ourselves,
The blood that we see shed, the tears that we
Shed, the wall, and the anonymous cross.

# Daniel Hoffman

*Daniel Hoffman, born 1923 in New York City, lives with
his wife and two children in Swarthmore, Pennsylvania;
he now teaches at the University of Pennsylvania.
He was educated at Columbia University, served
in the Army Air Force in World War II, and subsequently
taught at Columbia and at the University of Dijon, in
France. Beyond poetry, his works include several
scholarly studies of phases of American literature.*

## The seals in Penobscot Bay

hadn't heard of the atom bomb,
so I shouted a warning to them.

Our destroyer (on trial run) slid by
the rocks where they gamboled and played;

they must have misunderstood,
or perhaps not one of them heard

me over the engines and tides.
As I watched them over our wake

I saw their sleek skins in the sun
ripple, light-flecked, on the rock,

**Daniel Hoffman**   *191*

plunge, bubbling, into the brine,
and couple & laugh in the troughs

between the waves' whitecaps and froth.
Then the males clambered clumsily up

and lustily crowed like seacocks,
sure that their prowess held thrall

all the sharks, other seals, and seagulls.
And daintily flipped the females,

seawenches with musical tails;
each looked at the Atlantic as

though it were her looking-glass.
If my warning had ever been heard

it was sound none would now ever heed.
And I, while I watched those far seals,

tasted honey that buzzed in my ears
and saw, out to windward, the sails

of an obsolete ship with banked oars
that swept like two combs through the spray.

And I wished for a vacuum of wax
to ward away all those strange sounds,

yet I envied the sweet agony
of him who was tied to the mast,

when the boom, when the boom, when the boom
of guns punched dark holes in the sky.

**Daniel Hoffman**   *192*

**The seals in Penobscot Bay:** *The resolution of this poem is based directly on the story of Odysseus and the Sirens: Fearful that he and his men would be lulled into forgetfulness and death by the lovely songs of the sea-maidens, Odysseus devised a scheme by which his ship might safely pass the island from which they beckoned. He ordered every man in the crew to put wax in his ears and then commanded them to lash him to the mast so securely that, no matter how he might try, he could not get free. In this way, they escaped the fatal enchantment of the Sirens, with only Odysseus himself hearing, in a state of "sweet agony," the songs they sang.*

# John Hollander

*John Hollander, born 1929 in New York City, now lives and teaches there at Hunter College. He was educated at Columbia, Indiana, and Harvard, where he was a member of the Society of Fellows. Besides poetry he has written a scholarly study* The Untuning of the Sky: Ideas of Music in English Poetry 1500–1706 *and edited an anthology entitled* Poems of Our Moment.

## The lady's-maid song

When Adam found his rib was gone
He cursed and sighed and cried and swore,
And looked with cold resentment on
The creature God had used it for.
All love's delights were quickly spent
And soon his sorrows multiplied;
He learned to blame his discontent
On something stolen from his side.

And so in every age we find
Each Jack, destroying every Joan,
Divides and conquers womankind
In vengeance for the missing bone;
By day he spins out quaint conceits
With gossip, flattery and song
And then at night, between the sheets
He wrongs the girl to right the wrong.

Though shoulder, bosom, lip and knee
Are praised in every kind of art,
Here is Love's true anatomy:
His rib is gone; he'll have her heart.
So women bear the debt alone
And live eternally distressed,
For though we throw the dog his bone
He wants it back with interest.


## The great bear

Even on clear nights, lead the most supple children
Out onto hilltops, and by no means will
They make it out. Neither the gruff round image
From a remembered page nor the uncertain
Finger tracing that image out can manage
To mark the lines of what ought to be there,
Passing through certain bounding stars, until
The whole massive expanse of bear appear
Swinging, across the ecliptic; and, although
The littlest ones say nothing, others respond,
Making us thankful in varying degrees
For what we would have shown them: "There it is!"
"I see it now!" Even "Very like a bear!"
Would make us grateful. Because there is no bear

We blame our memory of the picture: trudging
Up the dark, starlit path, stooping to clutch
An anxious hand, perhaps the outline faded
Then; perhaps could we have retained the thing
In mind ourselves, with it we might have staged
Something convincing. We easily forget
The huge, clear, homely dipper that is such
An event to reckon with, an object set
Across the space the bear should occupy;
But even so, the trouble lies in pointing

At any stars. For one's own finger aims
Always elsewhere: the man beside one seems
Never to get the point. "No! The bright star
Just above my fingertip." The star,

If any, that he sees beyond one's finger
Will never be the intended one. To bring
Another's eye to bear in such a fashion
On any single star seems to require
Something very like a constellation
That both habitually see at night;
Not in the stars themselves, but in among
Their scatter, perhaps, some old familiar sight
Is always there to take a bearing from.
And if the smallest child of all should cry
Out on the wet, black grass because he sees
Nothing but stars, though claiming that there is
Some bear not there that frightens him, we need
Only reflect that we ourselves have need

Of what is fearful (being really nothing)
With which to find our way about the path
That leads back down the hill again, and with
Which to enable the older children standing
By us to follow what we mean by "This
Star," "That one," or "The other one beyond it."
But what of the tiny, scared ones?—Such a bear,
Who needs it? We can still make do with both
The dipper that we always knew was there
And the bright, simple shapes that suddenly
Emerge on certain nights. To understand
The signs that stars compose, we need depend
Only on stars that are entirely there
And the apparent space between them. There

Never need be lines between them, puzzling
Our sense of what is what. What a star does
Is never to surprise us as it covers

**John Hollander**  *197*

The center of its patch of darkness, sparkling
Always, a point in one of many figures.
One solitary star would be quite useless,
A frigid conjecture, true but trifling;
And any single sign is meaningless
If unnecessary. Crab, bull, and ram,
Or frosty, irregular polygons of our own
Devising, or finally the Great Dark Bear
That we can never quite believe is there—
Having the others, any one of them
Can be dispensed with. The bear, of all of them,

Is somehow most like any one, taken
At random, in that we always tend to say
That just because it might be there; because
Some Ancients really traced it out, a broken
And complicated line, webbing bright stars
And fainter ones together; because a bear
Habitually appeared—then even by day
It is for us a thing that should be there.
We should not want to train ourselves to see it.
The world is everything that happens to
Be true. The stars at night seem to suggest
The shapes of what might be. If it were best,
Even, to have it there (such a great bear!
All hung with stars!), there still would be no bear.

# Richard Howard

*Richard Howard, born 1929 in Cleveland, lives in New York City. Since his graduation from Columbia College, he has carried forward an active career as a translator of French literature and as a critic of contemporary poetry in English. His urbanity of outlook and accent make him something of a rarity in a period when some poets disguise their erudition as anxiously as others advertise their ignorance. He has published a critical study of contemporary American poets, Alone with America.*

## Crepuscular

Late in the afternoon the light
    at this tapering end
of Long Island not so much fails
    as filters out the sun,
and in a month amid stances
    restores the word twilight
to its original senses:
    the day between, or half
itself, as when Locke alluded
    to 'the twilight of probability.'

But if at this moment I see
    its application, still

the word comes hard, appalling me
      in poetry: it sounds
too much like toilet, and Verlaine
      becomes impossible
to translate, for instance, even
      when the real thing happens
around me, as at this moment.
      Should reality sound poetical?

I sit at the French window (why
      else worry about Verlaine?)
worrying too about Robert Frost
      who said either we write
out of a strong weakness (poets
      love oxymoronic forms)
for the Muse, or we write because
      it seems like a good idea
to write. As the day tapers off
      like the island, I wonder at my choice.

Indeed, have I chosen? Outside
      the open window, Max
the dog is staring in at me,
      I can still see him, pale
against the darkening lawn, now,
      for he is a white dog
that has just found out the difference
      between Inside and Outside,
the choice that always, when there is
      a door, even a French one, must be made.

Thresholds for Max have lately meant
      a problem: he lies across
the sill supposing, I suppose,
      he'll have the best of both—
whatever world looms on each side;
      why, as another French

**Richard Howard** *201*

romantic said, must a door be
    either open or shut?
Max whines if I go to the toilet
    and close him out—for him the word toilet

clearly suggests the twilight, some
    subliminal ending.
These French doors ajar (ah, Musset!)
    merely frustrate decision;
and as the moments modify
    each blade of grass, blossom,
bush and branch, suddenly showing,
    in a light committed
to impartiality, yet
    another aspect: the night side of things,

Max trots over to the window
    where I sit wondering
if I want to elope with her
    or just be good friends, more
like a brother to the Muse, and
    gravely—I guess it is
gravely, in fact I'll never know—
    shoves his white face against
the pane, nose flattened, of the door
    and barks at me for being inside it.

But if I join him on the lawn
    that is gray now, he will
only dash back to the table
    where I have been, and bark
at me out on the silver grass.
    The Muse indoors, or on
the road? Possessed, or befriended?
    Choice is impossible.
Robert Frost is impossible.
    Max and I know the truth, quite possibly,

that the light survives a long time
        here on Long Island as
elsewhere, and then will come to terms
        with darkness, and we call
the terms *evening,* our term for time
        when neither power has
dominion, the air balances,
        but just for now, and then
the odds are on the dark again.
        Max and I know this too: it will be night.

# Barbara Howes

Barbara Howes, born May 1, 1914, in Boston, lives with
her two sons in North Pownal, Vermont. After graduating
from Bennington, she founded and edited the literary
magazine Chimera. During the years when she was the
wife of the poet William Jay Smith, she lived for long
periods in Italy and in France. Her deep interest in the
literature of the Caribbean has led to her editorship of
a collection of writing entitled From the Green Antilles.

## Chimera

After a fearful maze where doubt
Crept at my side down the terrible lightless channel,
I came in my dream to a sandspit parting
Wind-tossed fields of ocean. There,
Lightstepping, appeared
A trio of moose or mules,
Ugly as peat,
Their trotters slim as a queen's.
"Hippocampi!" cried a voice as they sped
Over black water, their salty course,
And away. From the heaving sea
Then sprang a fabulous beast
For its evening gallop.
Head of a lion, goat's head rearing
Back, derisive, wild—the dragon

Body scaling the waves; each reckless
Nature in balance, flying apart
In one. How it sported
Across the water, how it ramped and ran!
My heart took heart. Awaking, I thought:
What was disclosed in this vision
Was good; phantom or real,
I have looked on a noble animal.


## Home leave

With seven matching calfskin cases for his new suits—
Wife and three children following up the plank—
The Colonel shepherds his brood on board.

As the band pumps out "Arrivederci
Roma," the airman's apple
Face bobs over the first-class rail;
Across the watery gap, Sicilian
Crowds like lemmings rush at the narrowing pier.

Poised on the balls of his feet, the athlete
Goes below. Headwaiters
Screen him with menus; sommeliers
Approach on the double; corks pop to the creaking
Of timbers, while he dreams
Of winning every ship's pool.

Florid, the airman bunts
Favors around the dance floor: sky-blue-pink
Balloons doze on the air. It is the Captain's
Dinner; haloed in streamers, he romps
With a Duchess and wins
At Musical Chairs.

Later, on the boat-deck, laced
Tight as a hammock by Irish
Whiskey, the athlete nuzzles the nurse. Collapsed
Like a tent around her, he rolls
With the ship.

After breakfast, the children on deck, New York
Near, balling his fists, the hero
Turns on his wife:
He hits out as if to do her honor.

With seven matching calfskin cases for his new suits—
Wife and children following down the plank—
The Colonel shepherds his brood ashore.

In forest-green sportcoat and desert brogans, he passes
Through Customs like quicksilver. His wife
Is heavily veiled; her three
Children follow like figures in effigy.

---

**Chimera:** *A chimera is a creature out of mythology that
breathes fire and has a lion's head, a goat's body, and a
serpent's tail. It is usually considered a horrible and unreal
figment of the imagination, but in this poem it is judged
differently. Hippocampi are sea horses with two forefeet and
bodies that end in tails like those of dolphins or of fish.*

# Ted Hughes

*Ted Hughes, born August 17, 1930, in Mytholmroyd,*
*Yorkshire, was married to the late Sylvia Plath by whom*
*he had two children. During World War II he served*
*with the Royal Air Force as a ground wireless mechanic*
*and then studied at Cambridge. During a long visit to*
*the United States, during which he lived in Northampton*
*and Boston, Massachusetts, his first book,* The Hawk in
the Rain, *was the winner of the First Publication Award*
*of the Poetry Center of the YM-YWHA in New York City.*

## Hawk roosting

I sit in the top of the wood, my eyes closed.
Inaction, no falsifying dream
Between my hooked head and hooked feet:
Or in sleep rehearse perfect kills and eat.

The convenience of the high trees!
The air's buoyancy and the sun's ray
Are of advantage to me;
And the earth's face upward for my inspection.

My feet are locked upon the rough bark.
It took the whole of Creation
To produce my foot, my each feather:
Now I hold Creation in my foot

Or fly up, and revolve it all slowly—
I kill where I please because it is all mine.
There is no sophistry in my body:
My manners are tearing off heads—

The allotment of death.
For the one path of my flight is direct
Through the bones of the living.
No arguments assert my right:

The sun is behind me.
Nothing has changed since I began.
My eye has permitted no change.
I am going to keep things like this.


## View of a pig

The pig lay on a barrow dead.
It weighed, they said, as much as three men.
Its eyes closed, pink white eyelashes.
Its trotters stuck straight out.

Such weight and thick pink bulk
Set in death seemed not just dead.
It was less than lifeless, further off.
It was like a sack of wheat.

I thumped it without feeling remorse.
One feels guilty insulting the dead,
Walking on graves. But this pig
Did not seem able to accuse.

It was too dead. Just so much
A poundage of lard and pork.
Its last dignity had entirely gone.
It was not a figure of fun.

**Ted Hughes**  *210*

Too dead now to pity.
To remember its life, din, stronghold
Of earthly pleasure as it had been,
Seemed a false effort, and off the point.

Too deadly factual. Its weight
Oppressed me—how could it be moved?
And the trouble of cutting it up!
The gash in its throat was shocking, but not pathetic.

Once I ran at a fair in the noise
To catch a greased piglet
That was faster and nimbler than a cat,
Its squeal was the rending of metal.

Pigs must have hot blood, they feel like ovens.
Their bite is worse than a horse's—
They chop a half-moon clean out.
They eat cinders, dead cats.

Distinctions and admirations such
As this one was long finished with.
I stared at it a long time. They were going to scald it,
Scald it and scour it like a doorstep.

# David Ignatow

*David Ignatow, born February 7, 1914, in Brooklyn, New York, now lives in East Hampton, New York. Married, with two children, he teaches at the School for the Arts, Columbia University, and is co-editor of the literary magazine Chelsea. Before taking up a teaching career that took him for short periods to the University of Kansas, the University of Kentucky, and Vassar College, he worked at a number of jobs that ranged from Western Union delivery boy to corporation president.*

## Simultaneously

Simultaneously, five thousand miles apart,
two telephone poles, shaking and roaring
and hissing gas, rose from their emplacements
straight up, leveled off and headed
for each other's land, alerted radar
and ground defense, passed each other
in midair, escorted by worried planes,
and plunged into each other's place,
steaming and silent and standing straight,
sprouting leaves.

## News report

At two A.M. a thing, jumping out of a manhole,
the cover flying, raced down the street,
emitting wild shrieks of merriment and lust.
Women on their way from work, chorus girls
or actresses, were accosted with huge leers
and made to run; all either brought down
from behind by its flying weight, whereat
it attacked blindly, or leaping ahead,
made them stop and lie down.
Each, hysterical, has described it in her way,
one giving the shaggy fur, the next the shank bone
of a beast, and a third its nature
from which, as it seemed, pus dribbled,
when she saw no more—
    all taking place
unnoticed until the first report, hours later
when consciousness was regained, and each
from diverse parts of the city has a tell-tale
sign, the red teeth marks sunk into the thigh
and the smell of a goat clinging tenaciously
through perfume and a bath.


## The bagel

I stopped to pick up the bagel
rolling away in the wind,
annoyed with myself
for having dropped it
as it were a portent.
Faster and faster it rolled,
with me running after it
bent low, gritting my teeth,
and I found myself doubled over
and rolling down the street

**David Ignatow**  *214*

head over heels, one complete somersault
after another like a bagel
and strangely happy with myself.

# Randall Jarrell

*Randall Jarrell, born May 6, 1914, in Nashville, Tennessee,
died after having been struck by an automobile in 1965.
With his wife and two daughters he lived in Greensboro,
North Carolina, where he was professor of English at
the Women's College of the University of North Carolina.
Educated at Vanderbilt University, he taught at the
University of Texas, Sarah Lawrence, Kenyon, and in
Europe at the Salzburg Seminar in American Civilization.
He served a term as Consultant in Poetry at the Library
of Congress and was literary editor of* The Nation. *During
World War II he spent more than three years with the
Army Air Force, mainly in the Pacific. His writings
include a novel,* Pictures from an Institution, *and two
influential volumes of essays,* Poetry and the Age *and*
A Sad Heart at the Supermarket.

## Nestus Gurley

Sometimes waking, sometimes sleeping,
Late in the afternoon, or early
In the morning, I hear on the lawn,
On the walk, on the lawn, the soft quick step,
The sound half song, half breath: a note or two
That with a note or two would be a tune.
It is Nestus Gurley.

It is an old
Catch or snatch or tune
In the Dorian mode: the mode of the horses
That stand all night in the field asleep
Or awake, the mode of the cold
Hunter, Orion, wheeling upside-down,
All space and stars, in cater-cornered Heaven.
When, somewhere under the east,
The great march begins, with birds and silence;
When, in the day's first triumph, dawn
Rides over the houses, Nestus Gurley
Delivers to me my lot.

As the sun sets, I hear my daughter say:
"He has four routes and makes a hundred dollars."
Sometimes he comes with dogs, sometimes with children,
Sometimes with dogs and children.
He collects, today.
I hear my daughter say:
"Today Nestus has got on his derby."
And he says, after a little: "It's two-eighty."
"How could it be two-eighty?"
"Because this month there's five Sundays: it's two-eighty."

He collects, delivers. Before the first, least star
Is lost in the paling east; at evening
While the soft, side-lit, gold-leafed day
Lingers to see the stars, the boy Nestus
Delivers to me the Morning Star, the Evening Star
—Ah no, only the Morning *News,* the Evening *Record*
Of what I have done and what I have not done
Set down and held against me in the Book
Of Death, on paper yellowing
Already, with one morning's sun, one evening's sun.

Sometimes I only dream him. He brings then
News of a different morning, a judgment not of men.
The bombers have turned back over the Pole,

**Randall Jarrell**  *218*

Having met a star. . . . I look at that new year
And, waking, think of our Moravian Star
Not lit yet, and the pure beeswax candle
With its red flame-proofed paper pompom
Not lit yet, and the sweetened
Bun we brought home from the love-feast, still not eaten,
And the song the children sang: *O Morning Star*—

And at this hour, to the dew-hushed drums
Of the morning, Nestus Gurley
Marches to me over the lawn; and the cat Elfie,
Furred like a musk-ox, coon-tailed, gold-leaf-eyed,
Looks at the paper boy without alarm
But yawns, and stretches, and walks placidly
Across the lawn to his ladder, climbs it, and begins to purr.

I let him in,
Go out and pick up from the grass the paper hat
Nestus has folded: this tricorne fit for a Napoleon
Of our days and institutions, weaving
Baskets, being bathed, receiving
Electric shocks, Rauwolfia. . . . I put it on
—Ah no, only unfold it.
There is dawn inside; and I say to no one
About—
       it is a note or two
That with a note or two would—
            say to no one
About nothing: "He delivers dawn."

When I lie coldly
—Lie, that is, neither with coldness nor with warmth—
In the darkness that is not lit by anything,
In the grave that is not lit by anything
Except our hope: the hope
That is not proofed against anything, but pure
And shining as the first, least star
That is lost in the east on the morning of Judgment—

**Randall Jarrell**   *219*

May I say, recognizing the step
Or tune or breath. . . .
      recognizing the breath,
May I say, "It is Nestus Gurley."


## The woman at the Washington zoo

The saris go by me from the embassies.

Cloth from the moon. Cloth from another planet.
They look back at the leopard like the leopard.

And I. . . .
      this print of mine, that has kept its color
Alive through so many cleanings; this dull null
Navy I wear to work, and wear from work, and so
To my bed, so to my grave, with no
Complaints, no comment: neither from my chief,
The Deputy Chief Assistant, nor his chief—
Only I complain. . . . this serviceable
Body that no sunlight dyes, no hand suffuses
But, dome-shadowed, withering among columns,
Wavy beneath fountains—small, far-off, shining
In the eyes of animals, these beings trapped
As I am trapped but not, themselves, the trap,
Aging, but without knowledge of their age,
Kept safe here, knowing not of death, for death—
Oh, bars of my own body, open, open!

The world goes by my cage and never sees me.
And there come not to me, as come to these,
The wild beast, sparrows pecking the llamas' grain,
Pigeons settling on the bears' bread, buzzards
Tearing the meat the flies have clouded. . . .
      Vulture,
When you come for the white rat that the foxes left,

Take off the red helmet of your head, the black
Wings that have shadowed me, and step to me as man:
The wild brother at whose feet the white wolves fawn,
To whose hand of power the great lioness
Stalks, purring. . . .
        You know what I was,
You see what I am: change me, change me!


## The snow-leopard

His pads furring the scarp's rime,
Weightless in greys and ecru, gliding
Invisibly, incuriously
As the crystals of the cirri wandering
A mile below his absent eyes,
The leopard gazes at the caravan.
The yaks groaning with tea, the burlaps
Lapping and lapping each stunned universe
That gasps like a kettle for its thinning life
Are pools in the interminable abyss
That ranges up through ice, through air, to night.
Raiders of the unminding element,
The last cold capillaries of their kind,
They move so slowly they are motionless
To any eye less stubborn than a man's. . . .
From the implacable jumble of the blocks
The grains dance icily, a scouring plume,
Into the breath, sustaining, unsustainable,
They trade to that last stillness for their death.
They sense with misunderstanding horror, with desire,
Behind the world their blood sets up in mist
The brute and geometrical necessity:
The leopard waving with a grating purr
His six-foot tail; the leopard, who looks sleepily—
Cold, fugitive, secure—at all he knows,
At all that he is: the heart of heartlessness.

**Randall Jarrell**  *221*

**Nestus Gurley:** *Nestus Gurley is only the boy who delivers the papers, but in this poem he looms as large as a character out of mythology. Dorian mode refers to the music of the Dorians, which the more sophisticated Athenians regarded as harsh and rough. Moravian Star is a decoration manufactured in Moravia, central Czechoslovakia. Rauwolfia is the original name for the medical extract known as snakeroot, sometimes used for treatment of mental patients.*

# Donald Justice

*Donald Justice, born August 12, 1925, in Miami, Florida, lives with his wife and son in Syracuse, New York, where he teaches English at Syracuse University. He studied at the Universities of Miami and North Carolina, then took a Ph.D. at the University of Iowa where he was an influential member of the Writers' Workshop.*

## Memo from the desk of X

Re: the question of poems.
Certainly your proposal
Merits consideration.

I myself recall fondly
Old friends among the poems—
Harmless, but to what purpose?

Some few indeed we might keep
Alive, in transparent tents,
As an example to youth

Of the great waste the past was.
The white face of a poem
Turned to the wall, the almost

Visible heartbeat, the deep
But irregular breathing—
No harm to the state in this.

The average citizen
Might be the healthier for
Some such exposure. Granted.

Nevertheless, we must weigh
The cost against the result.
Aside from supervision,

Frequent transfusions of blood—
And often of some rare type—
Would have to be provided,

And guides trained to interpret
Their curious expressions
For the new generation,

Those who have had no chance to
Learn much about suffering.
We of an older order

Should be prepared to refute
All charges of nostalgia.
We must look to the future.

I am told by our experts
That an esthetic response
To straight lines and to circles

May be acquired, with study.
This strikes me as promising.
Our landscapes already are

Shifting in that direction;
Likewise our lives. This approach
Is not unrealistic.

I therefore must recommend,
Though not without some regret,
The extinction of poems.

## The tourist from Syracuse

*One of those men who can be a car salesman or a*
*tourist from Syracuse or a hired assassin.*
                    JOHN D. MacDONALD

You would not recognize me.
Mine is the face which blooms in
The dank mirrors of washrooms
As you grope for the light switch.

My eyes have the expression
Of the cold eyes of statues
Watching their pigeons return
From the feed you have scattered,

And I stand on my corner
With the same marble patience.
If I move at all, it is
At the same pace precisely

As the shade of the awning
Under which I stand waiting
And with whose blackness it seems
I am already blended.

I speak seldom, and always
In a murmur as quiet

**Donald Justice**   226

As that of crowds which surround
The victims of accidents.

Shall I confess who I am?
My name is all names and none.
I am the used-car salesman,
The tourist from Syracuse,

The hired assassin, waiting.
I will stand here forever
Like one who has missed his bus—
Familiar, anonymous—

On my usual corner,
The corner at which you turn
To approach that place where now
You must not hope to arrive.

# Bob Kaufman

*Bob (Robert Cornell) Kaufman, born in San Francisco in 1940, is the son of a German Jew and a Martinique Roman Catholic who had thirteen other children. His maternal great-grandmother, brought to Louisiana on an African slave ship, was a great influence in his youth, as was his father's Orthodox Judaism and his mother's devout Roman Catholicism. He joined the Merchant Marine as a cabin boy when he was thirteen and worked at sea for many years. In the late 1950s he was one of the founders of Beatitudes, a poetry magazine of North Beach in San Francisco where he now lives.*

## Afterwards, they shall dance

In the city of St. Francis they have taken down the statue of
    St. Francis,
And the hummingbirds all fly forward to protest, humming
    feather poems.

Bodenheim denounced everyone and wrote. Bodenheim had
    no sweet marijuana dreams,
Patriotic muscateleer, did not die seriously, no poet love to
    end with, gone.

Dylan took the stone cat's nap at St. Vincent's, vaticaned
    beer, no defense;
That poem shouted from his nun-filled room, an insult to the
    brain, nerves,
Save now from Swansea, white horses, beer birds, snore
    poems, Wales-bird.

Billie Holiday got lost on the subway and stayed there
    forever,

Raised little peace-of-mind gardens in out of the way
    stations,
And will go on living in wrappers of jazz silence forever,
    loved.

My face feels like a living emotional relief map, forever wet.
My hair is curling in anticipation of my own wild gardening.

Poor Edgar Allan Poe died translated, in unpressed pants,
    ended in light,
Surrounded by ecstatic gold bugs, his hegira blessed
    by Baudelaire's orgy.

Whether I am a poet or not, I use fifty dollars' worth
    of air every day, cool.
In order to exist I hide behind stacks of red and blue poems
And open little sensuous parasols, singing the nail-in-
    the-foot song, drinking cool beatitudes.


## To my son Parker, asleep in the next room

On ochre walls in ice-formed caves shaggy Neanderthals
    marked their place in time.
On germinal trees in equatorial stands embryonic giants
    carved beginnings.
On Tasmanian flatlands mud-clothed first men hacked rock,
    still soft.
On Melanesian mountain peaks barked heads were reared
    in pride and beauty.
On steamy Java's cooling lava stooped humans raised stones
    to altar height.
On newborn China's plain mythless sons of Han acquired
    peaked gods with teak faces.
On holy India's sacred soil future gods carved worshipped
    reflections.
On Coptic Ethiopia's pimple rock pyramid builders tore
    volcanoes from earth.

**Bob Kaufman**   230

On death-loving Egypt's godly sands living sacrifices carved
    naked power.
On Sumeria's cliffs speechless artists gouged messages
    to men yet uncreated.
On glorious Assyria's earthen dens art priests chipped
    figures of awe and hidden dimensions.
On splendored Peru's gold-stained body filigreed temples
    were torn from severed hands.
On perfect Greece's bloody sites marble stirred
    under hands of men.
On degenerate Rome's trembling sod imitators sculpted lies
    into beauty.
On slave Europe's prostrate form chained souls shaped free
    men.
On wild America's green torso original men painted
    glacial languages.
On cold Arctica's snowy surface leathery men raised totems
    in frozen air.
On this shore, you are all men, before, forever, eternally
    free in all things.
On this shore, we shall raise our monuments of stones,
    of wood, of mud, of color, of labor, of belief, of being,
    of life, of love, of self, of man expressed
    in self-determined compliance, or willful revolt,
    secure in this avowed truth, that no man is our master,
    nor can any ever be, at any time in time to come.

---

**Afterwards, they shall dance:** *Maxwell Bodenheim, who died
in 1954, is a poet inevitably identified with the romantic
decades of Greenwich Village. In the last sad years of his
life he often traded his poems and his presence as poet
manqué for drinks from strangers in the bars of MacDougal
Street. At his death he was eulogized by one of his
contemporaries, Alfred Kreymborg, as a latter-day Poe.
St. Vincent's is the Roman Catholic hospital at Seventh
Avenue and Eleventh Street where Dylan Thomas died in
1953. Not long before her death in 1959, Billie Holiday, the
great black singer of blues, was convicted of violation of the
narcotics laws and served a sentence in the Women's Prison
of the City of New York which was then located in the Village.*

**Bob Kaufman**  231

# X. J. Kennedy

X. J. Kennedy, born 1930 in Dover, New Jersey, lives with
his wife and children in Bedford, Massachusetts, and
he teaches English at Tufts University. Educated at Seton
Hall and Columbia, he served four years in the United States Navy,
then spent a year in Paris studying at the Sorbonne.

## Artificer

Blessing his handiwork, his drawbridge closed,
    He sabbathed on a hill of hand-tooled wax.
On stainless steel chrysanthemums there posed
    Little gold bees with twist-keys in their backs.

Nothing could budge in this his country: lewd
    Leaves could go slither other people's hills.
    *His* thrushes tried tin whistles in their bills;
His oaks bore pewter acorns that unscrewed.

Increase perfection! So, he shaped a wife,
    Pleated the fabric of her chartered thigh,
Begat sons by excisions of a knife
    In camphorwood. He warned them not to die.

The moment flowed. So did his cellophane
    Brook over rollers. All obdurate day

His player-piano tunkled him its lay,
Though on its ivory dentures a profane

Tarnish kept ripening, and where high tide
    Slid on ballbearings ceaselessly to shore,
Red rust. All night, the world that lolled outside
    Kept slipping newborn rats under his door.


## Driving cross-country

Jack Giantkiller took and struck
    His harp and stalks sat up, all ears—
With wavelengths corn in Keokuk
    Comes on so hard it interferes.

Glass vacant, in the Stoplight Lounge,
    Expecting to be stood a meal,
Ella Ashhauler has to scrounge,
    Her slipper tilted, for some heel.

Where is the prince of yesteryear
    Beneath whose lip princesses roused?
Bourbon will add a gleam of cheer.
    The place has lately been deloused.

Prints of a bowling-ball-eyed child
    Brood over ornamental pewter.
A wand's been waved, the whole house styled
    To offend no one, by computer:

A room the same as last night's room,
    Exact same bath mat underfoot.
In thrall to some unlucky charm,
    We hurtle; but, it seems, stay put.

**X. J. Kennedy**  *234*

When, headlight-blind, we let fall head
    On pillows hard by right-hand lanes
In airconditioned gingerbread,
    It keeps on driving through our veins,

Some hag's black broth. At dawn we stare,
    Locked into lane by rule of lime.
We had a home. It was somewhere.
    We were there once upon a time.

# Galway Kinnell

*Galway Kinnell, born February 1, 1927, in Providence, Rhode Island, lives in Sheffield, Vermont, with his wife and two children. He was educated at Princeton and the University of Rochester and has taught at Alfred University, the University of Chicago, the University of Grenoble, New York University, and in Iran at the University of Teheran. Besides poetry he has published a novel, Black Light, and many translations from the French.*

## First song

Then it was dusk in Illinois, the small boy
After an afternoon of carting dung
Hung on the rail fence, a sapped thing
Weary to crying. Dark was growing tall
And he began to hear the pond frogs all
Calling upon his ear with what seemed their joy.

Soon their sound was pleasant for a boy
Listening in the smoky dusk and the nightfall
Of Illinois, and then from the field two small
Boys came bearing cornstalk violins
And rubbed three cornstalk bows with resins,
And they set fiddling with them as with joy.

It was now fine music the frogs and the boys
Did in the towering Illinois twilight make
And into dark in spite of a right arm's ache
A boy's hunched body loved out of a stalk
The first song of his happiness, and the song woke
His heart to the darkness and into the sadness of joy.


## Duck-chasing

I spied a very small brown duck
Riding the swells of the sea
Like a rocking-chair. "Little duck!"
I cried. It paddled away,
I paddled after it. When it dived,
Down I dived: too smoky was the sea,
We were lost. It surfaced
In the west, I torpedoed west
And when it dived I dived,
And we were lost and lost and lost
In the slant smoke of the sea.
When I came floating up on it
From the side, like a deadman,
And yelled suddenly, it took off,
It skimmed the swells as it ascended,
Brown wings burning and flashing
In the sun as the sea it rose over
Burned and flashed underneath it.
I did not see the little duck again.
Duck-chasing is a game like any game.
When it is over it is all over.

## To Christ our Lord

The legs of the elk punctured the snow's crust
And wolves floated lightfooted on the land
Hunting Christmas elk living and frozen;
Inside snow melted in a basin, and a woman basted
A bird spread over coals by its wings and head.

Snow had sealed the windows; candles lit
The Christmas meal. The Christmas grace chilled
The cooked bird, being long-winded and the room cold.
During the words a boy thought, is it fitting
To eat this creature killed on the wing?

He had killed it himself, climbing out
Alone on snowshoes in the Christmas dawn,
The fallen snow swirling and the snowfall gone,
Heard its throat scream as the rifle shouted,
Watched it drop, and fished from the snow the dead.

He had not wanted to shoot. The sound
Of wings beating into the hushed air
Had stirred his love, and his fingers
Froze in his gloves, and he wondered,
Famishing, could he fire? Then he fired.

Now the grace praised his wicked act. At its end
The bird on the plate
Stared at his stricken appetite.
There had been nothing to do but surrender,
To kill and to eat; he ate as he had killed, with wonder.

At night on snowshoes on the drifting field
He wondered again, for whom had love stirred?
The stars glittered on the snow and nothing answered.
Then the Swan spread her wings, cross of the cold north,
The pattern and mirror of the acts of earth.

**Galway Kinnell**   239

# Thomas Kinsella

*Thomas Kinsella, born May 4, 1928, in Dublin, Ireland,*
*teaches English at Southern Illinois University in*
*Carbondale. Before assuming a professorial career in*
*1965, he was for many years an Irish civil servant with*
*the Department of Finance. Profoundly concerned with*
*the past of his people, their language and myth, Kinsella,*
*according to the late Frank O'Connor is "the artistic*
*conscience" of the new poets of Ireland.*

## The secret garden

The place is growing difficult. Flails of bramble
Crawl into the lawn; on every hand
Glittering, toughened branches drink their dew.
Tiny worlds, drop by drop, tremble
On thorns and leaves; they will melt away.
The silence whispers around us:
Wither, wither, visible, invisible!

A child stands an instant at my knee.
His mouth smells of energy, light as light.
I touch my hand to his pearl flesh, taking strength.
He stands still, absorbing in return
The first taint. Immaculate, the waiting
Kernel of his brain.
How set him free, a son, toward the sour encounter?

Children's voices somewhere call his name.
He runs glittering into the sun, and is gone:
I cultivate my garden for the dew: . . .
A rasping boredom funnels into death!

The sun climbs, a creature of one day,
And the dew dries to dust.

My hand strays out and picks off one sick leaf.


## Folk wisdom

Each year for a short season
The toads stare and wait
And clutch in their being
A shrieking without breath.
There is nothing but the harrow—
Everything speaks its approach;
Even blades of grass,
Flower stems, are harrows' teeth,
Hideous, because they are
Parallel and in earth.

The men are shackling their horses
In the yard. They talk softly
About earth and seed.

Soon the toads will shriek—
Each, as he hears his neighbour,
Gathers all his strength.

And so the curse was lifted,
According to the tale;
One kiss, and a prince stood there
Where a toad had been.
It is possible . . . such a strain,

**Thomas Kinsella**  242

Under the kiss of the harrow,
Could suffice. As when a man
Clutches his ears, deafened
By his world, to find a jewel
Made of pain in his hands.

# Stanley Kunitz

*Stanley Kunitz, born July 29, 1905, in Worcester,*
*Massachusetts, lives in New York City with his third*
*wife, the painter Elise Asher. He was educated at*
*Harvard and then worked for many years as an editor of*
*biographical reference books. In World War II he was a*
*noncommissioned officer in charge of information and*
*education in the Air Transport Command. Subsequently*
*he taught at Bennington, at Brandeis, and, as a visiting*
*professor, at other American colleges. Although he had*
*been publishing for twenty years, his wide recognition*
*came suddenly when, in 1958, the publication of his*
*Selected Poems brought him the Pulitzer Prize and a*
*favorable revaluation of his career by many critics*
*and reviewers.*

## The science of the night

I touch you in the night, whose gift was you,
My careless sprawler,
And I touch you cold, unstirring, star-bemused,
That are become the land of your self-strangeness.
What long seduction of the bone has led you
Down the imploring roads I cannot take
Into the arms of ghosts I never knew,
Leaving my manhood on a rumpled field

To guard you where you lie so deep
In absent-mindedness,
Caught in the calcium snows of sleep?

And even should I track you to your birth
Through all the cities of your mortal trial,
As in my jealous thought I try to do,
You would escape me—from the brink of earth
Take off to where the lawless auroras run,
You with your wild and metaphysic heart.
My touch is on you, who are light-years gone.
We are not souls but systems, and we move
In clouds of our unknowing
                              like great nebulae.
Our very motives swirl and have their start
With father lion and with mother crab.

Dreamer, my own lost rib,
Whose planetary dust is blowing
Past archipelagoes of myth and light,
What far Magellans are you mistress of
To whom you speed the pleasure of your art?
As through a glass that magnifies my loss
I see the lines of your spectrum shifting red,
The universe expanding, thinning out,
Our worlds flying, oh flying, fast apart.

From hooded powers and from abstract flight
I summon you, your person and your pride.
Fall to me now from outer space,
Still fastened desperately to my side;
Through gulfs of streaming air
Bring me the mornings of the milky ways
Down to my threshold in your drowsy eyes;
And by the virtue of your honeyed word
Restore the liquid language of the moon,
That in gold mines of secrecy you delve.
Awake!

**Stanley Kunitz**   *246*

My whirling hands stay at the noon,
Each cell within my body holds a heart
And all my hearts in unison strike twelve.


**Father and son**

Now in the suburbs and the falling light
I followed him, and now down sandy road
Whiter than bone-dust, through the sweet
Curdle of fields, where the plums
Dropped with their load of ripeness, one by one.
Mile after mile I followed, with skimming feet,
After the secret master of my blood,
Him, steeped in the odor of ponds, whose indomitable love
Kept me in chains. Strode years; stretched into bird;
Raced through the sleeping country where I was young,
The silence unrolling before me as I came,
The night nailed like an orange to my brow.

How should I tell him my fable and the fears,
How bridge the chasm in a casual tone,
Saying, "The house, the stucco one you built,
We lost. Sister married and went from home,
And nothing comes back, it's strange, from where she goes.
I lived on a hill that had too many rooms:
Light we could make, but not enough of warmth,
And when the light failed, I climbed under the hill.
The papers are delivered every day;
I am alone and never shed a tear."

At the water's edge, where the smothering ferns lifted
Their arms, "Father!" I cried, "Return! You know
The way. I'll wipe the mudstains from your clothes;
No trace, I promise, will remain. Instruct
Your son, whirling between two wars,
In the Gemara of your gentleness,

**Stanley Kunitz** *247*

For I would be a child to those who mourn
And brother to the foundlings of the field
And friend of innocence and all bright eyes.
O teach me how to work and keep me kind."

Among the turtles and the lilies he turned to me
The white ignorant hollow of his face.

---

**The science of the night:** *Isolation, even at the pitch of love, is a recurrent theme of poets. The following lines may best be read as the meditation of a lover keenly aware of the proximity of his love and just as keenly aware of the terrible singleness of any human soul. The circumstance of the poem is focused in the line "My touch is on you, who are light-years gone."*

**Father and son:** *Dreams as a source of understanding have always figured importantly in poetry. The dream recorded here, which, actual or imagined, comes to the same thing, recapitulates a man's personal history and his arrival, just before waking, at wisdom that nevertheless involves the deepest sense of loss. Gemara is that part of the Talmud, the Jewish civil and canonical law, that serves as commentary on the Mishnah, or text.*

# Philip Larkin

*Philip Larkin, born August 9, 1922, in Coventry, England,
lives in Hull, where he is librarian of the university. He
was educated at the King Henry VIII School, Coventry,
and St. John's College, Oxford, and has published a
novel,* A Girl in Winter.

## Poetry of departures

Sometimes you hear, fifth-hand,
As epitaph:
*He chucked up everything*
*And just cleared off,*
And always the voice will sound
Certain you approve
This audacious, purifying,
Elemental move.

And they are right, I think.
We all hate home
And having to be there:
I detest my room,
Its specially-chosen junk,
The good books, the good bed,
And my life, in perfect order:
So to hear it said

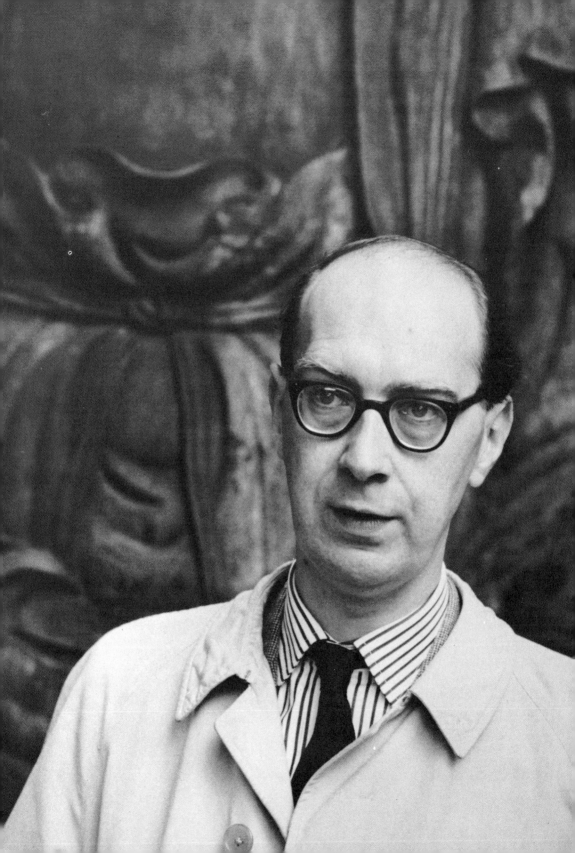

*He walked out on the whole crowd*
Leaves me flushed and stirred,
Like *Then she undid her dress*
Or *Take that you bastard;*
Surely I can, if he did?
And that helps me stay
Sober and industrious.
But I'd go today,

Yes, swagger the nut-strewn roads,
Crouch in the fo'c'sle
Stubbly with goodness, if
It weren't so artificial,
Such a deliberate step backwards
To create an object:
Books; china; a life
Reprehensibly perfect.


## Church going

Once I am sure there's nothing going on
I step inside, letting the door thud shut.
Another church: matting, seats, and stone,
And little books; sprawlings of flowers, cut
For Sunday, brownish now; some brass and stuff
Up at the holy end; the small neat organ;
And a tense, musty unignorable silence,
Brewed God knows how long. Hatless, I take off
My cycle-clips in awkward reverence,

Move forward, run my hand around the font.
From where I stand, the roof looks almost new—
Cleaned, or restored? Someone would know: I don't.
Mounting the lectern, I peruse a few
Hectoring large-scale verses, and pronounce
'Here endeth' much more loudly than I'd meant.

**Philip Larkin**  *251*

The echoes snigger briefly. Back at the door
I sign the book, donate an Irish sixpence,
Reflect the place was not worth stopping for.

Yet stop I did: in fact I often do,
And always end much at a loss like this,
Wondering what to look for; wondering, too,
When churches fall completely out of use
What we shall turn them into; if we shall keep
A few cathedrals chronically on show,
Their parchment, plate and pyx in locked cases,
And let the rest rent-free to rain and sheep.
Shall we avoid them as unlucky places?

Or, after dark, will dubious women come
To make their children touch a particular stone;
Pick simples for a cancer; or on some
Advised night see walking a dead one?
Power of some sort or other will go on
In games, in riddles, seemingly at random;
But superstition, like belief, must die,
And what remains when disbelief has gone?
Grass, weedy pavement, brambles, buttress, sky,

A shape less recognizable each week,
A purpose more obscure. I wonder who
Will be the last, the very last, to seek
This place for what it was; one of the crew
That tap and jot and know what rood-lofts were?
Some ruin-bibber, randy for antique,
Or Christmas-addict, counting on a whiff
Of gown-and-bands and organ-pipes and myrrh?
Or will he be my representative,

Bored, uninformed, knowing the ghostly silt
Dispersed, yet tending to this cross of ground
Through suburb scrub because it held unspilt
So long and equably what since is found

**Philip Larkin**  *252*

Only in separation—marriage, and birth,
And death, and thoughts of these—for whom was built
This special shell? For, though I've no idea
What this accoutred frowsty barn is worth,
It pleases me to stand in silence here;

A serious house on serious earth it is,
In whose blent air all our compulsions meet,
Are recognised, and robed as destinies.
And that much never can be obsolete,
Since someone will forever be surprising
A hunger in himself to be more serious,
And gravitating with it to this ground,
Which, he once heard, was proper to grow wise in,
If only that so many dead lie round.

**Philip Larkin** *253*

# Denise Levertov

*Denise Levertov, born October 24, 1923, lives in New York City and, during the summer, in Maine. She is the wife of Mitchell Goodman, a novelist and political activist, and they have one son. Miss Levertov's father was a Russian emigré who became an Anglican priest; her mother was Welsh. She came to the United States in 1948 and is an American citizen.*

## Bedtime

We are a meadow where the bees hum,
mind and body are almost one

as the fire snaps in the stove
and our eyes close,

and mouth to mouth, the covers
pulled over our shoulders,

we drowse as horses drowse afield,
in accord; though the fall cold

surrounds our warm bed, and though
by day we are singular and often lonely.

## Psalm concerning the castle

Let me be at the place of the castle.
Let the castle be within me.
Let it rise foursquare from the moat's ring.
Let the moat's waters reflect green plumage of ducks, let
    the shells of swimming turtles break the surface or be
    seen through the rippling depths.
Let horsemen be stationed at the rim of it, and a dog,
    always alert on the brink of sleep.
Let the space under the first storey be dark, let the water
    lap the stone posts, and vivid green slime glimmer
    upon them; let a boat be kept there.
Let the caryatids of the second storey be bears upheld on
    beams that are dragons.
On the parapet of the central room, let there be four archers,
    looking off to the four horizons. Within, let the
    prince be at home, let him sit in deep thought, at
    peace, all the windows open to the loggias.
Let the young queen sit above, in the cool air, her child in
    her arms; let her look with joy at the great circle, the
    pilgrim shadows, the work of the sun and the play of
    the wind. Let her walk to and fro. Let the columns
    uphold the roof, let the storeys uphold the columns,
    let there be dark space below the lowest floor, let the
    castle rise foursquare out of the moat, let the moat be a
    ring and the water deep, let the guardians guard it, let
    there be wide lands around it, let that country where it
    stands be within me, let me be where it is.

# Cecil Day Lewis

*Cecil Day Lewis, born April 27, 1904, in Beallintogher, Ireland, lives with his second wife near London, where he is a director of the publishing house Chatto and Windus. Educated at Oxford, he taught at schools in England and Scotland until 1935. During World War II he was an editor of books and pamphlets for the Ministry of Education and later returned to academic life first as a lecturer at Trinity College and then as professor of poetry at Oxford. He is widely known as the author of many expert detective stories which he publishes under the pseudonym Nicholas Blake. In 1968 he succeeded John Masefield as Poet Laureate of England.*

## Departure in the dark

Nothing so sharply reminds a man he is mortal
As leaving a place
In a winter morning's dark, the air on his face
Unkind as the touch of sweating metal:
Simple goodbyes to children or friends become
A felon's numb
Farewell, and love that was a warm, a meeting place—
Love is the suicide's grave under the nettles.

Gloomed and clemmed as if by an imminent ice-age
Lies the dear world

Of your street-strolling, field-faring. The senses, curled
At the dead end of a shrinking passage,
Care not if close the inveterate hunters creep,
And memories sleep
Like mammoths in lost caves. Drear, extinct is the world,
And has no voice for consolation or presage.

There is always something at such times of the passover,
When the dazed heart
Beats for it knows not what, whether you part
From home or prison, acquaintance or lover—
Something wrong with the time-table, something unreal
In the scrambled meal
And the bag ready packed by the door, as though the heart
Has gone ahead, or is staying here forever.

No doubt for the Israelites that early morning
It was hard to be sure
If home were prison or prison home: the desire
Going forth meets the desire returning.
This land, that had cut their pride down to the bone
Was now their own
By ancient deeds of sorrow. Beyond, there was nothing sure
But a desert of freedom to quench their fugitive yearnings.

At this blind hour the heart is informed of nature's
Ruling that man
Should be nowhere a more tenacious settler than
Among wry thorns and ruins, yet nurture
A seed of discontent in his ripest ease.
There's a kind of release
And a kind of torment in every goodbye for every man—
And will be, even to the last of his dark departures.

## Reconciliation

All day beside the shattered tank he'd lain
Like a limp creature hacked out of its shell,
Now shrivelling on the desert's grid,
Now floating above a sharp-set ridge of pain.

There came a roar, like water, in his ear.
The mortal dust was laid. He seemed to be lying
In a cool coffin of stone walls,
While memory slid towards a plunging weir.

The time that was, the time that might have been
Find in this shell of stone a chance to kiss
Before they part eternally:
He feels a world without, a world within

Wrestle like old antagonists, until each is
Balancing each. Then, in a heavenly calm,
The lock gates open, and beyond
Appear the argent, swan-assemblied reaches.


## The dead

They lie in the Sunday street
Like effigies thrown down after a fête
Among the bare-faced houses frankly yawning revulsion,
Fag-ends of fires, litter of rubble, stale
Confetti-sprinkle of blood. Was it defeat
With them, or triumph? Purification
Or All Fools' Day? On this they remain silent.
Their eyes are closed to honour and hate.

We cannot blame the great
Alone—the mad, the calculating or effete
Rulers. Whatever grotesque scuffle and piercing

**Cecil Day Lewis**  *260*

Indignant orgasm of pain took them,
All that enforced activity of death
Did answer and compensate
Some voluntary inaction, soft option, dream retreat.
Each man died for the sins of a whole world:
For the ant's self-abdication, the fat-stock's patience
Are sweet goodbye to human nations.

Still, they have made us eat
Our knowing words, who rose and paid
The bill for the whole party with their uncounted courage.
And if they chose the dearer consolations
Of living—the bar, the dog race, the discreet
Establishment—and let Karl Marx and Freud go hang,
Now they are dead, who can dispute their choice?
Not I, nor even Fate.

---

**Departure in the dark:** *In the third and fourth stanzas of this poem there is an extended allusion to the Biblical story of the delivery of the Israelites, under Moses, from imprisonment and bondage in Egypt to "a desert of freedom" and the Promised Land.*

**The dead:** *The dead here are ordinary people who lived ordinary lives, unaware of the life of the intellect as represented by such world-shaking figures as Karl Marx and Sigmund Freud, and died in anonymous multitudes in the bombing of London. Speaking as one who is aware of philosophies and scientific discoveries that shape history, the poet pays homage to those who keep the world going simply by enduring the hazards of existence and the darkness of their own ignorance.*

# Robert Lowell

*Robert Lowell, born March 1, 1917, in Boston, lives in New York City with his wife, the writer Elizabeth Hardwick, and his daughter. He went to Harvard for two years and then transferred to Kenyon College, where he was a student of John Crowe Ransom. During World War II he refused to register for the draft and was imprisoned as a conscientious objector. After his release, he lived with his first wife, the novelist Jean Stafford, in New York City and in Maine. In recent years he has taught in the English departments of Kenyon College and Boston University, and he is currently visiting professor at Harvard.*

## Ford Madox Ford

*1873–1939*

The lobbed ball plops, then dribbles to the cup . . . .
(a birdie Fordie!) But it nearly killed
the ministers. Lloyd George was holding up
the flag. He gabbled, 'Hop-toad, hop-toad, hop-toad!
Hueffer has used a niblick on the green;
it's filthy art, Sir, filthy art!'
You answered, 'What is art to me and thee?
Will a blacksmith teach a midwife how to bear?'
That cut the puffing statesman down to size,
Ford. You said, 'Otherwise,

I would have been general of a division.' Ah Ford!
Was it war, the sport of kings, that your *Good Soldier,*
the best French novel in the language, taught
those Georgian Whig magnificoes at Oxford,
at Oxford decimated on the Somme?
Ford, five times black-balled for promotion,
then mustard gassed voiceless some seven miles
behind the lines at Nancy or Belleau Wood:
you emerged in your 'worn uniform,
gilt dragons on the revers of the tunic,'
a Jonah—O divorced, divorced
from the whale-fat of post-war London! Boomed,
cut, plucked and booted! In Provence, New York . . .
marrying, blowing . . . nearly dying
at Boulder, when the altitude
pressed the world on your heart,
and your audience, almost football-size,
shrank to a dozen, while you stood
mumbling, with fish-blue eyes,
and mouth pushed out
fish-fashion, as if you gagged for air . . . .
Sandman! Your face, a childish O. The sun
is pernod-yellow and it gilds the heirs
of all the ages there on Washington
and Stuyvesant, your Lilliputian squares,
where writing turned your pockets inside out.
But master, mammoth mumbler, tell me why
the bales of your left-over novels buy
less than a bandage for your gouty foot.
Wheel-horse, O unforgetting elephant,
I hear you huffing at your old Brevoort,
Timon and Falstaff, while you heap the board
for publishers. Fiction! I'm selling short
your lies that made the great your equals. Ford,
you were a kind man and you died in want.

### Death from cancer

This Easter, Arthur Winslow, less than dead,
Your people set you up in Phillips' House
To settle off your wrestling with the crab—
The claws drop flesh upon your yachting blouse
Until longshoreman Charon come and stab
Through your adjusted bed
And crush the crab. On Boston Basin, shells
Hit water by the Union Boat Club wharf:
You ponder why the coxes' squeakings dwarf
The *resurrexit dominus* of all the bells.

Grandfather Winslow, look, the swanboats coast
That island in the Public Gardens, where
The bread-stuffed ducks are brooding, where with tub
And strainer the mid-Sunday Irish scare
The sun-struck shallows for the dusky chub
This Easter, and the ghost
Of risen Jesus walks the waves to run
Arthur upon a trumpeting black swan
Beyond Charles River to the Acheron
Where the wide waters and their voyager are one.

### For the Union dead

*Relinquunt omnia servare rem publicam.*

The old South Boston Aquarium stands
in a Sahara of snow now. Its broken windows are boarded.
The bronze weathervane cod has lost half its scales.
The airy tanks are dry.

Once my nose crawled like a snail on the glass;
my hand tingled
to burst the bubbles,
drifting from the noses of the cowed, compliant fish.

**Robert Lowell**   *265*

My hand draws back. I often sigh still
for the dark downward and vegetating kingdom
of the fish and reptile. One morning last March,
I pressed against the new barbed and galvanized

fence on the Boston Common. Behind their cage,
yellow dinosaur steam shovels were grunting
as they cropped up tons of mush and grass
to gouge their underworld garage.

Parking lots luxuriate like civic
sand piles in the heart of Boston.
A girdle of orange, Puritan-pumpkin-colored girders
braces the tingling Statehouse, shaking

over the excavations, as it faces Colonel Shaw
and his bell-cheeked Negro infantry
on St. Gaudens' shaking Civil War relief,
propped by a plank splint against the garage's earthquake.

Two months after marching through Boston,
half the regiment was dead;
at the dedication,
William James could almost hear the bronze Negroes breathe.

The monument sticks like a fishbone
in the city's throat.
Its colonel is as lean
as a compass needle.

He has an angry wrenlike vigilance,
a greyhound's gentle tautness;
he seems to wince at pleasure
and suffocate for privacy.

He is out of bounds. He rejoices in man's lovely,
peculiar power to choose life and die—

**Robert Lowell**  *266*

when he leads his black soldiers to death,
he cannot bend his back.

On a thousand small-town New England greens,
the old white churches hold their air
of sparse, sincere rebellion; frayed flags
quilt the graveyards of the Grand Army of the Republic.

The stone statues of the abstract Union Soldier
grow slimmer and younger each year—
wasp-waisted, they doze over muskets,
and muse through their sideburns.

Shaw's father wanted no monument
except the ditch,
where his son's body was thrown
and lost with his "niggers."

The ditch is nearer.
There are no statues for the last war here;
on Boylston Street, a commercial photograph
showed Hiroshima boiling

over a Mosler Safe, "the Rock of Ages,"
that survived the blast. Space is nearer.
When I crouch to my television set,
the drained faces of Negro school children rise like balloons.

Colonel Shaw
is riding on his bubble,
he waits
for the blessed break.

The Aquarium is gone. Everywhere,
giant finned cars nose forward like fish;
a savage servility
slides by on grease.

**Robert Lowell**   *267*

## Mr. Edwards and the spider

I saw the spiders marching through the air,
Swimming from tree to tree that mildewed day
   In latter August when the hay
   Came creaking to the barn. But where
    The wind is westerly,
Where gnarled November makes the spiders fly
Into the apparitions of the sky,
They purpose nothing but their ease and die
Urgently beating east to sunrise and the sea;

What are we in the hands of the great God?
It was in vain you set up thorn and briar
   In battle array against the fire
   And treason crackling in your blood;
    For the wild thorns grow tame
And will do nothing to oppose the flame;
Your lacerations tell the losing game
You play against a sickness past your cure.
How will the hands be strong? How will the heart endure?

A very little thing, a little worm,
Or hourglass-blazoned spider, it is said,
   Can kill a tiger. Will the dead
   Hold up his mirror and affirm
    To the four winds the smell
And flash of his authority? It's well
If God who holds you to the pit of hell,
Much as one holds a spider, will destroy,
Baffle and dissipate your soul. As a small boy

On Windsor Marsh, I saw the spider die
When thrown into the bowels of fierce fire:
   There's no long struggle, no desire
   To get up on its feet and fly—
    It stretches out its feet
And dies. This is the sinner's last retreat;

**Robert Lowell**  *268*

Yes, and no strength exerted on the heat
Then sinews the abolished will, when sick
And full of burning, it will whistle on a brick.

But who can plumb the sinking of that soul?
Josiah Hawley, picture yourself cast
   Into a brick-kiln where the blast
    Fans your quick vitals to a coal—
      If measured by a glass,
How long would it seem burning! Let there pass
A minute, ten, ten trillion; but the blaze
Is infinite, eternal: this is death,
To die and know it. This is the Black Widow, death.

---

**Ford Madox Ford:** *Ford Madox Ford was an Anglo-German writer who, in the fanatical anti-German climate of World War I, changed his name from Hueffer to Ford. He wrote one outstanding novel,* The Good Soldier, *which turned to advantage innovations made by Flaubert and other French naturalists, but most of his other novels were mere potboilers. He befriended and encouraged many writers at the beginnings of their careers, even when he himself had outlived his reputation and fallen into poverty and neglect. In his last years he was often in New York, a wheezing gourmand and failing bon vivant who was habitually seen at the Brevoort Hotel, the last resort of Edwardian grandeur in the city, in the neighborhood of both Washington Square and Stuyvesant Square.*

**Death from cancer:** *In the long view of this elegy, specific landmarks of the city of Boston are seen against a mythological background. Phillips House is a hospital. In Latin, the word cancer means crab, the fourth sign of the Zodiac. Charon is the mythical figure who ferried dead souls across the Styx, the chief river of the underworld. Acheron is the "river of woe" in Hades. This poem is one of four under the general title "In Memory of Arthur Winslow."*

**For the Union dead:** *The Latin motto is an adaptation of the inscription on St. Gaudens' Boston Civil War memorial to Robert Gould Shaw and his Union Negro troops. The* *original motto (of Shaw's club, the Society of the Cincinnati) says "He leaves everything to serve the republic." Here the subject and verb are made plural.*

**Mr. Edwards and the spider:** *Mr. Edwards, the speaker in this poem, is Jonathan Edwards, the great Calvinist theologian and preacher whose zeal was largely responsible for the religious revival in New England known as the Great Awakening. He was born in what is now Windsor, Connecticut, and as a child demonstrated his great aptitude as a naturalist by writing a series of scientific observations on the spider. In this poem, reminiscent of one of his famous sermons, Sinners in the Hands of an Angry God, he particularly addresses Josiah Hawley, a Revolutionary patriot who was one of the leaders of the opposition to Edwards' fiery revivalist preachings.*

# Edward Lucie-Smith

*Edward Lucie-Smith, born February 2, 1933, in Kingston,*
*Jamaica, was educated at the King's School, Canterbury,*
*and Merton College, Oxford, and now lives in London.*
*A free-lance writer, he is also well known as an art critic,*
*anthologist, and translator.*

## The lesson

'Your father's gone,' my bald headmaster said.
His shiny dome and brown tobacco jar
Splintered at once in tears. It wasn't grief.
I cried for knowledge which was bitterer
Than any grief. For there and then I knew
That grief has uses—that a father dead
Could bind the bully's fist a week or two;
And then I cried for shame, then for relief.

I was a month past ten when I learnt this:
I still remember how the noise was stilled
In school-assembly when my grief came in.
Some goldfish in a bowl quietly sculled
Around their shining prison on its shelf.
They were indifferent. All the other eyes
Were turned towards me. Somewhere in myself
Pride, like a goldfish, flashed a sudden fin.

## Poet in winter

A small room with one table and one chair,
This man who writes, then cancels what he writes,
Tears up the sheet, runs fingers through his hair;
His violent longing makes a fiercer chill
Than the sensed tilting of his hemisphere
Toward the frozen solstice, and he fights
A strange, oncoming ice-age of the will.

For him love does not burn, but chains him so:
The unspoken words lie heavy on his tongue,
Thoughts are like granite hurled into soft snow;
He holds a winter landscape in his mind;
Known tracks, habitual roads are covered now
By a blank sameness; he is caught and wrung,
Twists in the eddy of a polar wind.

And yet that wind grasps only at the man
Thus damned to strive; one opening the door
Would see him there, and casually would scan
His bent head and the slowly scribbled page
That's hidden at the sound; the draught would fan
Fragments of verses to the littered floor
As a false snowstorm falls upon a stage.

**Edward Lucie-Smith**  *273*

# Archibald MacLeish

*Archibald MacLeish, born May 7, 1892, in Glencoe,*
*Illinois, lives with his wife in Cambridge, Massachusetts—*
*where until recently he was Boylston Professor of*
*Rhetoric and Oratory at Harvard—and for part of each*
*year in Antigua, British West Indies. He was educated at*
*Yale and the Harvard Law School, served in the Field*
*Artillery in France during World War I, practiced law in*
*Boston, and later became an editor of* Fortune. *During*
*the administration of Franklin D. Roosevelt he was,*
*successively, Librarian of Congress and Undersecretary*
*of State. Among his writings are a number of radio and*
*television plays, the poetic dramas* Panic *and* J.B., *and*
*works of a documentary nature.*

## You, Andrew Marvell

And here face down beneath the sun
And here upon earth's noonward height
To feel the always coming on
The always rising of the night:

To feel creep up the curving east
The earthy chill of dusk and slow
Upon those under lands the vast
And ever climbing shadow grow

And strange at Ecbatan the trees
Take leaf by leaf the evening strange
The flooding dark about their knees
The mountains over Persia change

And now at Kermanshah the gate
Dark empty and the withered grass
And through the twilight now the late
Few travelers in the westward pass

And Baghdad darken and the bridge
Across the silent river gone
And through Arabia the edge
Of evening widen and steal on

And deepen on Palmyra's street
The wheel rut in the ruined stone
And Lebanon fade out and Crete
High through the clouds and overblown

And over Sicily the air
Still flashing with the landward gulls
And loom and slowly disappear
The sails above the shadowy hulls

And Spain go under and the shore
Of Africa the gilded sand
And evening vanish and no more
The low pale light across that land

Nor now the long light on the sea:

And here face downward in the sun
To feel how swift how secretly
The shadow of the night comes on . . .

## "Not marble nor the gilded monuments"

*for Adele*

The praisers of women in their proud and beautiful poems,
Naming the grave mouth and the hair and the eyes,
Boasted those they loved should be forever remembered:
These were lies.

The words sound but the face in the Istrian sun is forgotten.
The poet speaks but to her dead ears no more.
The sleek throat is gone—and the breast that was troubled to listen:
Shadow from door.

Therefore I will not praise your knees nor your fine walking
Telling you men shall remember your name as long
As lips move or breath is spent or the iron of English
Rings from a tongue.

I shall say you were young, and your arms straight, and your mouth
    scarlet:
I shall say you will die and none will remember you:
Your arms change, and none remember the swish of your garments,
Nor the click of your shoe.

Not with my hand's strength, not with difficult labor
Springing the obstinate words to the bones of your breast
And the stubborn line to your young stride and the breath to your
    breathing
And the beat to your haste
Shall I prevail on the hearts of unborn men to remember.

(What is a dead girl but a shadowy ghost
Or a dead man's voice but a distant and vain affirmation
Like dream words most)

Therefore I will not speak of the undying glory of women.
I will say you were young and straight and your skin fair

**Archibald MacLeish** 277

And you stood in the door and the sun was a shadow of leaves on your
    shoulders
And a leaf on your hair—

I will not speak of the famous beauty of dead women:
I will say the shape of a leaf lay once on your hair.
Till the world ends and the eyes are out and the mouths broken
Look! It is there!

---

**You, Andrew Marvell:** *The "cue" or point of departure for
this poem is Andrew Marvell's famous love poem "To His
Coy Mistress." Time and eternity, represented by the
movement of the sun, is a theme common to these poems, both
of which are otherwise concerned with human awareness.
Geographically, the point from which the westward passage
of night is observed is the southwestern shore of Lake
Michigan.*

# Louis MacNeice

*Louis MacNeice, born September 12, 1907, in Belfast, Ireland, died in 1964 in London where he was a program director for the British Broadcasting Company. He was educated at Merton College, Oxford, and later had a brief teaching career as lecturer in Greek in London. His early poetry is identified with that of his friends in the "English Group"—Spender, Lewis, and Auden—and with the last he is co-author of* Letters from Iceland. *He lived for extended periods in Greece; made a reading and concert tour in the United States in 1954 with his second wife, the singer Hedli Anderson; and at the time of his death was working on a manuscript later published as* The Strings Are False: An Unfinished Autobiography.

## The sunlight on the garden

The sunlight on the garden
Hardens and grows cold,
We cannot cage the minute
Within its nets of gold;
When all is told
We cannot beg for pardon.

Our freedom as free lances
Advances towards its end;
The earth compels, upon it

Sonnets and birds descend;
And soon, my friend,
We shall have no time for dances.

The sky was good for flying
Defying the church bells
And every evil iron
Siren and what it tells:
The earth compels,
We are dying, Egypt, dying

And not expecting pardon,
Hardened in heart anew,
But glad to have sat under
Thunder and rain with you,
And grateful too
For sunlight on the garden.


## Morning sun

Shuttles of trains going north, going south, drawing threads of blue,
The shining of the lines of trams like swords,
Thousands of posters asserting a monopoly of the good, the beautiful,
    the true,
Crowds of people all in the vocative, you and you,
The haze of the morning shot with words.

Yellow sun comes white off the wet streets but bright
Chromium yellows in the gay sun's light,
Filleted sun streaks the purple mist,
Everything is kissed and reticulated with sun
Scooped-up and cupped in the open fronts of shops
And bouncing on the traffic that never stops.

And the street fountain blown across the square
Rainbow-trellises the air and sunlight blazons

**Louis MacNeice**  *281*

The red butcher's and scrolls of fish on marble slabs,
Whistled bars of music crossing silver sprays
And horns of cars, touché, touché, rapiers' retort, a moving cage,
A turning page of shine and sound, the day's maze.

But when the sun goes out, the streets go cold, the hanging meat
And tiers of fish are colourless and merely dead,
And the hoots of cars neurotically repeat and the tiptoed feet
Of women hurry and falter whose faces are dead;
And I see in the air but not belonging there
The blown grey powder of the fountain grey as the ash
That forming on a cigarette covers the red.


## Prayer before birth

*Even poisons praise thee.*
GEORGE HERBERT

I am not yet born; O hear me.
Let not the bloodsucking bat or the rat or the stoat or the
        club-footed ghoul come near me.

I am not yet born, console me.
I fear that the human race may with tall walls wall me,
        with strong drugs dope me, with wise lies lure me,
            on black racks rack me, in blood-baths roll me.

I am not yet born; provide me
With water to dandle me, grass to grow for me, trees to talk
        to me, sky to sing to me, birds and a white light
            in the back of my mind to guide me.

I am not yet born; forgive me
For the sins that in me the world shall commit, my words
        when they speak me, my thoughts when they think me,
            my treason engendered by traitors beyond me,
                my life when they murder by means of my
                    hands, my death when they live me.

**Louis MacNeice**  *282*

I am not yet born; rehearse me
In the parts I must play and the cues I must take when
       old men lecture me, bureaucrats hector me, mountains
          frown at me, lovers laugh at me, the white
             waves call me to folly and the desert calls
                me to doom and the beggar refuses
                   my gift and my children curse me.
I am not yet born; O hear me,
Let not the man who is beast or who thinks he is God
       come near me.

I am not yet born; O fill me
With strength against those who would freeze my
       humanity, would dragoon me into a lethal automaton,
          would make me a cog in a machine, a thing with
             one face, a thing, and against all those
                who would dissipate my entirety, would
                   blow me like thistledown hither and
                  thither or hither and thither
                like water held in the
                  hands would spill me.
Let them not make me a stone and let them not spill me.
Otherwise kill me.

---

**The sunlight on the garden:** *An aspect of this poem not to be overlooked is its unusual rhyme scheme: while the stanzas follow a familiar pattern, the last words of lines 1 and 3 also rhyme with the first words in lines 2 and 4.*

*"Egypt" is a reference to Cleopatra as she is addressed by Mark Antony in Shakespeare's* Antony and Cleopatra *(IV:xv, 41). MacNeice's line echoes Shakespeare's "I am dying, Egypt, dying" and strengthens the point of the poem by supplying a famous instance of death faced with resignation and nobility.*

# James Merrill

*James Merrill, born March 3, 1926, in New York City,*
*lives in the old seaport village of Stonington, Connecticut.*
*He is a graduate of Amherst College and has for short*
*periods taught there and at other American colleges. He*
*has published two novels,* The Seraglio *and* The (Diblos)
Notebook; *his play* The Immortal Husband *was produced*
*off Broadway. A world traveler, he has spent many years*
*in residence abroad, particularly in Greece and in Italy.*

## Kite poem

"One is reminded of a certain person,"
Continued the parson, settling back in his chair
With a glass of port, "who sought to emulate
The sport of birds (it was something of a chore)
By climbing up on a kite. They found his coat
Two counties away; the man himself was missing."

His daughters tittered: it was meant to be a lesson
To them—they had been caught kissing, or some such nonsense,
The night before, under the crescent moon.
So, finishing his pheasant, their father began
This thirty-minute discourse, ending with
A story improbable from the start. He paused for breath,

Having shown but a few of the dangers. However, the wind
Blew out the candles and the moon wrought changes
Which the daughters felt along their stockings. Then,
Thus persuaded, they fled to their young men
Waiting in the sweet night by the raspberry bed,
And kissed and kissed, as though to escape on a kite.


## Laboratory poem

Charles used to watch Naomi, taking heart
    And a steel saw, open up turtles, live.
    While she swore they felt nothing, he would gag
    At blood, at the blind twitching, even after
    The murky dawn of entrails cleared, revealing
    Contours he knew, egg-yellows like lamps paling.

    Well then. She carried off the beating heart
    To the kymograph and rigged it there, a rag
    In fitful wind, now made to strain, now stopped
    By her solutions tonic or malign
    Alternately in which it would be steeped.
    What the heart bore, she noted on a chart,

    For work did not stop only with the heart.
    He thought of certain human hearts, their climb
    Through violence into exquisite disciplines
    Of which, as it now appeared, they all expired.
    Soon she would fetch another and start over,
    Easy in the presence of her lover.

## Voices from the other world

Presently at our touch the teacup stirred,
   Then circled lazily about
   From A to Z. The first voice heard
   (If they are voices, these mute spellers-out)
   Was that of an engineer

   Originally from Cologne.
   Dead in his 22nd year
   Of cholera in Cairo, he had 'known
   No happiness.' He once met Goethe, though.
   Goethe had told him: *Persevere.*

   Our blind hound whined. With that, a horde
   Of voices gathered above the Ouija board,
   Some childish and, you might say, blurred
   By sleep; one little boy
   Named Will, reluctant possibly in a ruff

   Like a large-lidded page out of El Greco, pulled
   Back the arras for that next voice,
   Cold and portentous: 'All is lost.
   Flee this house. Otto von Thurn und Taxis.
   Obey. You have no choice.'

   Frightened, we stopped; but tossed
   Till sunrise striped the rumpled sheets with gold.
   Each night since then, the moon waxes,
   Small insects flit round a cold torch
   We light, that sends them pattering to the porch . . .

   But no real Sign. New voices come,
   Dictate addresses, begging us to write;
   Some warn of lives misspent, and all of doom
   In ways that so exhilarate
   We are sleeping sound of late.

**James Merrill**   *287*

Last night the teacup shattered in a rage.
Indeed, we have grown nonchalant
Towards the other world. In the gloom here,
Our elbows on the cleared
Table, we talk and smoke, pleased to be stirred

Rather by buzzings in the jasmine, by the drone
Of our own voices and poor blind Rover's wheeze,
Than by those clamoring overhead,
Obsessed or piteous, for a commitment
We still have wit to postpone

Because, once looked at lit
By the cold reflections of the dead
Risen extinct but irresistible,
Our lives have never seemed more full, more real,
Nor the full moon more quick to chill.

# W. S. Merwin

*W. S. Merwin, born September 30, 1927, in Pennsylvania,*
*lives with his British wife in New York City and on a*
*farm in central France. The son of a Presbyterian*
*minister, he went to Princeton, where he majored in*
*Romance languages. After his graduation he spent several*
*years in France, Portugal, and Spain as a tutor and*
*eventually went to England, where his early reputation*
*as a poet was made. His translation of* The Cid *was*
*published in 1961.*

## Thorn leaves in March

Walking out in the late March midnight
With the old blind bitch on her bedtime errand
Of ease stumbling beside me, I saw

At the hill's edge, by the blue flooding
Of the arc-lamps, and the moon's suffused presence
The first leaves budding pale on the thorn trees,

Uncurling with that crass light coming through them,
Like the translucent wings of insects
Dilating in the dampness of birth;

And their green seemed already more ghostly
Than the hour drowned beneath bells, and the city sleeping,
Or even than the month with its round moon sinking.

As a white lamb the month's entrance had been:
The day warm, and at night unexpectedly
An hour of soft snow falling silently,

Soon ceasing, leaving transfigured all traceries,
These shrubs and trees, in white and white shadows; silk screens
Where were fences. And all restored again in an hour.

And as a lamb, I could see now, it would go,
Breathless, into its own ghostliness,
Taking with it more than its tepid moon.

And here there would be no lion at all that is
The beast of gold, and sought as an answer,
Whose pure sign in no solution is,

But between its two lambs the month would have run
As its varying moon, all silver,
That is the colour of questions.

Oh there as it went was such a silence
Before the water of April should be heard singing
Strangely as ever under the knowing ground

As fostered in me the motion of asking
In hope of no answer that fated leaves,
Sleep, or the sinking moon might proffer,

And in no words, but as it seemed in love only
For all breath, whose departing nature is
The spirit of question, whatever least I knew,

Whatever most I wondered. In which devotion
I stayed until the bell struck and the silver
Ebbed before April, and might have stood unseizing

Among answers less ghostly than the first leaves
On the thorn trees, since to seize had been
Neither to love nor to possess;

**W. S. Merwin**  *291*

While the old bitch nosed and winded, conjuring
A congenial spot, and the constellations
Sank nearer already, listing toward summer.


**The drunk in the furnace**

  For a good decade
The furnace stood in the naked gulley, fireless
And vacant as any hat. Then when it was
No more to them than a hulking black fossil
To erode unnoticed with the rest of the junk-hill
By the poisonous creek, and rapidly to be added
  To their ignorance,

  They were afterwards astonished
To confirm, one morning, a twist of smoke like a pale
Resurrection, staggering out of its chewed hole,
And to remark then other tokens that someone,
Cosily bolted behind the eye-holed iron
Door of the drafty burner, had there established
  His bad castle.

  Where he gets his spirits
It's a mystery. But the stuff keeps him musical:
Hammer-and-anvilling with poker and bottle
To his jugged bellowings, till the last groaning clang
As he collapses onto the rioting
Springs of a litter of car-seats ranged on the grates,
  To sleep like an iron pig.

  In their tar-paper church
On a text about stoke-holes that are sated never
Their Reverend lingers. They nod and hate trespassers.
When the furnace wakes, though, all afternoon
Their witless offspring flock like piped rats to its siren
Crescendo, and agape on the crumbling ridge
  Stand in a row and learn.


**W. S. Merwin**  *292*

# Christopher Middleton

*Christopher Middleton, born June 10, 1926, in Truro,
Cornwall, England, was educated at Merton College,
Oxford, and is a teacher of German literature. While he
makes his home in England, he travels widely and is
acquainted with the United States through a year spent
at the University of Texas. As a translator he has been
concerned mainly with twentieth-century German poetry.*

## In some seer's cloud car

Eyes of slain stag,
Borges the Argentinian,
62, being blind,
flew up to Austin
on tiger's breath, I think,
in some seer's cloud car.

Borges' mother
is 86.
She can't darn or cook.
She feeds him canned soup,
with what tenderness,
and sends the laundry out.

Borges the poet,
by her escorted, steered,
quotes by the yard in living rooms

English saga, German song.
He has it all by heart.
He's honeycombed.

And robust bread
browns in our oven.
We zoom down streets to shop
detergent, checked by signs.
And behold, way below,
the dark town sparkle.

Me, my table groans
under Arp and dictionaries.
60 ungraded exercises,
treatises, a score—when
Borges asks 'What was that word?'
there's not one I remember.

By whale I came here, it seems.
On whale back, past Labrador.
On the nth day,
spotted dawn over Dallas
in skies of purple steam,
and ate an egg.


## Edward Lear in February

Since last September I've been trying to describe
two moonstone hills,
and an ochre mountain, by candlelight, behind.
But a lizard has been sick into the ink,
a cat keeps clawing at me, you should see my face,
I'm too intent to dodge.

Out of the corner of my eye,
an old man (he's putting almonds into a bag)
stoops in sunlight, closer than the hills.

**Christopher Middleton**  *295*

But all the time these bats flick at me
and plop, like foetuses, all over the blotting paper.
Someone began playing a gong outside, once.
I liked that, it helped; but in a flash
neighbours were pelting him with their slippers and things,
bits of coke and old railway timetables.

I have come unstuck in this cellar. Help.
Pacing up and down in my own shadow
has stopped me liking the weight it falls from.
That lizard looks like being sick again. The owls
have built a stinking nest on the Eighteenth Century.

So much for two moonstone hills,
ochre mountain, old man
cramming all those almonds into a bag.

---

**In some seer's cloud car:** *Jorge Luis Borges, born 1899, is one
of the greatest contemporary Latin American writers. The
twentieth-century painter and sculptor Hans Arp was
noted for his revolutionary dispositions of space and his
unconventional use of texture.*

# Marianne Moore

*Marianne Moore, born November 15, 1887, in St. Louis,
Missouri, lives in Brooklyn, New York. She is a graduate
of Bryn Mawr and for a brief time after college taught
commercial subjects at the United States Indian school in
Carlisle, Pennsylvania. For a number of years she was
employed in the New York Public Library system and,
from 1925 to 1929, was editor of* The Dial, *the most
distinguished literary magazine of its time. She is the
most honored of women poets in America and in recent
years has made many reading appearances at colleges and
universities. About her own work she has said: "To be
trusted is an ennobling experience; and poetry is a
peerless proficiency of the imagination. I prize it, but am
myself an observer; I can see no reason for calling my
work poetry except that there is no other category in
which to put it."*

## A carriage from Sweden

They say there is a sweeter air
    where it was made, than we have here;
    a Hamlet's castle atmosphere.
At all events there is in Brooklyn
something that makes me feel at home.

No one may see this put-away
    museum-piece, this country cart

that inner happiness made art;
and yet, in this city of freckled
integrity it is a vein

of resined straightness from north-wind
  hardened Sweden's once-opposed-to-
  compromise archipelago
of rocks. Washington and Gustavus
Adolphus, forgive our decay.

Seats, dashboard and sides of smooth gourd-
  rind texture, a flowered step, swan-
  dart brake, and swirling crustacean-
tailed equine amphibious creatures
that garnish the axle-tree! What

a fine thing! What unannoying
  romance! And how beautiful, she
  with the natural stoop of the
snowy egret, gray-eyed and straight-haired,
for whom it should come to the door,—

of whom it reminds me. The split
  pine fair hair, steady gannet-clear
  eyes and the pine-needled-path deer-
swift step; that is Sweden, land of the
free and the soil for a spruce-tree—

vertical though a seedling—all
  needles: from a green trunk, green shelf
  on shelf fanning out by itself.
The deft white-stockinged dance in thick-soled
shoes! Denmark's sanctuaried Jews!

The puzzled-jugs and hand-spun rugs,
  the root-legged kracken shaped like dogs,
  the hanging buttons and the frogs
that edge the Sunday jackets! Sweden,
you have a runner called the Deer, who

**Marianne Moore** *299*

When he's won a race, likes to run
        more; you have the sun-right gable-
        ends due east and west, the table
spread as for a banquet; and the put-
in twin vest-pleats with a fish-fin

effect when you need none. Sweden,
        what makes the people dress that way
        and those who see you wish to stay?
The runner, not too tired to run more
at the end of the race? And that

cart, dolphin-graceful? A Dalgrén
        lighthouse, self-lit? responsive and
        responsible, I understand;
it's not pine-needle-paths that give spring
when they're run on, it's a Sweden

of moated white castles,—the bed
        of densely grown flowers in an S
        meaning Sweden and stalwartness,
skill, and a surface that says
Made in Sweden: carts are my trade.

## The student

"In America," began
the lecturer, "everyone must have a
degree. The French do not think that
all can have it, they don't say everyone
        must go to college." We
do incline to feel
        that although it may be unnecessary

to know fifteen languages,
one degree is not too much. With us, a

school—like the singing tree of which
the leaves were mouths singing in concert—is
    both a tree of knowledge
and of liberty,—
    seen in the unanimity of college

mottoes, *lux et veritas,*
*Christo et ecclesiae, sapiet*
*felici.* It may be that we
have not knowledge, just opinions, that we
    are undergraduates,
not students; we know
    we have been told with smiles, by expatriates

of whom we had asked "When will
your experiment be finished?" "Science
is never finished." Secluded
from domestic strife, Jack Bookworm led a
    college life, says Goldsmith;
and here also as
    in France or Oxford, study is beset with

dangers,—with bookworms, mildews,
and complaisancies. But someone in New
England has known enough to say
the student is patience personified,
    is a variety
of hero, "patient
    of neglect and of reproach,"—who can "hold by

himself." You can't beat hens to
make them lay. Wolf's wool is the best of wool,
but it cannot be sheared because
the wolf will not comply. With knowledge as
    with the wolf's surliness,
the student studies
    voluntarily, refusing to be less

**Marianne Moore** *301*

than individual. He
"gives his opinion and then rests on it";
he renders service when there is
no reward, and is too reclusive for
      some things to seem to touch
him, not because he
      has no feeling but because he has so much.


## Four quartz crystal clocks

There are four vibrators, the world's exactest clocks;
      and these quartz time-pieces that tell
time intervals to other clocks,
      these workless clocks work well;
and all four, independently the
      same, are there in the cool Bell
          Laboratory time

vault. Checked by a comparator with Arlington,
      they punctualize the "radio,
cinéma," and "presse,"—a group the
      Giraudoux truth-bureau
of hoped-for accuracy has termed
      "instruments of truth." We know—
          as Jean Giraudoux says

certain Arabs have not heard—that Napoleon
      is dead; that a quartz prism when
the temperature changes, feels
      the change and that the then
electrified alternate edges
      oppositely charged, threaten
          careful timing; so that

this water-clear crystal as the Greeks used to say,
      this "clear ice" must be kept at the

**Marianne Moore**   *302*

same coolness. Repetition, with
      the scientist, should be
synonymous with accuracy.
The lemur-student can see
      that an aye-aye is not

an angwan-tíbo, potto, or loris. The sea-
      side burden should not embarrass
the bell-buoy with the buoy-ball
      endeavoring to pass
hotel patronesses; nor could a
      practiced ear confuse the glass
            eyes for taxidermists

with eye-glasses from the optometrist. And as
      MEridian-7 1, 2
1, 2 gives, each fifteenth second
      in the same voice, the new
data—"The time will be" so and so—
      you realize that "when you
            hear the signal," you'll be

hearing Jupiter or jour pater, the day god—
      the salvaged son of Father Time—
telling the cannibal Chronos
      (eater of his proxime
newborn progeny) that punctual-
      ity is not a crime.

---

**A carriage from Sweden:** *A Swedish country cart in Brooklyn,
New York, "this city of freckled integrity," provides the
anomaly on which this lively meditation is based. Gustavus
Adolphus is the name of several kings of Sweden, one of
whom was a contemporary of George Washington. Kracken,
usually spelled* kraken, *is a fabulous Scandinavian sea
monster. Dalgrén was a Swedish inventor who contributed
to the improvement of lighthouses.*

**Marianne Moore**   *303*

**The student:** *In the following annotations, Marianne Moore suggests how phrases from her reading and observation are fitted, in the manner of mosaics, into the text of her poem:*

"In America." Les Idéals de l'Éducation Française; lecture, December 3, 1931, by M. Auguste Desclos, Director-adjoint, Office National des Universités et Écoles Françaises de Paris.

The singing tree. Each leaf was a mouth and every leaf joined in concert. *Arabian Nights.*

"Science is never finished." Professor Einstein to an American student; *New York Times.*

Jack Bookworm in Goldsmith's *The Double Transformation.*

A variety of hero: Emerson in *The American Scholar;* "there can be no scholar without the heroic mind"; "let him hold by himself; . . . patient of neglect, patient of reproach."

The wolf. Edmund Burke, November, 1781, in reply to Fox: "there is excellent wool on the back of a wolf and therefore he must be sheared. . . . But will he comply?"

"Gives his opinion." Henry McBride in the *New York Sun,* December 12, 1931: "Dr. Valentiner . . . has the typical reserve of the student. He does not enjoy the active battle of opinion that invariably rages when a decision is announced that can be weighed in great sums of money. He gives his opinion firmly and rests upon that."

**Four quartz crystal clocks:** *The following are the author's own notes to her poem:*

Bell T. leaflet, 1939, *"The World's Most Accurate Clocks:* In the Bell Telephone Laboratories in New York, in a 'time vault' whose temperature is maintained within 1/100 of a degree, at 41° centigrade, are the most accurate clocks in the world—the four quartz crystal clocks. . . . When properly cut and inserted in a suitable circuit, they will control the rate of electric vibration to an accuracy of one part in a million. . . . When you call MEridian 7-1212 for correct time you get it every 15 seconds."

Jean Giraudoux: "Appeler à l'aide d'un camouflage ces instruments fait pour la vérité qui sont la radio, le cinéma, la presse?" "J'ai traversé voilà un an des pays arabes où l'on ignorait encore que Napoléon était mort." *Une allocation radiodiffusée de M. Giraudoux aux Françaises à propos de Sainte Catherine;* the *Figaro,* November, 1939.

The cannibal Chronos. Rhea, mother of Zeus, hid him from Chronos who "devoured all his children except Jupiter (air), Neptune (water), and Pluto (the grave). These Time cannot consume." Brewer's *Dictionary of Phrase and Fable.*

# Howard Moss

*Howard Moss, born January 22, 1922, in New York,*
*has been a lifelong resident of his native city and, for*
*many years, an editor of* The New Yorker. *He was*
*educated at the University of Michigan and the University*
*of Wisconsin and then, for two years, taught at Vassar*
*College. His play* The Folding Green *was produced by*
*The Poets' Theatre in Cambridge, Massachusetts. He is*
*the author of* The Magic Lantern of Marcel Proust *and of a*
*collection of critical essays entitled* Writing Against Time.

## The gift to be simple

Breathing something German at the end,
Which no one understood, he died, a friend,
    Or so he meant to be, to all of us.
    Only the stars defined his radius;
His life, restricted to a wooden house,
Was in his head. He saw a fledgling fall.
    Two times he tried to nest it, but it fell
    Once more, and died; he wandered home again—
We save so plain a story for great men.
      An angel in ill-fitting sweaters,
      Writing children naive letters,
    A violin player lacking vanities,
    A giant wit among the homilies—
We have no parallel to that immense
      Intelligence.

But if he were remembered for the Bomb,
As some may well remember him, such a tomb,
    For one who hated violence and ceremony
    Equally, would be a wasted irony.
He flew to formal heavens from his perch,
A scientist become his own research,
    And even if the flames were never gold
    That lapped his body to an ash gone cold,
    Even if his death no trumpets tolled,
      There is enough of myth inside the truth
      To make a monument to fit him with;
    And since the universe is in a jar,
    There is no weeping where his heavens are,
And I would remember, now the world is less,
    His gentleness.

## Underwood

From the thin slats of the Venetian blinds
The sun has plucked a sudden metaphor:
A harp of light, reflected on the floor,
Disorients the chair and desk and door.
Those much too delicate hands still tapping
The Underwood seem now Hindu dancers
Or five or ten young Balinese children
Hopping up and down in a clearing where
The striped light scrapes through bamboo seedlings
And moves from skinny shade to thin veneer
And changes as the harp of light is changing
Its twanging image on the office floor,
Being so remarkably the blinding heir
Of something that is not, and yet is, there.

Once I watched at the water cooler
A face bent over the jet-thin water:

**Howard Moss**   *308*

The iris of the bent eye changed its color
As if the water jet had stained it green;
I saw the animal head's slight shudder,
Lifted from the surface of that running stream.
Tall branches then grew green in the hallway,
Arching above a green-ferned pathway;
A screen of green leaves hung in the doorway.
Was that a mirror where I saw the beaked birds,
The sluggish coffin of the alligator,
The monkeys climbing up the sunlit tree trunks?
Or did imagination, in that corridor,
Create, like the harp, its sudden metaphor?

Inside that drawer, among the blotters, folders,
Memos, carbons, pencils, papers,
Is the youngest animal of all awaking
In that coarse nest where he's been sleeping?
If I should reach into that dangerous drawer,
What singular teeth might pierce my skin?
Of if he should leap, should I then kill him,
And watch, where the harp had set its lightness,
The marvelous animal blood go thin?

**Great spaces**

I would worship if I could
Man, woman, child, or dog,
Strip the desert from my back,
Spill an ocean from each eye,
And like those saints who trust to luck

Sit for years under a tree.
I live now in a dirty city
That prowls the sky and is my shade;
Only a low, uneasy light
Gathers there, a light low-keyed

**Howard Moss** *309*

Amid great spaces and great times.
They soon grow smaller. I forget
What months and years once swam through me
As I walked into their great rooms,
Forgotten rooms, forgotten scenes,

And out in space a statue stands
That will not gloss its meaning. Near
Its pedestal, and on its hands
And knees, a figure, wild, unshorn,
Lifts its head to speak. It says,

"Nothing is unwilling to be born."

**The gift to be simple:** *This poem is a tribute written on the death of Albert Einstein, the great modern physicist whose theories, especially in their relevance to the development of the atomic bomb and its more lethal variations, have influenced the life of everyone on earth. His own life was one of endearing simplicity, and yet it was shadowed by the irony that he who hated the misuses of science should have been largely responsible for making atomic warfare possible.*

**Underwood:** *Underwood is the brand name of a famous typewriter, and in this poem the word is used punningly to suggest that, beyond the office world of "blotters, folders,/ Memos, carbons, pencils, papers" is the world of the imagination and jungle freedom. All of this has been evoked by the sun through Venetian blinds, the sudden creation of a "harp of light" that transforms the pedestrian activity of an office and makes it lively with hazards and surprises.*

# Howard Nemerov

*Howard Nemerov, born March 1, 1920, in New York City,
lives with his wife and three children in Lexington,
Massachusetts, and is on the faculty of Brandeis
University. He is a graduate of Harvard and, during
World War II, served with the Royal Canadian Air Force
and the United States Army Air Force in Canada and in
England. In 1963 he was appointed to a term as Consultant
in Poetry at the Library of Congress. He has published
three novels and Journal of the Fictive Life, a "complex
psychological narrative" describing the "conflict within
a writer caught between the modes of poetry and fiction."
His volume of poems The Blue Swallows was awarded
the first Theodore Roethke Memorial Prize in 1968.*

## Learning by doing

They're taking down a tree at the front door,
The power saw is snarling at some nerves,
Whining at others. Now and then it grunts,
And sawdust falls like snow or a drift of seeds.

Rotten, they tell us, at the fork, and one
Big wind would bring it down. So what they do
They do, as usual, to do us good.
Whatever cannot carry its own weight
Has got to go, and so on; you expect

To hear them talking next about survival
And the values of a free society.
For in the explanations people give
On these occasions there is generally some
Mean-spirited moral point, and everyone
Privately wonders if his neighbors plan
To saw him up before he falls on them.

Maybe a hundred years in sun and shower
Dismantled in a morning and let down
Out of itself a finger at a time
And then an arm, and so down to the trunk,
Until there's nothing left to hold on to
Or snub the splintery holding rope around,
And where those big green divagations were
So loftily with shadows interleaved
The absent-minded blue rains in on us.

Now that they've got it sectioned on the ground
It looks as though somebody made a plain
Error in diagnosis, for the wood
Looks sweet and sound throughout. You couldn't know,
Of course, until you took it down. That's what
Experts are for, and these experts stand round
The giant pieces of tree as though expecting
An instruction booklet from the factory
Before they try to put it back together.

Anyhow, there it isn't, on the ground.
Next come the tractor and the crowbar crew
To extirpate what's left and fill the grave.
Maybe tomorrow grass seed will be sown.
There's some mean-spirited moral point in that
As well: you learn to bury your mistakes,
Though for a while at dusk the darkening air
Will be with many shadows interleaved,
And pierced with a bewilderment of birds.

## Mousemeal

My son invites me to witness with him
a children's program, a series of cartoons,
on television. Addressing myself to share
his harmless pleasures, I am horrified
by the unbridled violence and hostility
of the imagined world he takes in stride,
where human beings dressed in the skins of mice
are eaten by portcullises and cowcatchers,
digested through the winding corridors
of organs, overshoes, boa constrictors
and locomotive boilers, to be excreted
in waters where shark and squid and abalone
wait to employ their tentacles and jaws.
It seems there is no object in this world
unable to become a gullet with great lonely teeth;
sometimes a set of teeth all by itself
comes clacking over an endless plain
after the moving mouse; and though the mouse
wins in the end, the tail of one cartoon
is spliced into the mouth of the next, where his
rapid and trivial agony repeats itself
in another form. My son has seen these things
a number of times, and knows what to expect;
he does not seem disturbed or anything more
than mildly amused. Maybe these old cartoons
refer to my childhood and not to his
(The ogres in them wear Mussolini's face),
so that when mice are swallowed by skeletons
or empty suits of armor, when a tribe
of savage Negro mice is put through a wringer
and stacked flat in the cellar, he can take
the objective and critical view, while I
am shaken to see the giant picassoid
parents eating and voiding their little mice
time and again. And when the cheery announcer
cries, "Well, kids, that's the end," my son gets up

obediently and runs outside to play.
I hope he will ride over this world as well,
and that his crudest and most terrifying dreams
will not return with such wide publicity.

# Marge Piercy

*Marge Piercy, born 1936 in Detroit, lives in New York
City with her husband, who is a mathematician. She
attended the University of Michigan, then took a master's
degree at Northwestern University where, she says,
"I began to do too well in graduate school too easily—
began to get ideas for PMLA papers instead of poems—
and left school abruptly. . . . Then I sat in a condemned
building in Chicago learning my craft."*

## The peaceable kingdom

*A painting by Edward Hicks, 1780–1849, hung in the Brooklyn Museum*

Creamcheese babies square and downy as bolsters
in nursery clothing nestle among curly lions and lowing cattle,
a wolf of scythe and ashes, a bear smiling in sleep.
The paw of a leopard with spots and eyes of headlights
rests near calf and vanilla child.
In the background under the yellow autumn tree
Indians and settlers sign a fair treaty.
The mist of dream cools the lake.

On the first floor of the museum Indian remains
are artfully displayed. Today is August sixth.
man eats man with sauces of newsprint.

The vision of that kingdom of satisfaction
where all bellies are round with sweet grasses
blows on my face pleasantly
though I have eaten five of those animals.
We are fat and busy as maggots.

All the rich flat black land,
the wide swirlmarked browngreen rivers,
leafy wheat baking tawny, corn's silky spikes,
sun bright kettles of steel and crackling wires, turn into
infinite shining weapons that scorch the earth.
The pride of our hive
packed into hoards of murderous sleek bombs.

We glitter and spark righteousness.
We are blinding as a new car in the sunshine.
Gasoline rains from our fluffy clouds.
Everywhere our evil froths polluting the waters—
in what stream on what mountain do you miss
the telltale redbrown sludge and rim of suds?

Peace: the word lies like a smooth turd
on the tongues of politicians ordering
the sweet flesh seared on the staring bone.
Guilt is added to the municipal water,
guilt is deposited in the marrow and teeth.
In my name they are stealing from people with nothing
their slim bodies. When did I hire these assassins?

My mild friend no longer paints mysteries of doors and mirrors.
On her walls the screams of burning children coagulate.
The mathematician with his webspangled language
of shadow and substance half spun
sits in an attic playing the flute all summer
for fear of his own brain, for fear that the baroque
arabesque of his joy will be turned to a weapon.
Five P.M. in Brooklyn: night all over my country.
Watch the smoke of guilt drift out of dreams.

**Marge Piercy**  *319*

When did I hire these killers? one day in anger
in seaslime hatred at the duplicity of flesh?
eating steak in a suave restaurant, did I give the sign?
sweating like a melon in bed, did I murmur consent?
did I contract it in Indiana for a teaching job?
was it something I signed for a passport or a loan?
Now in my name blood burns like oil day and night.

This nation is founded on blood like a city on swamps
yet its dream has been beautiful and sometimes just
that now grows brutal and heavy as a burned out star.

# Sylvia Plath

*Sylvia Plath, born October 27, 1932, in Boston,*
*Massachusetts, died in London in 1963 by suicide. She*
*was married to the English poet Ted Hughes by whom*
*she had two children. Her death abruptly ended a brief*
*and brilliant career as a poet which began at Smith*
*College and continued at Newnham College, Cambridge,*
*where she met her husband while she was spending a*
*year abroad on a Fulbright fellowship.*

## The applicant

First, are you our sort of a person?
Do you wear
A glass eye, false teeth or a crutch,
A brace or a hook,
Rubber breasts or a rubber crotch,

Stitches to show something's missing? No, no? Then
How can we give you a thing?
Stop crying.
Open your hand.
Empty? Empty. Here is a hand

To fill it and willing
To bring teacups and roll away headaches
And do whatever you tell it.

Will you marry it?
It is guaranteed

To thumb shut your eyes at the end
And dissolve of sorrow.
We make new stock from the salt.
I notice you are stark naked.
How about this suit—

Black and stiff, but not a bad fit.
Will you marry it?
It is waterproof, shatterproof, proof
Against fire and bombs through the roof.
Believe me, they'll bury you in it.

Now your head, excuse me, is empty.
I have the ticket for that.
Come here, sweetie, out of the closet.
Well, what do you think of *that*?
Naked as paper to start

But in twenty-five years she'll be silver,
In fifty, gold.
A living doll, everywhere you look.
It can sew, it can cook,
It can talk, talk, talk.

It works, there is nothing wrong with it.
You have a hole, it's a poultice.
You have an eye, it's an image.
My boy, it's your last resort.
Will you marry it, marry it, marry it.

**Sylvia Plath**  322

# Daddy

You do not do, you do not do
Any more, black shoe
In which I have lived like a foot
For thirty years, poor and white,
Barely daring to breathe or Achoo.

Daddy, I have had to kill you.
You died before I had time—
Marble-heavy, a bag full of God,
Ghastly statue with one grey toe
Big as a Frisco seal

And a head in the freakish Atlantic
Where it pours bean green over blue
In the waters off beautiful Nauset.
I used to pray to recover you.
Ach, du.

In the German tongue, in the Polish town
Scraped flat by the roller
Of wars, wars, wars.
But the name of the town is common.
My Polack friend

Says there are a dozen or two.
So I never could tell where you
Put your foot, your root,
I never could talk to you.
The tongue stuck in my jaw.

It stuck in a barb wire snare.
Ich, ich, ich, ich,
I could hardly speak.
I thought every German was you
And the language obscene.

**Sylvia Plath**  324

An engine, an engine
Chuffing me off like a Jew.
A Jew to Dachau, Auschwitz, Belsen.
I began to talk like a Jew.
I think I may well be a Jew.

The snows of the Tyrol, the clear beer of Vienna
Are not very pure or true.
With my gypsy ancestress and my weird luck
And my Taroc pack and my Taroc pack
I may be a bit of a Jew.

I have always been scared of you,
With your Luftwaffe, your gobbledygoo.
And your neat moustache
And your Aryan eye, bright blue.
Panzer-man, panzer-man, O You—

Not God but a swastika
So black no sky could squeak through.
Every woman adores a Fascist,
The boot in the face, the brute
Brute heart of a brute like you.

You stand at the blackboard, daddy,
In the picture I have of you,
A cleft in your chin instead of your foot
But no less a devil for that, no not
Any less the black man who

Bit my pretty red heart in two.
I was ten when they buried you.
At twenty I tried to die
And get back, back, back to you.
I thought even the bones would do.

But they pulled me out of the sack,
And they stuck me together with glue.

**Sylvia Plath**   325

And then I knew what to do.
I made a model of you,
A man in black with a Meinkampf look

And a love of the rack and the screw.
And I said I do, I do.
So daddy, I'm finally through.
The black telephone's off at the root,
The voices just can't worm through.

If I've killed one man, I've killed two—
The vampire who said he was you
And drank my blood for a year,
Seven years, if you want to know.
Daddy, you can lie back now.

There's a stake in your fat black heart
And the villagers never liked you.
They are dancing and stamping on you.
They always *knew* it was you.
Daddy, daddy, you bastard, I'm through.

# Ezra Pound

*Ezra Pound, born October 30, 1885, in Hailey, Idaho, has lived most of his life in Italy, at first in Rapallo and lately in Venice. He attended the University of Pennsylvania and Hamilton College, taught Romance languages for a brief time at Pennsylvania and at Wabash College in Indiana, and then went to Europe to begin a long and famous career as an expatriate. He first settled in London, where his acuteness as an editor and his zeal as a promoter of new forces in literature were given wide exercise. In 1924 he went to live in Italy and eventually became a propagandist for the Fascist regime, an activity that led to his being brought back to the United States in 1945 as a prisoner of the American Army on a charge of treason. When psychiatrists declared him mentally incompetent to stand trial, he was committed to St. Elizabeth's Hospital in Washington, where he continued to work on his magnum opus, The Cantos. On the intercession of Robert Frost and others, he was released in 1958 and allowed to return to Italy. His dramatic personal history has been given wide publicity; yet he will most likely be remembered, not for his political judgments, but for his widely felt influence as a great craftsman on the course of poetry and the history of the language.*

## Further instructions

Come, my songs, let us express our baser passions,
Let us express our envy of the man with a steady job and no worry
      about the future.
You are very idle, my songs.
I fear you will come to a bad end.
You stand about in the streets,
You loiter at the corners and bus-stops,
You do next to nothing at all.

You do not even express our inner nobilities,
You will come to a very bad end.

And I?
I have gone half cracked,
I have talked to you so much that
                        I almost see you about me,
Insolent little beasts, shameless, devoid of clothing!

But you, newest song of the lot,
You are not old enough to have done much mischief,
I will get you a green coat out of China
With dragons worked upon it,
I will get you the scarlet silk trousers
From the statue of the infant Christ in Santa Maria Novella,
Lest they say we are lacking in taste,
Or that there is no caste in this family.


## Commission

Go, my songs, to the lonely and the unsatisfied,
Go also to the nerve-racked, go to the enslaved-by-convention,
Bear to them my contempt for their oppressors.
Go as a great wave of cool water,
Bear my contempt of oppressors.

**Ezra Pound**  329

Speak against unconscious oppression,
Speak against the tyranny of the unimaginative,
Speak against bonds.
Go to the bourgeoise who is dying of her ennuis,
Go to the women in suburbs.
Go to the hideously wedded,
Go to them whose failure is concealed,
Go to the unluckily mated,
Go to the bought wife,
Go to the woman entailed.

Go to those who have delicate lust,
Go to those whose delicate desires are thwarted,
Go like a blight upon the dullness of the world;
Go with your edge against this,
Strengthen the subtle cords,
Bring confidence upon the algae and the tentacles of the soul.

Go in a friendly manner,
Go with an open speech.
Be eager to find new evils and new good,
Be against all forms of oppression.
Go to those who are thickened with middle age,
To those who have lost their interest.

Go to the adolescent who are smothered in family—
Oh how hideous it is
To see three generations of one house gathered together!
It is like an old tree with shoots,
And with some branches rotted and falling.

Go out and defy opinion,
Go against this vegetable bondage of the blood.
Be against all sorts of mortmain.

## The garden

*En robe de parade.*
        SAMAIN

Like a skein of loose silk blown against a wall
She walks by the railing of a path in Kensington Gardens,
And she is dying piece-meal
        of a sort of emotional anaemia.

And round about there is a rabble
Of the filthy, sturdy, unkillable infants of the very poor.
They shall inherit the earth.

In her is the end of breeding.
Her boredom is exquisite and excessive.
She would like some one to speak to her,
And is almost afraid that I
        will commit that indiscretion.

## Portrait d'une femme

Your mind and you are our Sargasso Sea,
London has swept about you this score years
And bright ships left you this or that in fee:
Ideas, old gossip, oddments of all things,
Strange spars of knowledge and dimmed wares of price.
Great minds have sought you—lacking someone else.
You have been second always. Tragical?
No. You preferred it to the usual thing:
One dull man, dulling and uxorious,
One averaged mind—with one thought less, each year.
Oh, you are patient, I have seen you sit
Hours, where something might have floated up.
And now you pay one. Yes, you richly pay.
You are a person of some interest, one comes to you
And takes strange gain away:

**Ezra Pound**   *331*

Trophies fished up; some curious suggestion;
Fact that leads nowhere; and a tale or two,
Pregnant with mandrakes, or with something else
That might prove useful and yet never proves,
That never fits a corner or shows use,
Or finds its hour upon the loom of days:
The tarnished, gaudy, wonderful old work;
Idols and ambergris and rare inlays,
These are your riches, your great store; and yet
For all this sea-hoard of deciduous things,
Strange woods half sodden, and new brighter stuff:
In the slow float of differing light and deep,
No! there is nothing! In the whole and all,
Nothing that's quite your own.
        Yet this is you.


## The river-merchant's wife: a letter

While my hair was still cut straight across my forehead
I played about the front gate, pulling flowers.
You came by on bamboo stilts, playing horse,
You walked about my seat, playing with blue plums.
And we went on living in the village of Chokan:
Two small people, without dislike or suspicion.

At fourteen I married My Lord you.
I never laughed, being bashful.
Lowering my head, I looked at the wall.
Called to, a thousand times, I never looked back.

At fifteen I stopped scowling,
I desired my dust to be mingled with yours
Forever and forever and forever.
Why should I climb the look out?

At sixteen you departed.
You went into far Ku-to-yen, by the river of swirling eddies,
And you have been gone five months.
The monkeys make sorrowful noise overhead.

You dragged your feet when you went out.
By the gate now, the moss is grown, the different mosses,
Too deep to clear them away!
The leaves fall early this autumn, in wind.
The paired butterflies are already yellow with August
Over the grass in the West garden;
They hurt me. I grow older.
If you are coming down through the narrows of the river Kiang,
Please let me know beforehand,
And I will come out to meet you
    As far as Cho-fu-sa.

By Rihaku

---

**Portrait d'une femme:** *The Sargasso Sea, an area in the
Atlantic Ocean stretching northeast from the West Indies to
the Azores, cradles the wreckage of thousands of ships that
have sunk there as well as wreckage carried there by its
far-ranging currents. This poem is based on one extended
metaphor—a detailed comparison of the Sargasso Sea with
the character and behavior of a London hostess.*

# John Crowe Ransom

*John Crowe Ransom, born April 30, 1888, in Pulaski,*
*Tennessee, lives in Gambier, Ohio, where he has for*
*many years been professor of English at Kenyon College.*
*He was educated at Vanderbilt University, where he was*
*one of the group of poets who became known as the*
*"Fugitives." He also attended Oxford as a Rhodes scholar.*
*His several books of criticism have been widely*
*influential, and he has been mentor to many distinguished*
*young poets, among them Robert Lowell, Randall Jarrell,*
*and the late Edgar Bogardus.*

## Survey of literature

In all the good Greek of Plato
I lack my roastbeef and potato.

A better man was Aristotle,
Pulling steady on the bottle.

I dip my hat to Chaucer,
Swilling soup from his saucer,

And to Master Shakespeare
Who wrote big on small beer.

The abstemious Wordsworth
Subsisted on a curd's-worth,

But a slick one was Tennyson,
Putting gravy on his venison.

What these men had to eat and drink
Is what we say and what we think.

The influence of Milton
Came wry out of Stilton.

Sing a song for Percy Shelley,
Drowned in pale lemon jelly,

And for precious John Keats,
Dripping blood of pickled beets.

Then there was poor Willie Blake,
He foundered on sweet cake.

God have mercy on the sinner
Who must write with no dinner,

No gravy and no grub,
No pewter and no pub,

No belly and no bowels,
Only consonants and vowels.


## Dead boy

The little cousin is dead, by foul subtraction,
A green bough from Virginia's aged tree,
And none of the county kin like the transaction,
Nor some of the world of outer dark, like me.

**John Crowe Ransom**   *336*

A boy not beautiful, nor good, nor clever,
A black cloud full of storms too hot for keeping,
A sword beneath his mother's heart—yet never
Woman bewept her babe as this is weeping.

A pig with a pasty face, so I had said,
Squealing for cookies, kinned by poor pretense
With a noble house. But the little man quite dead,
I see the forebears' antique lineaments.

The elder men have strode by the box of death
To the wide flag porch, and muttering low send round
The bruit of the day. O friendly waste of breath!
Their hearts are hurt with a deep dynastic wound.

He was pale and little, the foolish neighbors say;
The first-fruits, saith the Preacher, the Lord hath taken;
But this was the old tree's late branch wrenched away,
Grieving the sapless limbs, the shorn and shaken.

## Captain Carpenter

Captain Carpenter rose up in his prime
Put on his pistols and went riding out
But had got wellnigh nowhere at that time
Till he fell in with ladies in a rout.

It was a pretty lady and all her train
That played with him so sweetly but before
An hour she'd taken a sword with all her main
And twined him of his nose for evermore.

Captain Carpenter mounted up one day
And rode straightway into a stranger rogue
That looked unchristian but be that as may
The Captain did not wait upon prologue.

**John Crowe Ransom** *337*

But drew upon him out of his great heart
The other swung against him with a club
And cracked his two legs at the shinny part
And let him roll and stick like any tub.

Captain Carpenter rode many a time
From male and female took he sundry harms
He met the wife of Satan crying "I'm
The she-wolf bids you shall bear no more arms."

Their strokes and counters whistled in the wind
I wish he had delivered half his blows
But where she should have made off like a hind
The bitch bit off his arms at the elbows.

And Captain Carpenter parted with his ears
To a black devil that used him in this wise
O Jesus ere his threescore and ten years
Another had plucked out his sweet blue eyes.

Captain Carpenter got up on his roan
And sallied from the gate in hell's despite
I heard him asking in the grimmest tone
If any enemy yet there was to fight?

"To any adversary it is fame
If he risk to be wounded by my tongue
Or burnt in two beneath my red heart's flame
Such are the perils he is cast among.

"But if he can he has a pretty choice
From an anatomy with little to lose
Whether he cut my tongue and take my voice
Or whether it be my round red heart he choose."

It was the neatest knave that ever was seen
Stepping in perfume from his lady's bower
Who at this word put in his merry mien
And fell on Captain Carpenter like a tower.

I would not knock old fellows in the dust
But there lay Captain Carpenter on his back
His weapons were the old heart in his bust
And a blade shook between rotten teeth alack.

The rogue in scarlet and grey soon knew his mind
He wished to get his trophy and depart
With gentle apology and touch refined
He pierced him and produced the Captain's heart.

God's mercy rest on Captain Carpenter now
I thought him Sirs an honest gentleman
Citizen husband soldier and scholar enow
Let jangling kites eat of him if they can.

But God's deep curses follow after those
That shore him of his goodly nose and ears
His legs and strong arms at the two elbows
And eyes that had not watered seventy years.

The curse of hell upon the sleek upstart
That got the Captain finally on his back
And took the red red vitals of his heart
And made the kites to whet their beaks clack clack.

**John Crowe Ransom**   *339*

# Alastair Reid

*Alastair Reid was born March 22, 1926, in Whithorn, Scotland. He spent his childhood in a fishing village on the island of Arran, attended the University of St. Andrews, and then served with the British Navy in World War II, mainly in the East Indies. After the war, he lived for a number of years in the United States, teaching at Sarah Lawrence College, then returned to Europe to live first in Spain and then in London on a houseboat on the Thames with his son Jasper. He has been a correspondent for The New Yorker and is now on the faculty of Antioch College in Yellow Springs, Ohio.*

## Pigeons

On the crooked arm of Columbus, on his cloak,
they mimic his blind and statuary stare,
and the chipped profiles of his handmaidens
they adorn with droppings. Over the loud square,
from all the arms and ledges of their rest,
only a bread crust or a bell unshelves them.
Adding to Atlas' globe, they dispose themselves
with a fat propriety, and pose as garlands
importantly about his burdened shoulders.
Occasionally a lift of wind uncarves them.

Stone becomes them; they, in their turn, become it.
Their opal eyes have a monumental cast.
And, in a maze of noise,
their quiet *croomb croomb* dignifies the spaces,
suggesting the sound of silence. On cobbled islands,
marooned in tantrums of traffic, they know their place,
faithful and anonymous, like servants,
and never beg, but properly receive.

Arriving in rainbows of oil-and-water feathers,
they fountain down from buttresses and outcrops,
from Fontainebleau and London,
and, squat on the margins of roofs, with a gargoyle look,
they note, from an edge of air, with hooded eyes,
the city slowly lessening the sky.

All praise to them who nightly in the parks
keep peace for us; who, cosmopolitan,
patrol and people all cathedral places,
and easily, lazily haunt and inhabit
St. Paul's, St. Peter's, or the Madeleine,
the paved courts of the past, pompous as keepers—
a sober race of messengers and custodians,
neat in their international uniforms,
alighting with a word perhaps from Rome.
Permanence is their business, space and time
their special preservations; and wherever
the great stone men we save from death are stationed,
appropriately on the head of each is perched,
as though forever, his appointed pigeon.

# Theodore Roethke

*Theodore Roethke, born May 25, 1908, in Saginaw,
Michigan, died suddenly in 1963 in Seattle where he was
professor of English at the University of Washington.
When he was young he was constantly in the greenhouse
of his father and his uncle, an experience which
illuminates many of his poems which dramatize the
consciousness of childhood. He was educated at the
University of Michigan and at Harvard; and his teaching
career included positions at Lafayette, Penn State, where
he was also coach of tennis, and at Bennington. He
worked on his first book of poems, Open House, for ten
years; after that his output was comparatively prolific,
and the range of his style and subject matter were greatly
extended as he passed through several distinct phases of
development.*

## I knew a woman

I knew a woman, lovely in her bones,
When small birds sighed, she would sigh back at them;
Ah, when she moved, she moved more ways than one:
The shapes a bright container can contain!
Of her choice virtues only gods should speak,
Or English poets who grew up on Greek
(I'd have them sing in chorus, cheek to cheek).

How well her wishes went! She stroked my chin,
She taught me Turn, and Counter-turn, and Stand;
She taught me Touch, that undulant white skin;
I nibbled meekly from her proffered hand;
She was the sickle; I, poor I, the rake,
Coming behind her for her pretty sake
(But what prodigious mowing we did make).

Loves like a gander, and adores a goose:
Her full lips pursed, the errant note to seize;
She played it quick, she played it light and loose;
My eyes, they dazzled at her flowing knees;
Her several parts could keep a pure repose,
Or one hip quiver with a mobile nose
(She moved in circles, and those circles moved).

Let seed be grass, and grass turn into hay:
I'm martyr to a motion not my own;
What's freedom for? To know eternity.
I swear she cast a shadow white as stone.
But who would count eternity in days?
These old bones live to learn her wanton ways:
(I measure time by how a body sways).


**Prayer**

If I must of my Senses lose,
I pray Thee, Lord, that I may choose
Which of the Five I shall retain
Before oblivion clouds the brain.
My Tongue is generations dead,
My Nose defiles a comely head;
For hearkening to carnal evils
My Ears have been the very devil's.
And some have held the Eye to be
The instrument of lechery,

**Theodore Roethke**   345

More furtive than the Hand in low
And vicious venery—Not so!
Its rape is gentle, never more
Violent than a metaphor.
In truth, the Eye's the abettor of
The holiest platonic love:
Lip, Breast and Thigh cannot possess
So singular a blessedness.
Therefore, O Lord, let me preserve
The Sense that does so fitly serve,
Take Tongue and Ear—all else I have—
Let Light attend me to the grave!

## A field of light

1

Came to lakes; came to dead water,
Ponds with moss and leaves floating,
Planks sunk in the sand.

A log turned at the touch of a foot;
A long weed floated upward;
An eye tilted.

> Small winds made
> A chilly noise;
> The softest cove
> Cried for sound.

> Reached for a grape
> And the leaves changed;
> A stone's shape
> Became a clam.

> A fine rain fell
> On fat leaves;

**Theodore Roethke**  *346*

I was there alone
In a watery drowse.

2

Angel within me, I asked,
Did I ever curse the sun?
Speak and abide.

Under, under the sheaves,
Under the blackened leaves,
Behind the green viscid trellis,
In the deep grass at the edge of a field,
Along the low ground dry only in August,—

Was it dust I was kissing?
A sigh came far.
Alone, I kissed the skin of a stone;
Marrow-soft, danced in the sand.

3

The dirt left my hand, visitor.
I could feel the mare's nose.
A path went walking.
The sun glittered on a small rapids.
Some morning thing came, beating its wings.
The great elm filled with birds.

Listen, love,
The fat lark sang in the field;
I touched the ground, the ground warmed by the killdeer,
The salt laughed and the stones;
The ferns had their ways, and the pulsing lizards,
And the new plants, still awkward in their soil,
The lovely diminutives.

I could watch! I could watch!
I saw the separateness of all things!
My heart lifted up with the great grasses;

**Theodore Roethke**   *347*

The weeds believed me, and the nesting birds.
There were clouds making a rout of shapes crossing a windbreak of
   cedars,
And a bee shaking drops from a rain-soaked honeysuckle.
The worms were delighted as wrens.
And I walked, I walked through the light air;
I moved with the morning.


## Elegy for Jane

*My student, thrown by a horse*

I remember the neckcurls, limp and damp as tendrils;
And her quick look, a sidelong pickerel smile;
And how, once startled into talk, the light syllables leaped for her,
And she balanced in the delight of her thought,
A wren, happy, tail into the wind,
Her song trembling the twigs and small branches.
The shade sang with her;
The leaves, their whispers turned to kissing;
And the mould sang in the bleached valleys under the rose.

Oh, when she was sad, she cast herself down into such a pure depth,
Even a father could not find her:
Scraping her cheek against straw;
Stirring the clearest water.

My sparrow, you are not here,
Waiting like a fern, making a spiney shadow.
The sides of wet stones cannot console me,
Nor the moss, wound with the last light.

If only I could nudge you from this sleep,
My maimed darling, my skittery pigeon.
Over this damp grave I speak the words of my love:
I, with no rights in this matter,
Neither father nor lover.

**Theodore Roethke**   *348*

## The waking

I wake to sleep, and take my waking slow.
I feel my fate in what I cannot fear.
I learn by going where I have to go.

We think by feeling. What is there to know?
I hear my being dance from ear to ear.
I wake to sleep, and take my waking slow.

Of those so close beside me, which are you?
God bless the Ground! I shall walk softly there,
And learn by going where I have to go.

Light takes the Tree; but who can tell us how?
The lowly worm climbs up a winding stair;
I wake to sleep, and take my waking slow.

Great Nature has another thing to do
To you and me; so take the lively air,
And, lovely, learn by going where to go.

This shaking keeps me steady. I should know.
What falls away is always. And is near.
I wake to sleep, and take my waking slow.
I learn by going where I have to go.

---

**A field of light:** *This poem, written from the point of view
of a child as he encounters the world of nature, has the air
of an epiphany—a showing forth of things of a divine order.
Emphasis is placed strictly upon the reality, the particularity,
of things observed, and in the process a sense of curiosity
gives way to a sense of harmony.*

**Theodore Roethke** 349

# Muriel Rukeyser

*Muriel Rukeyser, born December 15, 1913, in New York, lives in her native city. She studied at Vassar College and later taught there and at other colleges for brief periods as lecturer or as poet-in-residence. She was in Spain as a reporter at the outbreak of the Civil War, and her experiences there have been recorded in a number of her poems. Her writings include, besides poetry, biographical studies of Willard Gibbs and Wendell Willkie and a novel,* The Orgy.

## Boy with his hair cut short

Sunday shuts down on this twentieth-century evening.
The L passes. Twilight and bulb define
the brown room, the overstuffed plum sofa,
the boy, and the girl's thin hands above his head.
A neighbor's radio sings stocks, news, serenade.

He sits at the table, head down, the young clear neck exposed,
watching the drugstore sign from the tail of his eye;
tattoo, neon, until the eye blears, while his
solicitous tall sister, simple in blue, bending
behind him, cuts his hair with her cheap shears.

The arrow's electric red always reaches its mark,
successful neon! He coughs, impressed by that precision.

His child's forehead, forever protected by his cap,
is bleached against the lamplight as he turns head
and steadies to let the snippets drop.

Erasing the failure of weeks with level fingers,
she sleeks the fine hair, combing: "You'll look fine tomorrow!
You'll surely find something, they can't keep turning you down;
the finest gentleman's not so trim as you!" Smiling, he raises
the adolescent forehead wrinkling ironic now.

He sees his decent suit laid out, new-pressed,
his carfare on the shelf. He lets his head fall, meeting
her earnest hopeless look, seeing the sharp blades splitting,
the darkened room, the impersonal sign, her motion,
the blue vein, bright on her temple, pitifully beating.


## Effort at speech between two people

:      Speak to me.     Take my hand.     What are you now?
       I will tell you all.     I will conceal nothing.
       When I was three, a little child read a story about a rabbit
       who died, in the story, and I crawled under a chair     :
       a pink rabbit     :   it was my birthday, and a candle
       burnt a sore spot on my finger, and I was told to be happy.

:      Oh, grow to know me.     I am not happy.     I will be open:
       Now I am thinking of white sails against a sky like music,
       like glad horns blowing, and birds tilting, and an arm about me.
       There was one I loved, who wanted to live, sailing.

:      Speak to me.     Take my hand.     What are you now?
       When I was nine, I was fruitily sentimental,
       fluid     :   and my widowed aunt played Chopin,
       and I bent my head on the painted woodwork, and wept.
       I want now to be close to you.     I would
       link the minutes of my days close, somehow, to your days.

I am not happy.     I will be open.
I have liked lamps in evening corners, and quiet poems.
There has been fear in my life.     Sometimes I speculate
on what a tragedy his life was, really.

Take my hand.     First my mind in your hand.     What are
        you now?
When I was fourteen, I had dreams of suicide,
and I stood at a steep window, at sunset, hoping toward death
if the light had not melted clouds and plains to beauty,
if light had not transformed that day, I would have leapt.
I am unhappy.     I am lonely.     Speak to me.

I will be open.     I think he never loved me:
he loved the bright beaches, the little lips of foam
that ride small waves, he loved the veer of gulls:
he said with a gay mouth: I love you.     Grow to know me.

What are you now?     If we could touch one another,
if these our separate entities could come to grips,
clenched like a Chinese puzzle . . . yesterday
I stood in a crowded street that was live with people,
and no one spoke a word, and the morning shone.
Everyone silent, moving. . . . Take my hand.     Speak to me.

# Delmore Schwartz

*Delmore Schwartz, born December 8, 1913, in Brooklyn,*
*died in New York City in 1966. He was educated at the*
*University of Wisconsin, New York University, and*
*Harvard University, where from 1940 to 1947 he taught*
*in the English department as a Briggs-Copeland Fellow.*
*From 1943 to 1955 he was an editor of the* Partisan
Review. *Besides poetry, his writings include many*
*influential essays on literary themes and a number of*
*short stories, some of which are gathered in a volume*
*entitled* The World is A Wedding.

## The ballet of the fifth year

Where the sea gulls sleep or indeed where they fly
Is a place of different traffic. Although I
Consider the fishing bay (where I see them dip and curve
And purely glide) a place that weakens the nerve
Of will, and closes my eyes, as they should not be
(They should burn like the street-light all night quietly,
So that whatever is present will be known to me),
Nevertheless the gulls and the imagination
Of where they sleep, which comes to creation
In strict shape and color, from their dallying
Their wings slowly, and suddenly rallying
Over, up, down the arabesque of descent,
Is an old act enacted, my fabulous intent

When I skated, afraid of policemen, five years old,
In the winter sunset, sorrowful and cold,
Hardly attained to thought, but old enough to know
Such grace, so self-contained, was the best escape to know.


## The heavy bear who goes with me

*"the withness of the body"*
WHITEHEAD

The heavy bear who goes with me,
A manifold honey to smear his face,
Clumsy and lumbering here and there,
The central ton of every place,
The hungry beating brutish one
In love with candy, anger, and sleep,
Crazy factotum, dishevelling all,
Climbs the building, kicks the football,
Boxes his brother in the hate-ridden city.
Breathing at my side, that heavy animal,
That heavy bear who sleeps with me,
Howls in his sleep for a world of sugar,
A sweetness intimate as the water's clasp,
Howls in his sleep because the tight-rope
Trembles and shows the darkness beneath.
—The strutting show-off is terrified,
Dressed in his dress-suit, bulging his pants,
Trembles to think that his quivering meat
Must finally wince to nothing at all.

That inescapable animal walks with me,
Has followed me since the black womb held,
Moves where I move, distorting my gesture,
A caricature, a swollen shadow,
A stupid clown of the spirit's motive,
Perplexes and affronts with his own darkness,
The secret life of belly and bone,

**Delmore Schwartz** *356*

Opaque, too near, my private, yet unknown,
Stretches to embrace the very dear
With whom I would walk without him near,
Touches her grossly, although a word
Would bare my heart and make me clear,
Stumbles, flounders, and strives to be fed
Dragging me with him in his mouthing care,
Amid the hundred million of his kind,
The scrimmage of appetite everywhere.


## Baudelaire

When I fall asleep, and even during sleep,
I hear, quite distinctly, voices speaking
Whole phrases, commonplace and trivial,
Having no relation to my affairs.

Dear Mother, is any time left to us
In which to be happy? My debts are immense.
My bank account is subject to the court's judgment.
I know nothing. I cannot know anything.
I have lost the ability to make an effort.
But now as before my love for you increases.
You are always armed to stone me, always:
It is true. It dates from childhood.

For the first time in my long life
I am almost happy. The book, almost finished,
Almost seems good. It will endure, a monument
To my obsessions, my hatred, my disgust.

Debts and inquietude persist and weaken me.
Satan glides before me, saying sweetly:
"Rest for a day! You can rest and play today.
Tonight you will work." When night comes,
My mind, terrified by the arrears,

Bored by sadness, paralyzed by impotence,
Promises: "Tomorrow: I will tomorrow."
Tomorrow the same comedy enacts itself
With the same resolution, the same weakness.

I am sick of this life of furnished rooms.
I am sick of having colds and headaches:
You know my strange life. Every day brings
Its quota of wrath. You little know
A poet's life, dear Mother: I must write poems,
The most fatiguing of occupations.

I am sad this morning. Do not reproach me.
I write from a café near the post office,
Amid the click of billiard balls, the clatter of dishes,
The pounding of my heart. I have been asked to write
"A History of Caricature." I have been asked to write
"A History of Sculpture." Shall I write a history
Of the caricatures of the sculptures of you in my heart?

Although it costs you countless agony,
Although you cannot believe it necessary,
And doubt that the sum is accurate,
Please send me money enough for at least three weeks.

# James Scully

*James Scully, born February 23, 1937, in New Haven,*
*lives with his wife and children in Mansfield, Connecticut,*
*and teaches English at the University of Connecticut*
*where he studied as an undergraduate and went on to*
*take his Ph.D. degree. His first volume of poems, The*
*Marches, won the Lamont Poetry Prize for 1967, and he*
*is editor of a collection of essays by poets entitled*
Modern Poetics.

## Midsummer

*(Coventry, Connecticut)*

That the high sheen of death could blot
this green away, or life survive
the great ice age, is almost not

to be believed. Clearly, today's
raw sunlight ripens into grass
and grazing cows, as though always

it has been so. Still, glacial rock,
like giant bone, breaks through the earth
and weighs the age-old walls that block

these fields, the livestock locked within.
a herd of clear-cut whites and blacks,
the cows browse in oblivion,

their muscles ruffling under veils
of gaudy, violet-winged black flies
aswarm their hides—and swish their tails—

thickset, but limber as bullwhips
perpetually in motion, long
quick lengths unravelled at the tips,

from side to side. Nearby, a brace
of mules tethered to buried stakes
stand stock-still. And out through space,

at times, too far away to hear,
a flashing Sabre-jet transcends
the mules, the massive cows—a mere

slow-motioned slip of silver light—
and wakes a ghostly rainbow arc
flatly across far hills, its slight

exhaustion burning through the blue
useless sky, trailing away,
its destination out of view.

The glacier's gone. The cows assent
grassward, earmarked with metal tags,
delicacies of ornament

that glint and tick away the sun
as their ears twitch, as they remain
one pulsing mass—as if each one

had undergone the bull, the calf,
the frost-bit rains, and now held out
for nothing less than life itself:

such middle-aging gaiety
as knows not what it was, nor is,
nor what it is about to be,

**James Scully**  *361*

nor cares that space thins out, goes dumb,
that time may cease to come—as if,
rockbound, this were the kingdom come,

and the hunched fields were crystal-clear
Jerusalem, and life was judged
vibration in the summer air.


## The glass blower

Canaries were his hobby.
Upstairs in the attic, with his knobby
hands, he put up small-gauge wire stalls;
copper gauze, from the slant roof to the floor,
huddled the birdflock in their drowsy ark.
There were a hundred or more
that sat on crusted bars, their claws locked tight—
upright albino bats, until the night-
time came. When he groped up the stairs, the light
blazed and they awoke.
The hungry bodies quickened.
A few flew at the screen, but every dark
reflection glided skillfully on the walls
behind the gold wheelings—wheels of a clock
chirping every second on the second.

Gradually it unwound.
And going to work, a Jonah's underground,
he'd disappear into a warehouse: punch in,
check orders, stir a batch of sand, start
the wheel grinding out his daily payload
of undistracted art—
and shape a universe, a toy glass ball
one shakes, seeing the plastic snowflakes fall
within a pool, upon a parasol
of plastic (underneath,

**James Scully**  *362*

a woman and a man
were frozen in their strolling). And the haloed,
high-stooled glass blower, leaning over a Bunsen
burner, at a wooden bench, would breathe
glass straws into strings of glass balloons.

They were sold—the rare
canaries, then pigeons, chickens, and a pair
of guinea pigs. Experiments, they arrived
and left, like courses in their covered dish.
He even bred, in an aquarium,
rainbow-colored fish:
then, streaked with orange scars, the slim swordtails
cut a wakeless way, and the milky sails
of angelfish, razor-thin, edged trails
of tendril over rock;
the snails neither sank
nor swam, but stuffed their pinkish horns with scum.
He also stocked black mollies. Short-lived,
their bulbous heads and tapering bodies, black
tear-shapes, cruised the bottom of the tank.

Lightheaded bubbles swirled
surfacewise. Wound in a filmy world,
a fetus feeding on its inmost part,
he'd circle bar to bar each night, without
going far, but staggering home stone blind,
his pockets inside-out.
Fleeced, he made the cellar workshop a cage
of pipes and copper coils, trying to gauge
the distillation and advancing age
of alcohol. Ferment-
ing, dribbling from the lips,
he would sit wall-eyed with his wheeling mind
among odd junk. Near a dog-eared sea chart,
a bottle made a toppled monument
preserving remnants of a model ship.

# Anne Sexton

*Anne Sexton, born November 9, 1928, in Newton,*
*Massachusetts, lives with her husband and two daughters*
*in Weston, Massachusetts, not far from her birthplace.*
*She attended local schools, lived for periods in Baltimore*
*and San Francisco, and was a student of Robert Lowell*
*during the years he was at Boston University. She has*
*spent many summers on Cape Cod and in Maine at*
*her family home.*

## Letter written on a ferry
## crossing Long Island Sound

I am surprised to see
that the ocean is still going on.
Now I am going back
and I have ripped my hand
from your hand as I said I would
and I have made it this far
as I said I would
and I am on the top deck now,
holding my wallet, my cigarettes,
and my car keys
at two o'clock on a Tuesday
in August of 1960.

Dearest,
although everything has happened,
nothing has happened.
The sea is very old.
The sea is the face of Mary,
without miracles or rage
or unusual hope,
grown rough and wrinkled
with incurable age.

Still,
I have eyes.
These are my eyes:
the orange letters that spell
"ORIENT" on the life preserver
that hangs by my knees,
the cement lifeboat that wears
its dirty canvas coat,
the faded sign that sits on its shelf
saying "KEEP OFF."
Oh, all right, I say,
I'll save myself.

Over my right shoulder
I see four nuns
who sit like a bridge club,
their faces poked out
from under their habits,
as good as good babies who
have sunk into their carriages.
Without discrimination,
the wind pulls the skirts
of their arms.
Almost undressed,
I see what remains:
that holy wrist,
that ankle,
that chain.

**Anne Sexton**   *366*

Oh, God,
although I am very sad,
could you please
let these four nuns
loosen from their leather boots
and their wooden chairs
to rise out
over this greasy deck,
out over this iron rail,
nodding their pink heads to one side,
flying four abreast
in the old-fashioned side stroke,
each mouth open and round,
breathing together
as fish do,
singing without sound.

Dearest,
see how my dark girls sally forth,
over the passing lighthouse of Plum Gut,
its shell as rusty
as a camp dish,
as fragile as a pagoda
on a stone,
out over the little lighthouse
that warns me of drowning winds
that rub over its blind bottom
and its blue cover—
winds that will take the toes
and the ears of the rider
or the lover.

There go my dark girls;
their dresses puff
in the leeward air.
Oh, they are lighter than flying dogs
or the breath of dolphins;
each mouth opens gratefully,

**Anne Sexton**  *367*

wider than a milk cup.
My dark girls sing for this:
They are going up.

Here are my four dark girls.
See them rise
on black wings, drinking
the sky, without smiles
or hands
or shoes.
They call back to us
from the gauzy edge of paradise,
*good news, good news.*


## Her kind

I have gone out, a possessed witch,
haunting the black air, braver at night;
dreaming evil, I have done my hitch
over the plain houses, light by light:
lonely thing, twelve-fingered, out of mind.
A woman like that is not a woman, quite.
I have been her kind.

I have found the warm caves in the woods,
filled them with skillets, carvings, shelves,
closets, silks, innumerable goods;
fixed the suppers for the worms and the elves:
whining, rearranging the disaligned.
A woman like that is misunderstood.
I have been her kind.

I have ridden in your cart, driver,
waved my nude arms at villages going by,
learning the last bright routes, survivor

**Anne Sexton**   *368*

where your flames still bite my thigh
and my ribs crack where your wheels wind.
A woman like that is not ashamed to die.
I have been her kind.

# Karl Shapiro

*Karl Shapiro, born November 10, 1913, in Baltimore,*
*Maryland, is professor of English at the University of*
*California at Davis. He attended the University of Virginia*
*for a brief and unhappy period and graduated from Johns*
*Hopkins University. He served with the Army in the*
*South Pacific for four years in World War II, during*
*which his first books were published; and on his return*
*he was appointed Consultant in Poetry at the Library of*
*Congress. He taught at Johns Hopkins for several years,*
*then went to Chicago to serve as editor of* Poetry: A
Magazine of Verse *from 1950 to 1956. His critical attitudes*
*are stated in a volume of poetry,* Essay on Rime, *and*
*in a volume of essays,* In Defense of Ignorance.

## Nostalgia

My soul stands at the window of my room,
 And I ten thousand miles away;
My days are filled with Ocean's sound of doom,
 Salt and cloud and the bitter spray.
Let the wind blow, for many a man shall die.

My selfish youth, my books with gilded edge,
 Knowledge and all gaze down the street;
The potted plants upon the window ledge

Gaze down with selfish lives and sweet.
Let the wind blow, for many a man shall die.

My night is now her day, my day her night,
    So I lie down, and so I rise;
The sun burns close, the star is losing height,
    The clock is hunted down the skies.
Let the wind blow, for many a man shall die.

Truly a pin can make the memory bleed,
    A world explode the inward mind
And turn the skulls and flowers never freed
    Into the air, no longer blind.
Let the wind blow, for many a man shall die.

Laughter and grief join hands. Always the heart
    Clumps in the breast with heavy stride;
The face grows lined and wrinkled like a chart,
    The eyes bloodshot with tears and tide.
Let the wind blow, for many a man shall die.

## Haircut

O wonderful nonsense of lotions of Lucky Tiger,
Of savory soaps and oils of bottle-bright green,
The gold of liqueurs, the unguents of Newark and Niger,
Powders and balms and waters washing me clean,

In mirrors of marble and silver I see us forever
Increasing, decreasing the puzzles of luminous spaces
As I turn, am revolved and am pumped in the air on a lever,
With the backs of my heads in chorus with all of my faces.

Scissors and comb are mowing my hair into neatness,
Now pruning my ears, now smoothing my neck like a plain;

**Karl Shapiro** 372

In the harvest of hair and the chaff of powdery sweetness
My snow-covered slopes grow dark with the wooly rain.

And the little boy cries, for it hurts to sever the curl,
And we too are quietly bleating to part with our coat.
Does the barber want blood in a dish? I am weak as a girl,
I desire my pendants, the fatherly chin of a goat.

I desire the pants of a bear, the nap of a monkey
Which trousers of friction have blighted down to my skin.
I am bare as a tusk, as jacketed up as a flunkey,
With the chest of a moth-eaten camel growing within.

But in death we shall flourish, you summer-dark leaves of my head,
While the flesh of the jaw ebbs away from the shores of my teeth;
You shall cover my sockets and soften the boards of my bed
And lie on the flat of my temples as proud as a wreath.


## Drug store

*I do remember an apothecary,*
*And hereabouts 'a dwells*

It baffles the foreigner like an idiom,
And he is right to adopt it as a form
Less serious than the living-room or bar;
        For it disestablishes the cafe,
Is a collective, and on basic country.

Not that it praises hygiene and corrupts
The ice-cream parlor and the tobacconist's
Is it a center; but that the attractive symbols
        Watch over puberty and leer
Like rubber bottles waiting for sick-use.

Youth comes to jingle nickels and crack wise;
The baseball scores are his, the magazines

**Karl Shapiro**   *373*

Devoted to lust, the jazz, the Coca-Cola,
    The lending-library of love's latest.
He is the customer; he is heroized.

And every nook and cranny of the flesh
Is spoken to by packages with wiles.
"Buy me, buy me," they whimper and cajole;
    The hectic range of lipsticks pouts,
Revealing the wicked and the simple mouth.

With scarcely any evasion in their eye
They smoke, undress their girls, exact a stance;
But only for a moment. The clock goes round;
    Crude fellowships are made and lost;
They slump in booths like rags, not even drunk.

---

**Nostalgia:** *World War II took hundreds of thousands of
American soldiers to the other side of the world. This poem,
written in 1942, when its author was on military duty in the
Indian Ocean, makes particular use of geography and time to
suggest the topsy-turvy quality of a life interrupted by
global conflict.*

# Jon Silkin

*Jon Silkin, born December 2, 1930, in London, was educated at the University of Leeds, worked for years as a manual laborer, then returned to his alma mater as Gregory Fellow in Poetry for a period of seven years. Recently he has been living in the United States, as poet-in-residence at Denison University in Ohio and as a member of the faculty of the Writers' Workshop at the State University of Iowa. He is founder and co-editor of the literary quarterly Stand.*

## Death of a son

*(who died in a mental hospital aged one)*

Something has ceased to come along with me.
Something like a person: something very like one.
And there was no nobility in it
Or anything like that.

Something was there like a one year
Old house, dumb as stone. While the near buildings
Sang like birds and laughed
Understanding the pact

They were to have with silence. But he
Neither sang nor laughed. He did not bless silence
Like bread, with words.
He did not forsake silence.

But rather, like a house in mourning
Kept the eye turned in to watch the silence while
    The other houses like birds
      Sang around him.

And the breathing silence neither
Moved nor was still.

    I have seen stones: I have seen brick
But this house was made up of neither bricks nor stone
    But a house of flesh and blood
      With flesh of stone

    And bricks for blood. A house
Of stones and blood in breathing silence with the other
    Birds singing crazy on its chimneys.
    But this was silence,

    This was something else, this was
Hearing and speaking though he was a house drawn
    Into silence, this was
      Something religious in his silence,

    Something shining in his quiet,
This was different this was altogether something else:
    Though he never spoke, this
      Was something to do with death.

    And then slowly the eye stopped looking
Inward. The silence rose and became still.
The look turned to the outer place and stopped,
    With the birds still shrilling around him.
    And as if he could speak

He turned over on his side with his one year
Red as a wound
He turned over as if he could be sorry for this
And out of his eyes two great tears rolled, like stones,
    and he died.

**Jon Silkin**  *376*

# Louis Simpson

*Louis Simpson, born March 27, 1923, in Jamaica, British West Indies, lives with his wife and three children in Port Jefferson, Long Island, and is on the faculty of the State University of New York at Stony Brook. He was educated in British schools in Jamaica and took his Ph.D. from Columbia University. He has published a novel* Riverside Drive; *his book of poems* At the End of the Open Road *was awarded the Pulitzer Prize for 1964.*

## Hot night on Water Street

A hot midsummer night on Water Street—
The boys in jeans were combing their blonde hair,
Watching the girls go by on tired feet;
And an old woman with a witch's stare
Cried "Praise the Lord!" She vanished on a bus
With hissing air brakes, like an incubus.

Three hardware stores, a barbershop, a bar,
A movie playing Westerns—where I went
To see a dream of horses called *The Star* . . . .
Some day, when this uncertain continent
Is marble, and men ask what was the good
We lived by, dust may whisper "Hollywood."

Then back along the river bank on foot
By moonlight . . . . On the West Virginia side
An owlish train began to huff and hoot;
It seemed to know of something that had died.
I didn't linger—sometimes when I travel
I think I'm being followed by the Devil.

At the newsstand in the lobby, a cigar
Was talkative: "Since I've been in this town
I've seen one likely woman, and a car
As she was crossing Main Street, knocked her down."
I was a stranger here myself, I said,
And bought the *New York Times,* and went to bed.

**My father in the night commanding No**

My father in the night commanding No
Has work to do. Smoke issues from his lips;
    He reads in silence.
The frogs are croaking and the street lamps glow.

And then my mother winds the gramophone—
The Bride of Lammermoor begins to shriek—
    Or reads a story
About a prince, a castle, and a dragon.

The moon is glittering above the hill.
I stand before the gateposts of the King—
    So runs the story—
Of Thule, at midnight when the mice are still.

And I have been in Thule! It has come true—
The journey and the danger of the world,
    All that there is
To bear and to enjoy, endure and do.

**Louis Simpson**   *380*

Landscapes, seascapes . . . Where have I been led?
The names of cities—Paris, Venice, Rome—
    Held out their arms.
A feathered god, seductive, went ahead.

Here is my house. Under a red rose tree
A child is swinging; another gravely plays.
    They are not surprised
That I am here; they were expecting me.

And yet my father sits and reads in silence,
My mother sheds a tear, the moon is still,
    And the dark wind
Is murmuring that nothing ever happens.

Beyond his jurisdiction as I move,
Do I not prove him wrong? And yet, it's true
    *They* will not change
There, on the stage of terror and of love.

The actors in that playhouse always sit
In fixed positions—father, mother, child
    With painted eyes.
How sad it is to be a little puppet!

Their heads are wooden. And you once pretended
To understand them! Shake them as you will,
    They cannot speak.
Do what you will, the comedy is ended.

Father, why did you work? Why did you weep,
Mother? Was the story so important?
    *"Listen!"* the wind
Said to the children, and they fell asleep.

**Louis Simpson**   *381*

# L. E. Sissman

*L. E. Sissman, born 1928 in Detroit, lives with his second
wife in the village of Still River, Massachusetts, and
commutes to his work as vice-president and creative
director of the advertising firm of Kenyon and Eckhardt
in Boston. As a precocious youngster he was a winner
of the National Spelling Bee and later became one of
radio's Quiz Kids. Expelled from Harvard "for laziness
and insubordination," he was readmitted and graduated
with honors. More overtly autobiographical than most
poets, he writes with a sophisticated awareness of the
symbols and totems of his own Depression generation as,
in middle age, it experiences an American world of
affluence it neither made nor could imagine.*

## A disappearance in West Cedar Street

Did Shriner die or make it to New York?
In his side room, across the hall from mine,
Wide windows air bare ticking. On a line
Outside, clean sheets flap. Samples of his work

Litter the closet: a barbed, wiry nude
In his hirsute pen line; a sketch of me
In ink and wash; a torn gouache of three
Pears on a windowsill. A cache of food—

Saltines, Velveeta Cheese, dried apricots—
Hid in a cairn of bags is now laid bare.
Also a bathrobe belt, one sock, a pair
Of sneakers with frayed laces tied in knots,

A paperback "Candide." Did Shriner die
While I was on the Cape? Did his cough stop
Dead in the welfare ward? Did a blue cop
Wheel Shriner out under the summer sky?

Did absolutely nobody appear
When they interred his box in Potter's Field?
(I would have been there.) Did nobody yield
A summer hat, a winter thought, a tear?

Or did he make it to New York? Did his
Ship dock at last at Fifty-Seventh Street?
Did angels, agents, and collectors meet
His price for life? Is that where Shriner is?

Does he sit down now in Minetta's late
With mistresses and models on each hand?
And is he now an icon in the land
Of mind and matter southward of Hell Gate?

Grey curtains flutter. A tall smell of pork
Ascends the stairs. The landlady below
Tells me in broken English she don't know.
Did Shriner die or make it to New York?

**In and out: severance of connections, 1946**

   1  CIVIS

Walking the town as if I owned it all—
Each lilac leafing out in Brattle Street,
Each green vane in the hollow square guarding
The gargoyles on Memorial Hall, each inch

Of rubber tubing in the Mallinckrodt
Chemical Laboratory, each
Particle who would learn and gladly teach,
Each English bicycle chained to its rack,
Each green bag humping on its scholar's back,
Each tally for a Cambridge traffic death,
Each boyish girl who makes you catch your breath,
Each Argyle sock, each Bursar's bill, each ounce
Of shag, each brick, each doctorate—as if
I owned the entire spring-wound town, I walk
Up the north path to University Hall.

### 2 MAGISTER

The Master's teeth squeak as he sprinkles me
(Too hot to handle) with a mist of spit
That dries quite coolly. "Edwards, I've got some
Rough news for you." In his glazed, padded, blue
Old double-breasted serge suit and his bat-
Wing bow tie (navy, with pink polka dots),
He lets me have it right between the eyes,
His aces on the table, man to boy.
"Look, if there's one thing I can't tolerate
It's smart guys that won't work. The deans are soft
On geniuses. Not me. What we need more
Of is Midwestern athletes who get C's."
He stands up to reveal that his brown vest
Is perfectly misbuttoned. "Now, don't think
That I'm the least bit sorry about you.
I'm sorry for your mother and your dad.
You let them down. Now, you get out of here
And do something worthwhile. Work with your hands.
Stick with it two years. Maybe they'll take you back.
Okay, fella? That's it. Now let's shake."
We shake. I shake in secret with the shame of it.

### 3 EXILIUM

The ghost goes south, avoiding well-worn ways
Frequented by his friends. Instead, he slips

**L. E. Sissman**   *385*

Into loose shadows on the sunless side
Of the least-travelled street. But even there,
One with a bony finger points him out
And pierces him with questions. Zigzagging,
He hedges hastily back to his route,
Which leads on past his windows, tendrilly
Embraced already by the outriders
Of summer's ivy, past his pipes and books
And dirty shirts and mother's picture, past
The dining hall where his name is still good
For a square meal, no questions asked, and past
The common room which is too good for him.
Across the Drive his beast heaves into view:
A monster boathouse lolling on the bank
Of the high river, backside in the water.
Inside, he greets the landlord's black-haired daughter,
Miss Jacobs, with a nod, and goes upstairs
To put his chamois-seated crew pants on.
Then, past the ranks of Compromises, he
Walks out to the land's end of the long float,
Selects his Single, and stands out to sea.

# Edith Sitwell

*Edith Sitwell, born September 7, 1887, in Scarborough,*
*Yorkshire, died in 1964 in London where, except for parts*
*of each year spent at her ancestral home, Renishaw,*
*Derbyshire, and at her brother Osbert's castle in*
*Montegufoni, Italy, she had lived most of her life. The*
*three Sitwells—Dame Edith, Sir Osbert (who died in*
*1969) and Sacheverell—were the most famous family of*
*writers in the contemporary world. Known for her*
*distinctive mode of costume, which often suggested the*
*medieval, she had a deep interest in English literary and*
*social history. This led her to the writing of such books*
*as Bath, Alexander Pope, The English Eccentrics, and a*
*biography of Elizabeth I. Late in her life she was*
*converted to Roman Catholicism, made several visits to*
*the United States, and wrote an acerb volume of memoirs*
*entitled Taken Care Of.*

## Heart and mind

Said the Lion to the Lioness—'When you are amber dust—
No more a raging fire like the heat of the Sun
(No liking but all lust)—
Remember still the flowering of the amber blood and bone,
The rippling of bright muscles like a sea,
Remember the rose-prickles of bright paws,
Though we shall mate no more
Till the fire of that sun the heart and the moon-cold bone are one.'

Said the Skeleton lying upon the sands of Time—
'The great gold planet that is the mourning heat of the Sun
Is greater than all gold, more powerful
Than the tawny body of a Lion that fire consumes
Like all that grows or leaps . . . so is the heart
More powerful than all dust. Once I was Hercules
Or Samson, strong as the pillars of the seas:
But the flames of the heart consumed me, and the mind
Is but a foolish wind.'

Said the Sun to the Moon—'When you are but a lonely white crone,
And I, a dead King in my golden armor somewhere in a dark wood,
Remember only this of our hopeless love:
That never till Time is done
Will the fire of the heart and the fire of the mind be one.'


## Still falls the rain

*The Raids, 1940. Night and Dawn*

Still falls the Rain—
Dark as the world of man, black as our loss—
Blind as the nineteen hundred and forty nails
Upon the Cross.

Still falls the Rain
With a sound like the pulse of the heart that is changed to the hammer-
        beat
In the Potter's Field, and the sound of the impious feet

On the Tomb:
            Still falls the Rain
In the Field of Blood where the small hopes breed and the human brain
Nurtures its greed, that worm with the brow of Cain.

Still falls the Rain
At the feet of the Starved Man hung upon the Cross.

**Edith Sitwell**   *389*

Christ that each day, each night, nails there, have mercy on us—
On Dives and on Lazarus:
Under the Rain the sore and the gold are as one.

Still falls the Rain—
Still falls the Blood from the Starved Man's wounded Side:
He bears in His Heart all wounds—those of the light that died,
The last faint spark
In the self-murdered heart, the wounds of the sad uncomprehending
    dark,
The wounds of the baited bear—
The blind and weeping bear whom the keepers beat
On his helpless flesh . . . the tears of the hunted hare.

Still falls the Rain—
Then—O Ile leape up to my God: who pulles me doune—
See, see where Christ's blood streames in the firmament:
It flows from the Brow we nailed upon the tree
Deep to the dying, to the thirsting heart
That holds the fires of the world—dark-smirched with pain
As Caesar's laurel crown.

Then sounds the voice of One who like the heart of man
Was once a child who among beasts has lain—
'Still do I love, still shed my innocent light, my Blood, for thee.'


## Scotch rhapsody

'Do not take a bath in Jordan,
                  Gordon,
On the holy Sabbath, on the peaceful day!'
Said the huntsman, playing on his old bagpipe,
Boring to death the pheasant and the snipe—
Boring the ptarmigan and grouse for fun—
Boring them worse than a nine-bore gun.
Till the flaxen leaves where the prunes are ripe

**Edith Sitwell**  *390*

Heard the tartan wind a-droning in the pipe,
And they heard MacPherson say:
'Where do the waves go? What hotels
Hide their bustles and their gay ombrelles?
And would there be room?—Would there be *room*?
    *Would* there be room for me?'
There is a hotel at Ostend
Cold as the wind, without an end,
Haunted by ghostly poor relations
Of Bostonian conversations
(Bagpipes rotting through the walls).
And there the pearl-ropes fall like shawls
With a noise like marine waterfalls.
And 'Another little drink wouldn't do us any harm'
Pierces through the Sabbatical calm.
And that is the place for me!
So do not take a bath in Jordan,
                Gordon,
On the holy Sabbath, on the peaceful day—
Or you'll never go to heaven, Gordon MacPherson,
And speaking purely as a private person
That is the place—*that* is the place—that is the *place* for me!

---

**Still falls the rain:** *The particular "occasion" of this poem is
the Battle of Britain, when air raids by massive squadrons
of Nazi bombers devastated much of London and killed scores
of thousands of people. The larger perspective of the poem is
the murderous history of mankind under the benign, suffering,
eyes of Christ crucified. Dives is the rich man in the parable
of the rich man and Lazarus told by St. Luke. The lines "O
Ile leape up to my God: who pulles me doune—/See, see
where Christ's blood streames in the firmament," taken from
the last soliloquy of Doctor Faustus in Marlowe's play,
express the hero's terror and possible hope as he tries to
evade the penalty of eternal damnation for having sold
his soul to the devil.*

# William Jay Smith

*William Jay Smith, born 1918 in Winnfield, Louisiana, is on the faculty of Hollins College, Virginia. He was educated at Washington University, Columbia, and Oxford, which he attended as a Rhodes scholar. During World War II he was Navy personnel officer of a Pacific air base and, for two years, liaison officer aboard a French war vessel in the Atlantic and Pacific. He has taught at Columbia and at Williams College, was an active member of the Vermont legislature, and later Consultant in Poetry at the Library of Congress.*

## American primitive

Look at him there in his stovepipe hat,
His high-top shoes, and his handsome collar;
Only my Daddy could look like that,
And I love my Daddy like he loves his Dollar.

The screen door bangs, and it sounds so funny—
There he is in a shower of gold;
His pockets are stuffed with folding money,
His lips are blue, and his hands feel cold.

He hangs in the hall by his black cravat,
The ladies faint, and the children holler:
Only my Daddy could look like that,
And I love my Daddy like he loves his Dollar.

## Independence Day

Life is inadequate, but there are many real
    Things of beauty here: the flower peddler's cart
Adrift like an island in the city streets,
    The peddler's mare, lifting her mighty hoof
Aware of all that beauty. And the slate
    Where the schoolboy draws his forty-eight
States, ready to make room for the world.
    The sea's enormous wealth; societies
Commemorating blizzards in the North; the small
    White birds in the South where trees are tall
And the hoopsnake bounces downhill like a wagon wheel.

There are real things of beauty; all
    These things were yours. The shadowy
And fabulous quality of the imaginary
    Is presumed; we know it shall
One day take the world. Now the sea
    Has but poor mimic in the shell; a bell
Must free itself of sound, must break with freedom
    To be free. And so you broke, and so you waved
Farewell to us, and turned away
    To a mirror of completion and of certainty,
To clocks that tick, and have no time to tell.

Poems are praise, and poems cannot end.
    There is no answer for we do not ask.
Upon a cliff of sadness the trees bend
    Strangely toward the sea; the end
Is in oneself. O our unsuffering, suffering
    Sick friend, so life is adequate
And you are whole? There are real things of beauty
    Here, and sorrow is our praise. The day
Is bright, the cloud bank white with gulls.
    And while we lie, and watch the ocean roll,
The wind, an Indian paintbrush, sweeps the sky.

**William Jay Smith**   *394*

### The closing of the rodeo

The lariat snaps; the cowboy rolls
    His pack, and mounts and rides away.
Back to the land the cowboy goes.

Plumes of smoke from the factory sway
    In the setting sun. The curtain falls,
A train in the darkness pulls away.

Goodbye, says the rain on the iron roofs.
    Goodbye, say the barber poles.
Dark drum the vanishing horses' hooves.

# W. D. Snodgrass

*W. D. Snodgrass, born January 5, 1926, in Wilkinsburg,
Pennsylvania, lives with his second wife and his two
children in Syracuse, New York, where he is on the
faculty of the University. He attended Geneva College for
a year, joined the Navy as an apprentice seaman and,
three years later, entered the University of Iowa, from
which he graduated. He has taught at Cornell, the
University of Rochester, and Wayne University. The
first book he published, Heart's Needle, was awarded
the Pulitzer Prize in 1960.*

## The campus on the hill

Up the reputable walks of old established trees
They stalk, children of the *nouveaux riches;* chimes
Of the tall Clock Tower drench their heads in blessing:
"I don't wanna play at your house;
I don't like you any more."
My house stands opposite, on the other hill,
Among meadows, with the orchard fences down and falling;
Deer come almost to the door.
You cannot see it, even in this clearest morning.
White birds hang in the air between
Over the garbage landfill and those homes thereto adjacent,
Hovering slowly, turning, settling down
Like the flakes sifting imperceptibly onto the little town

In a waterball of glass.
And yet, this morning, beyond this quiet scene,
The floating birds, the backyards of the poor,
Beyond the shopping plaza, the dead canal, the hillside
    lying tilted in the air,
Tomorrow has broken out today:
Riot in Algeria, in Cyprus, in Alabama;
Aged in wrong, the empires are declining,
And China gathers, soundlessly, like evidence.
What shall I say to the young on such a morning?—
Mind is the one salvation?—also grammar?—
No; my little ones lean not toward revolt. They
Are the Whites, the vaguely furiously driven, who resist
Their souls with such passivity
As would make Quakers swear. All day, dear Lord, all day
They wear their godhead lightly.
They look out from their hill and say,
To themselves, "We have nowhere to go but down;
The great destination is to stay."
Surely the nations will be reasonable;
They look at the world—don't they?—the world's way?
The clock just now has nothing more to say.


### April inventory

The green catalpa tree has turned
All white; the cherry blooms once more.
In one whole year I haven't learned
A blessed thing they pay you for.
The blossoms snow down in my hair;
The trees and I will soon be bare.

The trees have more than I to spare.
The sleek, expensive girls I teach,
Younger and pinker every year,
Bloom gradually out of reach.

**W. D. Snodgrass**  *398*

The pear tree lets its petals drop
Like dandruff on a tabletop.

The girls have grown so young by now
I have to nudge myself to stare.
This year they smile and mind me how
My teeth are falling with my hair.
In thirty years I may not get
Younger, shrewder, or out of debt.

The tenth time, just a year ago,
I made myself a little list
Of all the things I'd ought to know,
Then told my parents, analyst,
And everyone who's trusted me
I'd be substantial, presently.

I haven't read one book about
A book or memorized one plot.
Or found a mind I did not doubt.
I learned one date. And then forgot.
And one by one the solid scholars
Get the degrees, the jobs, the dollars.

And smile above their starchy collars.
I taught my classes Whitehead's notions;
One lovely girl, a song of Mahler's.
Lacking a source-book or promotions,
I showed one child the colors of
A luna moth and how to love.

I taught myself to name my name,
To bark back, loosen love and crying;
To ease my woman so she came,
To ease an old man who was dying.
I have not learned how often I
Can win, can love, but choose to die.

**W. D. Snodgrass**   399

I have not learned there is a lie
Love shall be blonder, slimmer, younger;
That my equivocating eye
Loves only by my body's hunger;
That I have forces, true to feel,
Or that the lovely world is real.

While scholars speak authority
And wear their ulcers on their sleeves,
My eyes in spectacles shall see
These trees procure and spend their leaves.
There is a value underneath
The gold and silver in my teeth.

Though trees turn bare and girls turn wives,
We shall afford our costly seasons;
There is a gentleness survives
That will outspeak and has its reasons.
There is a loveliness exists,
Preserves us, not for specialists.

# Stephen Spender

*Stephen Spender, born February 28, 1909, in London, now*
*lives for part of the year in his native city and in a village*
*in southern France. He is married to the pianist Natasha*
*Litvin, and they have two children. He was educated at*
*Oxford, where he became a friend of W. H. Auden and*
*with whom he was popularly associated as joint leader*
*of the "English Group," whose other members were*
*Cecil Day Lewis and Louis MacNeice. He is often*
*regarded as a sort of roving ambassador of modern*
*letters, an honorary title attendant upon his lifelong*
*editorial and political activities and his wide travels as*
*lecturer and cultural representative in America, Europe,*
*and Asia. He is a frequent lecturer and visiting professor*
*at American universities, most recently at Northwestern*
*and the University of Connecticut.*

## The express

After the first powerful plain manifesto
The black statement of pistons, without more fuss
But gliding like a queen, she leaves the station.
Without bowing and with restrained unconcern
She passes the houses which humbly crowd outside,
The gasworks and at last the heavy page
Of death, printed by gravestones in the cemetery.

Beyond the town there lies the open country
Where, gathering speed, she acquires mystery,
The luminous self-possession of ships on ocean.
It is now she begins to sing—at first quite low
Then loud, and at last with a jazzy madness—
The song of her whistle screaming at curves,
Of deafening tunnels, brakes, innumerable bolts.
And always light, aerial, underneath
Goes the elate metre of her wheels.
Steaming through metal landscape on her lines
She plunges new eras of wild happiness
Where speed throws up strange shapes, broad curves
And parallels clean like the steel of guns.
At last, further than Edinburgh or Rome,
Beyond the crest of the world, she reaches night
Where only a low streamline brightness
Of phosphorus on the tossing hills is white.
Ah, like a comet through flame she moves entranced
Wrapt in her music no bird song, no, nor bough
Breaking with honey buds, shall ever equal.

## An elementary school class room in a slum

Far far from gusty waves, these children's faces.
Like rootless weeds the torn hair round their paleness.
The tall girl with her weighed-down head. The paper-seeming boy with
     rat's eyes. The stunted unlucky heir
Of twisted bones, reciting a father's gnarled disease,
His lesson from his desk. At back of the dim class,
One unnoted, sweet and young: his eyes live in a dream
Of squirrels' game, in tree room, other than this.

On sour cream walls, donations. Shakespeare's head
Cloudless at dawn, civilized dome riding all cities.
Belled, flowery, Tyrolese valley. Open-handed map

Awarding the world its world. And yet, for these
Children, these windows, not this world, are world,
Where all their future's painted with a fog,
A narrow street sealed in with a lead sky,
Far far from rivers, capes, and stars of words.

Surely Shakespeare is wicked, the map a bad example
With ships and sun and love tempting them to steal—
For lives that slyly turn in their cramped holes
From fog to endless night? On their slag heap, these children
Wear skins peeped through by bones and spectacles of steel
With mended glass, like bottle bits on stones.
All of their time and space are foggy slum
So blot their maps with slums as big as doom.

Unless, governor, teacher, inspector, visitor,
This map becomes their window and these windows
That open on their lives like crouching tombs
Break, O break open, till they break the town
And show the children to the fields and all their world
Azure on their sands, to let their tongues
Run naked into books, the white and green leaves open
The history theirs whose language is the sun.


## Port Bou

As a child holds a pet
Arms clutching but with hands that do not join
And the coiled animal watches the gap
To outer freedom in animal air,
So the earth-and-rock flesh arms of this harbour
Embrace but do not enclose the sea
Which, through a gap, vibrates to the open sea
Where ships and dolphins swim and above is the sun.
In the bright winter sunlight I sit on the stone parapet

Of a bridge; my circling arms rest on a newspaper
Empty in my mind as the glittering stone
Because I search for an image
And seeing an image I count out the coined words
To remember the childish headlands of this harbour.
A lorry halts beside me with creaking brakes
And I look up at warm waving flag-like faces
Of militiamen staring down at my French newspaper.
'How do they speak of our struggle, over the frontier?'
I hold out the paper, but they refuse,
They did not ask for anything so precious
But only for friendly words and to offer me cigarettes.
In their smiling faces the war finds peace, the famished mouths
Of the rusty carbines brush against their trousers
Almost as fragilely as reeds;
And wrapped in a cloth—old mother in a shawl—
The terrible machine-gun rests.
They shout, salute back as the truck jerks forward
Over the vigorous hill, beyond the headland.
An old man passes, his running mouth,
With three teeth like bullets, spits out 'pom-pom-pom.'
The children run after; and, more slowly, the women
Clutching their clothes, follow over the hill;
Till the village is empty, for the firing practice,
And I am left alone on the bridge at the exact centre
Where the cleaving river trickles like saliva.
At the exact centre, solitary as a target,
Where nothing moves against a background of cardboard houses
Except the disgraceful skirring dogs; and the firing begins,
Across the harbour mouth from headland to headland,
White flecks of foam gashed by lead in the sea;
And the echo trails over its iron lash
Whipping the flanks of the surrounding hills.
My circling arms rest on the newspaper,
My mind seems paper where dust and ink fall,
I tell myself the shooting is only for practice,
And my body seems a cloth which the machine-gun stitches

**Stephen Spender**   405

Like a sewing machine, neatly, with cotton from a reel;
And the solitary, irregular, thin 'paffs' from the carbines
Draw on long needles white threads through my navel.

---

**Port Bou:** *During the Spanish Civil War, Port Bou was a main point of entry into Spain from France. This poem is the meditation of a sympathetic stranger, enisled in a remote seaside village, as he encounters the forces of the peasant militia and observes, first with detachment, finally with a grotesque sense of physical involvement, their practice for war.*

# George Starbuck

*George Starbuck, born June 15, 1931, in Columbus, Ohio,
studied at the California Institute of Technology, the
University of Chicago, and Harvard. After the publication
of his first book,* Bone Thoughts, *he spent a year in
Europe as winner of the Prix de Rome. He now lives in
Iowa City where he teaches in the creative writing
program of the State University of Iowa.*

## Bone thoughts on a dry day

*Walking to the museum
over the Outer Drive,
I think, before I see them
dead, of the bones alive.*

How perfectly the snake smooths over the fact
he strings sharp beads around that charmer's neck.

Bird bone may be breakable, but
have you ever held a cat's jaw shut?
Brittle as ice.

Take mice:
the mouse is a berry, his bones mere seeds:
step on him once and see.

You mustn't think that the fish
choke on those bones, or that chickens wish.

The wise old bat
hangs his bones in a bag.

Two chicks ride a bike,
unlike
that legless swinger of crutches, the ostrich.

Only the skull of a man is much of an ashtray.

Each owl
turns on a dowel.

When all the other tents are struck, an old
elephant pitches himself on his own poles.

But as for my bones—
tug of a toe, blunt-bowed barge of a thighbone,
gondola-squadron of ribs, and the jaw scow—
they weather the swing and storm of the flesh they plow,
out of conjecture of shore, one jolt from land.

*I climb the museum steps like a beach.*
*There, on squared stone, some cast-up keels bleach.*
*Here, a dark sea speaks with white hands.*


**New strain**

You should see these musical mice.
    When we start the device
they rise on their haunches and sniff
    the air as if
they remembered all about dancing.
    Soon they are chancing

**George Starbuck**   409

a step or two, and a turn.
      How quickly they learn
The rest, and with leaps and spins
      master the ins
and outs of it, round and round
      and round. We found
the loudest music best
      and now we test
with a kind of electric bell
      which works as well.

In two to two-and-a-quarter
      minutes, a shorter
rhythm captures the front
      legs, and they stunt
in somersaults until
      they become still
and seem to have lost their breath.
      But the sign of death
is later: the ears, which have been
      flat, like a skin
skullcap, relax and flare
      as if the air
might hold some further thing
      for the listening.

# Wallace Stevens

*Wallace Stevens, born October 2, 1879, in Reading,*
*Pennsylvania, died in 1955. He was educated at Harvard*
*and the New York Law School and, in 1904, began to*
*practice law in New York City. From 1916 until his death,*
*he lived with his wife and daughter in Hartford,*
*Connecticut, where he was associated with the Hartford*
*Accident and Indemnity Company, of which he became*
*vice-president in 1934. He did not publish his first book*
*of poems, Harmonium, until he was forty years old. As a*
*businessman, he kept his writing career a strictly private*
*preoccupation and lived wholly apart from literary society.*

## The poems of our climate

I

Clear water in a brilliant bowl,
Pink and white carnations. The light
In the room more like a snowy air,
Reflecting snow. A newly-fallen snow
At the end of winter when afternoons return.
Pink and white carnations—one desires
So much more than that. The day itself
Is simplified: a bowl of white,
Cold, a cold porcelain, low and round,
With nothing more than the carnations there.

II

Say even that this complete simplicity
Stripped one of all one's torments, concealed
The evilly compounded, vital I
And made it fresh in a world of white,
A world of clear water, brilliant-edged,
Still one would want more, one would need more,
More than a world of white and snowy scents.

III

There would still remain the never-resting mind,
So that one would want to escape, come back
To what had been so long composed.
The imperfect is our paradise.
Note that, in this bitterness, delight,
Since the imperfect is so hot in us,
Lies in flawed words and stubborn sounds.

## The sense of the sleight-of-hand man

One's grand flights, one's Sunday baths,
One's tootings at the weddings of the soul
Occur as they occur. So bluish clouds
Occurred above the empty house and the leaves
Of the rhododendrons rattled their gold,
As if someone lived there. Such floods of white
Came bursting from the clouds. So the wind
Threw its contorted strength around the sky.

Could you have said the bluejay suddenly
Would swoop to earth? It is a wheel, the rays
Around the sun. The wheel survives the myths.
The fire eye in the clouds survives the gods.

To think of a dove with an eye of grenadine
And pines that are cornets, so it occurs,

**Wallace Stevens**  *413*

And a little island full of geese and stars:
It may be that the ignorant man, alone,
Has any chance to mate his life with life
That is the sensual, pearly spouse, the life
That is fluent in even the wintriest bronze.


## Mrs. Alfred Uruguay

So what said the others and the sun went down
And, in the brown blues of evening, the lady said,
In the donkey's ear, "I fear that elegance
Must struggle like the rest." She climbed until
The moonlight in her lap, mewing her velvet,
And her dress were one and she said, "I have said no
To everything, in order to get at myself.
I have wiped away moonlight like mud. Your innocent ear
And I, if I rode naked, are what remain."

The moonlight crumbled to degenerate forms,
While she approached the real, upon her mountain,
With lofty darkness. The donkey was there to ride,
To hold by the ear, even though it wished for a bell,
Wished faithfully for a falsifying bell.
Neither the moonlight could change it. And for her,
To be, regardless of velvet, could never be more
Than to be, she could never differently be,
Her no and no made yes impossible.

Who was it passed her there on a horse all will,
What figure of capable imagination?
Whose horse clattered on the road on which she rose,
As it descended, blind to her velvet and
The moonlight? Was it a rider intent on the sun,
A youth, a lover with phosphorescent hair,
Dressed poorly, arrogant of his streaming forces,
Lost in an integration of the martyrs' bones,
Rushing from what was real; and capable?

The villages slept as the capable man went down,
Time swished on the village clocks and dreams were alive,
The enormous gongs gave edges to their sounds,
As the rider, no chevalere and poorly dressed,
Impatient of the bells and midnight forms,
Rode over the picket rocks, rode down the road,
And, capable, created in his mind,
Eventual victor, out of the martyrs' bones,
The ultimate elegance: the imagined land.


## Peter Quince at the clavier

I

Just as my fingers on these keys
Make music, so the selfsame sounds
On my spirit make a music, too.

Music is feeling, then, not sound;
And thus it is that what I feel,
Here in this room, desiring you,

Thinking of your blue-shadowed silk,
Is music. It is like the strain
Waked in the elders by Susanna.

Of a green evening, clear and warm,
She bathed in her still garden, while
The red-eyed elders watching, felt

The basses of their beings throb
In witching chords, and their thin blood
Pulse pizzicati of Hosanna.

II

In the green water, clear and warm,
Susanna lay.

**Wallace Stevens**   *415*

She searched
The touch of springs,
And found
Concealed imaginings.
She sighed,
For so much melody.

Upon the bank, she stood
In the cool
Of spent emotions.
She felt, among the leaves,
The dew
Of old devotions.

She walked upon the grass,
Still quavering.
The winds were like her maids,
On timid feet,
Fetching her woven scarves,
Yet wavering.

A breath upon her hand
Muted the night.
She turned—
A cymbal crashed,
And roaring horns.

III

Soon, with a noise like tambourines,
Came her attendant Byzantines.

They wondered why Susanna cried
Against the elders by her side;

And as they whispered, the refrain
Was like a willow swept by rain.

**Wallace Stevens**   *416*

Anon, their lamps' uplifted flame
Revealed Susanna and her shame.

And then, the simpering Byzantines
Fled, with a noise like tambourines.

IV

Beauty is momentary in the mind—
The fitful tracing of a portal;
But in the flesh it is immortal.

The body dies; the body's beauty lives.
So evenings die, in their green going,
A wave, interminably flowing.
So gardens die, their meek breath scenting
The cowl of winter, done repenting.

So maidens die, to the auroral
Celebration of a maiden's choral.

Susanna's music touched the bawdy strings
Of those white elders; but, escaping,
Left only Death's ironic scraping.
Now, in its immortality, it plays
On the clear viol of her memory,
And makes a constant sacrament of praise.

---

**The poems of our climate:** *The central issue of this poem is
the contrast between the radiant simplicity of a bowl of
carnations and the restlessness of the mind that observes it.
The issue is closely examined and then resolved in one
forthright statement. The true and final paradise for modern
man is not the static perfection of a still life, however
beautiful it may be, however persuasively it may invite
him to emulation, because "The imperfect is our paradise."*

**Wallace Stevens**   417

**The sense of the sleight-of-hand man:** *Beginning with random notations on any man's emotions and on a variety of natural phenomena, the speaker delights in the accidents by which the mind and the natural world are made congruent. This sense of participation, he implies, is not dependent upon myths, gods, religions, but is open to everyone since "ignorant man, alone" has the capacity to see metaphors in nature and to feel that his life is one with the energy that flows through all things.*

**Mrs. Alfred Uruguay:** *A grand, well-upholstered, dowager-like lady on a bored donkey rides laboriously upward through the moonlight of imagination to reach the summit of reality; a poor figure of a knight on horseback goes clattering downhill, seeking the sun and the magical realm of the imagination. The lady's mission is hopeless: she already possesses as much reality as her limited mind can accommodate. The man on horseback is more capable. By directing his search into life instead of away from it, he achieves the victory denied her—"The ultimate elegance: the imagined land."*

**Peter Quince at the clavier:** *This poem is a poetic retelling of a story from the Apocrypha: Susanna, the beautiful wife of Joachim, was spied upon by two Hebrew elders as she bathed. When they attempted to seduce her, she drove them off and soon brought charges against them. They, in turn, charged that it was she who had attempted to seduce them. Their word was accepted against hers and Susanna was condemned to death. But just as she was about to be executed, the prophet Daniel proved her innocence, and the elders were put to death instead. Peter Quince is a fictitious name given to an individual who, moved by passion for a woman who is absent, recreates the story of Susanna in terms of a musical composition played on a clavier, a delicate forerunner of the piano.*

# Mark Strand

*Mark Strand, born April 11, 1934, in Summerside, Prince Edward Island, is another American poet who, like Elizabeth Bishop and John Malcolm Brinnin, spent many formative years in the Maritime Provinces of Canada. He is married and lives in New York City. Educated at Antioch College and Yale University, he later spent one year in Italy on a Fulbright Scholarship and another at the University of Brazil in Rio de Janeiro as a Fulbright lecturer. His spare, dream-oriented poems recall modes of perception and being made familiar by Franz Kafka and other writers who tend to scant descriptive or programmatic methods in favor of the experiential.*

## The tunnel

A man has been standing
in front of my house
for days. I peek at him
from the living room
window and at night,
unable to sleep,
I shine my flashlight
down on the lawn.
He is always there.

After a while
I open the front door

**Mark Strand**   *419*

just a crack and order
him out of my yard.
He narrows his eyes
and moans. I slam
the door and dash back
to the kitchen, then up
to the bedroom, then down.

I weep like a schoolgirl
and make obscene gestures
through the window. I
write large suicide notes
and place them so he
can read them easily.
I destroy the living
room furniture to prove
I own nothing of value.

When he seems unmoved
I decide to dig a tunnel
to a neighboring yard.
I seal the basement off
from the upstairs with
a brick wall. I dig hard
and in no time the tunnel
is done. Leaving my pick
and shovel below,

I come out in front of a house
and stand there too tired to
move or even speak, hoping
someone will help me.
I feel I'm being watched
and sometimes I hear
a man's voice,
but nothing is done
and I have been waiting for days.

**Mark Strand**   *420*

**The last bus**

*(Rio de Janeiro, 1966)*

It is dark.
A slight rain
dampens the streets.
Nothing moves

in Lota's park.
The palms hang
over the matted grass,
and the voluminous bushes,

bundled in sheets,
billow beside the walks.
The world is out of reach.
The ghosts of bathers rise

slowly out of the surf and turn
high in the spray.
They walk on the beach
and their eyes burn

like stars.
And Rio sleeps:
the sea is a dream
in which it dies and is reborn.

The bus speeds.
A violet cloud
unravels in its wake.
My legs begin to shake.

My lungs fill up with steam.
Sweat covers my face
My neck and shoulders ache.
and falls to my chest.

**Mark Strand**   422

Not even sure
that I am awake,
I grip the hot
edge of the seat.

The driver smiles.
His pants are rolled above his knees
and his bare calves
gleam in the heat.

A woman tries to comfort me.
She puts her hand under my shirt
and writes the names of flowers
on my back.

Her skirt is black.
She has a tiny skull
and crossbones on each knee.
There is a garden in her eyes

where rows of dull,
white tombstones crowd the air
and people stand,
waving goodbye.

I have the feeling I am there.
She whispers through her teeth
and puts her lips
against my cheek.

The driver turns.
His eyes are closed and he is combing
back his hair.
He tells me to be brave.

I feel my heartbeat
growing fainter as he speaks.

**Mark Strand**   *423*

The woman kisses me again.
Her jaw creaks

and her breath clings
to my neck like mist.
I turn to the window's
cracked pane

streaked with rain.
Where have I been?
I look toward Rio—
nothing is the same.

The Christ who stood
in a pool of electric light
high on his hill
is out of sight.

And the bay is black.
And the black city
sinks into its grave.
And I shall never come back.

# May Swenson

*May Swenson, born 1919, in Logan, Utah, lives on Long Island. She attended Utah State University, then worked for a year as a reporter on Salt Lake City's Deseret News before going to New York. Recognized by many fellowships and awards, her poetry is particularly notable for its close notations of natural phenomena and its often unorthodox shapes.*

## The centaur

The summer that I was ten—
Can it be there was only one
summer that I was ten? It must

have been a long one then—
each day I'd go out to choose
a fresh horse from my stable

which was a willow grove
down by the old canal.
I'd go on my two bare feet.

But when, with my brother's jack-knife,
I had cut me a long limber horse
with a good thick knob for a head,

and peeled him slick and clean
except a few leaves for the tail,
and cinched my brother's belt

around his head for a rein,
I'd straddle and canter him fast
up the grass bank to the path,

trot along in the lovely dust
that talcumed over his hoofs,
hiding my toes, and turning

his feet to swift half-moons.
The willow knob with the strap
jouncing between my thighs

was the pommel and yet the poll
of my nickering pony's head.
My head and my neck were mine,

yet they were shaped like a horse.
My hair flopped to the side
like the mane of a horse in the wind.

My forelock swung in my eyes,
my neck arched and I snorted.
I shied and skittered and reared,

stopped and raised my knees,
pawed at the ground and quivered.
My teeth bared as we wheeled

and swished through the dust again.
I was the horse and the rider,
and the leather I slapped to his rump

spanked my own behind.
Doubled, my two hoofs beat
a gallop along the bank,

the wind twanged in my mane,
my mouth squared to the bit.
And yet I sat on my steed

quiet, negligent riding,
my toes standing the stirrups,
my thighs hugging his ribs.

At a walk we drew up to the porch.
I tethered him to a paling.
Dismounting, I smoothed my skirt

and entered the dusky hall.
My feet on the clean linoleum
left ghostly toes in the hall.

*Where have you been?* said my mother,
*Been riding,* I said from the sink,
and filled me a glass of water.

*What's that in your pocket?* she said.
*Just my knife.* It weighted my pocket
and stretched my dress awry.

*Go tie back your hair,* said my mother,
and *Why is your mouth all green?*
*Rob Roy, he pulled some clover
as we crossed the field,* I told her.

# Allen Tate

*Allen Tate, born November 19, 1899, in Winchester,*
*Kentucky, lives in Minneapolis, where he is professor*
*of English at the University of Minnesota. A graduate of*
*Vanderbilt University, he was one of the founders of The*
*Fugitive, the magazine which served as the mouthpiece*
*of a movement in Southern letters that deeply influenced*
*the careers of a number of writers identified with the*
*"new criticism." One of America's leading literary critics,*
*he has published highly regarded studies of modern*
*literature and has otherwise contributed his talents to a*
*number of editorial and academic positions.*

## Mr. Pope

When Alexander Pope strolled in the city
Strict was the glint of pearl and gold sedans.
Ladies leaned out more out of fear than pity
For Pope's tight back was rather a goat's than man's.

Often one thinks the urn should have more bones
Than skeletons provide for speedy dust,
The urn gets hollow, cobwebs brittle as stones
Weave to the funeral shell a frivolous rust.

And he who dribbled couplets like a snake
Coiled to a lithe precision in the sun

Is missing. The jar is empty; you may break
It only to find that Mr. Pope is gone.

What requisitions of a verity
Prompted the wit and rage between his teeth
One cannot say. Around a crooked tree
A moral climbs whose name should be a wreath.


## Death of little boys

When little boys grown patient at last, weary,
Surrender their eyes immeasurably to the night,
The event will rage terrific as the sea;
Their bodies fill a crumbling room with light.

Then you will touch at the bedside, torn in two,
Gold curls now deftly intricate with gray
As the windowpane extends a fear to you
From one peeled aster drenched with the wind all day.

And over his chest the covers in an ultimate dream
Will mount to the teeth, ascend the eyes, press back
The locks—while round his sturdy belly gleam
The suspended breaths, white spars above the wreck:

Till all the guests, come in to look, turn down
Their palms, and delirium assails the cliff
Of Norway where you ponder, and your little town
Reels like a sailor drunk in his rotten skiff.

The bleak sunshine shrieks its chipped music then
Out to the milkweed amid the fields of wheat.
There is a calm for you where men and women
Unroll the chill precision of moving feet.

# James Tate

*James Tate, born December 8, 1943, in Kansas City, Missouri, studied at Kansas State College, then took a Master of Fine Arts degree from Iowa. His first book of poems,* The Lost Pilot, *was awarded the Yale Series of Younger Poets Award in 1967. He is currently teaching at Columbia University.*

## The lost pilot

*for my father, 1922–1944*

Your face did not rot
like the others—the co-pilot,
for example, I saw him

yesterday. His face is corn-
mush: his wife and daughter,
the poor ignorant people, stare

as if he will compose soon.
He was more wronged than Job.
But your face did not rot

like the others—it grew dark,
and hard like ebony;
the features progressed in their

distinction. If I could cajole
you to come back for an evening,
down from your compulsive

orbiting, I would touch you,
read your face as Dallas,
your hoodlum gunner, now,

with the blistered eyes, reads
his braille editions. I would
touch your face as a disinterested

scholar touches an original page.
However frightening, I would
discover you, and I would not

turn you in; I would not make
you face your wife, or Dallas,
or the co-pilot, Jim. You

could return to your crazy
orbiting, and I would not try
to fully understand what

it means to you. All I know
is this: when I see you,
as I have seen you at least

once every year of my life,
spin across the wilds of the sky
like a tiny, African god,

I feel dead. I feel as if I were
the residue of a stranger's life,
that I should pursue you.

My head cocked toward the sky,
I cannot get off the ground,
and, you, passing over again,

fast, perfect, and unwilling
to tell me that you are doing
well, or that it was mistake

that placed you in that world,
and me in this; or that misfortune
placed these worlds in us.

# Dylan Thomas

*Dylan Thomas, born October 27, 1914, in Swansea, Wales, died in New York City on November 9, 1953. He received no formal education beyond secondary school, and his first professional writing was done as a journalist in his native town. Until his death, which occurred during the fourth of the extensive reading tours he made in the United States, he lived with his wife and three children in the village of Laugharne, on the southwest coast of Wales. His "play for voices," Under Milk Wood, has been widely produced in the United States and in Europe, and his recorded readings of his own poems have had an unparalleled success with a large public.*

## The hunchback in the park

The hunchback in the park
A solitary mister
Propped between trees and water
From the opening of the garden lock
That lets the trees and water enter
Until the Sunday sombre bell at dark

Eating bread from a newspaper
Drinking water from the chained cup
That the children filled with gravel
In the fountain basin where I sailed my ship

Slept at night in a dog kennel
But nobody chained him up.

Like the park birds he came early
Like the water he sat down
And Mister they called Hey mister
The truant boys from the town
Running when he had heard them clearly
On out of sound

Past lake and rockery
Laughing when he shook his paper
Hunchbacked in mockery
Through the loud zoo of the willow groves
Dodging the park keeper
With his stick that picked up leaves.

And the old dog sleeper
Alone between nurses and swans
While the boys among willows
Made the tigers jump out of their eyes
To roar on the rockery stones
And the groves were blue with sailors

Made all day until bell time
A woman figure without fault
Straight as a young elm
Straight and tall from his crooked bones
That she might stand in the night
After the locks and chains

All night in the unmade park
After the railings and shrubberies
The birds the grass the trees the lake
And the wild boys innocent as strawberries
Had followed the hunchback
To his kennel in the dark.

**Dylan Thomas**  *438*

## A refusal to mourn the death, by fire, of a child in London

Never until the mankind making
Bird beast and flower
Fathering and all humbling darkness
Tells with silence the last light breaking
And the still hour
Is come of the sea tumbling in harness

And I must enter again the round
Zion of the water bead
And the synagogue of the ear of corn
Shall I let pray the shadow of a sound
Or sow my salt seed
In the least valley of sackcloth to mourn

The majesty and burning of the child's death.
I shall not murder
The mankind of her going with a grave truth
Nor blaspheme down the stations of the breath
With any further
Elegy of innocence and youth.

Deep with the first dead lies London's daughter,
Robed in the long friends,
The grains beyond age, the dark veins of her mother,
Secret by the unmourning water
Of the riding Thames.
After the first death, there is no other.

## Do not go gentle into that good night

Do not go gentle into that good night,
Old age should burn and rave at close of day;
Rage, rage against the dying of the light.

**Dylan Thomas** *439*

Though wise men at their end know dark is right,
Because their words had forked no lightning they
Do not go gentle into that good night.

Good men, the last wave by, crying how bright
Their frail deeds might have danced in a green bay,
Rage, rage against the dying of the light.

Wild men who caught and sang the sun in flight,
And learn, too late, they grieved it on its way,
Do not go gentle into that good night.

Grave men, near death, who see with blinding sight
Blind eyes could blaze like meteors and be gay,
Rage, rage against the dying of the light.

And you, my father, there on the sad height,
Curse, bless, me now with your fierce tears, I pray.
Do not go gentle into that good night.
Rage, rage against the dying of the light.


**Fern Hill**

Now as I was young and easy under the apple boughs
About the lilting house and happy as the grass was green,
    The night above the dingle starry,
      Time let me hail and climb
    Golden in the heydays of his eyes,
And honoured among wagons I was prince of the apple towns
And once below a time I lordly had the trees and leaves
      Trail with daisies and barley
    Down the rivers of the windfall light.

And as I was green and carefree, famous among the barns
About the happy yard and singing as the farm was home,

In the sun that is young once only,
    Time let me play and be
Golden in the mercy of his means,
And green and golden I was huntsman and herdsman, the calves
Sang to my horn, the foxes on the hills barked clear and cold,
    And the sabbath rang slowly
In the pebbles of the holy streams.

All the sun long it was running, it was lovely, the hay
Fields high as the house, the tunes from the chimneys, it was air
    And playing, lovely and watery
      And fire green as grass.
    And nightly under the simple stars
As I rode to sleep the owls were bearing the farm away,
All the moon long I heard, blessed among stables, the nightjars
    Flying with the ricks, and the horses
      Flashing into the dark.

And then to awake, and the farm, like a wanderer white
With the dew, come back, the cock on his shoulder: it was all
    Shining, it was Adam and maiden,
      The sky gathered again
    And the sun grew round that very day.
So it must have been after the birth of the simple light
In the first, spinning place, the spellbound horses walking warm
    Out of the whinnying green stable
      On to the fields of praise.

And honoured among foxes and pheasants by the gay house
Under the new made clouds and happy as the heart was long,
    In the sun born over and over,
      I ran my heedless ways,
    My wishes raced through the house high hay
And nothing I cared, at my sky blue trades, that time allows
In all his tuneful turning so few and such morning songs
    Before the children green and golden
      Follow him out of grace.

Nothing I cared, in the lamb white days, that time would take me
Up to the swallow thronged loft by the shadow of my hand,
    In the moon that is always rising,
      Nor that riding to sleep
    I should hear him fly with the high fields
And wake to the farm forever fled from the childless land.
Oh as I was young and easy in the mercy of his means,
      Time held me green and dying
    Though I sang in my chains like the sea.

---

**A refusal to mourn the death, by fire, of a child in London:**
*This poem, one of a number that reflect Dylan Thomas's
experience when he served as a fire warden during the
bombings of London, is based upon a solemn irony. Whereas
its title states a firm reluctance to honor the child's death
with an elegy, the poem proceeds to do precisely that. To
celebrate the event with an elegy, the poet implies, would
be to accept it, and this he refuses to do. "I shall not
murder/The mankind of her going with a grave truth," he
says, since grave truths are the same old homilies and clichés
that have always been spoken at burial ceremonies. He
would prefer to honor this death by refusing to see it not as
a single tragedy but as another frightful reminder of the
murderous history of mankind.*

**Do not go gentle into that good night:** *David Thomas, a quiet,
gentle, dignified man, was for many years a dedicated
schoolteacher who, in his youth, had hoped to become a poet.
This poem, written as a tribute by his son as he watched the
progress of his father's fatal illness, was completed barely
a year before the death of Dylan Thomas himself.*

**Fern Hill:** *On the map, Fern Hill is located near the village
of Laugharne (pronounced larn), in southwestern Wales,
where Dylan Thomas lived. In this poem, he gives the name
to another location—a hillside farm where, as a child, he
spent many summers with his aunt and uncle. This farm
has pasture lands overlooking the estuary of the river Towy.
The old whitewashed house is surrounded by a number of
barns, high mounds of hay, and an apple orchard of great age.*

# Charles Tomlinson

*Charles Tomlinson, born January 8, 1927, in Stoke-on-Trent, Staffordshire, England, now lives in a village in Gloucestershire with his wife and two daughters. A frequent visitor to the United States, he enjoys the southwest particularly and says that if he had two lives he would spend one of them there. He is also a painter, and has translated poetry and prose from German, Spanish, Russian, Italian, and Hungarian.*

## Las Trampas U.S.A.

I go through hollyhocks
in a dry garden, up
to the house,
knock, then ask
in English for the key
to Las Trampas church.
The old woman
says in Spanish: I
do not speak English
so I say: Where
is the church key
in Spanish.
—You see those
three men working: you
ask them. She
goes in, I
go on

preparing to ask
them in Spanish:
Hi, they say
in American. Hello
I say and ask
them in English
where is the key
to the church and they
say: He has it
gesturing to a fourth
man working
hoeing a corn-field
nearby, and to him
(in Spanish): Where is
the church key? And he:
I have it.—O.K.
they say in
Spanish-American:
You bring it (and
to me in English)
He'll bring it. You
wait for him
by the church door.
Thank you, I say and they
reply in American
You're welcome. I go
once more and
await in shadow
the key: he
who brings it is not
he of the hoe, but
one of the three
men working, who
with a Castilian grace
ushers me in
to this place
of coolness out
of the August sun.

**Charles Tomlinson**   445

## At Barstow

Nervy with neons, the main drag
was all there was. A placeless place.
A faint flavour of Mexico in the tacos
tasting of gasoline. Trucks refuelled
before taking off through space. Someone lived
in the houses with their houseyards wired
like tiny Belsens. The Gotterdammerung
would be like this. No funeral pyres, no choirs
of lost trombones. An Untergand
without a clang, without
a glimmer of gone glory
however dimmed. At the motel desk
was a photograph of Roy Rogers
signed. It was here
he made a stay. He did not
ride away on Trigger
through the high night, the tilted
Pleiades overhead, the polestar low, no
going off until
the eyes of beer-cans
had ceased to glint at him
and the desert darknesses
had quenched the neons. He was spent.
He was content. Down he lay.
The passing trucks patrolled his sleep,
the shifted gears contrived
a muffled fugue against the fading of his day
and his dustless, undishonoured stetson rode
beside the bed,
glowed in the pulsating, never-final twilight
there, at that execrable conjunction
of gasoline and desert air.

# Derek Walcott

*Derek Walcott, born January 23, 1930, in Castries, St.*
*Lucia, lives with his wife and three children in Trinidad*
*where he has worked variously as a teacher, a journalist,*
*and an art critic. Educated at St. Mary's College and the*
*University of the West Indies, he has lived for brief*
*periods in the United States and in England, where his*
*plays have been produced by the British Broadcasting*
*Corporation.*

## Ruins of a great house

*Though our longest sun sets at right declensions and makes*
*but winter arches, it cannot be long before we lie down in darkness,*
*and have our light in ashes . . .*

BROWNE: *Urn Burial*

Stones only, the *disjecta membra* of this Great House,
Whose moth-like girls are mixed with candledust,
Remain to file the lizard's dragonish claws;
The mouths of those gate cherubs streaked with stain.
Axle and coachwheel silted under the muck
Of cattle droppings.

        Three crows flap for the trees,
And settle, creaking the eucalyptus boughs.
A smell of dead limes quickens in the nose
The leprosy of Empire.

'Farewell, green fields'
'Farewell, ye happy groves!'

Marble as Greece, like Faulkner's south in stone,
Deciduous beauty prospered and is gone;
But where the lawn breaks in a rash of trees
A spade below dead leaves will ring the bone
Of some dead animal or human thing
Fallen from evil days, from evil times.

It seems that the original crops were limes
Grown in that silt that clogs the river's skirt;
The imperious rakes are gone, their bright girls gone,
The river flows, obliterating hurt.

I climbed a wall with the grill ironwork
Of exiled craftsmen, protecting that great house
From guilt, perhaps, but not from the worm's rent,
Nor from the padded cavalry of the mouse.
And when a wind shook in the limes I heard
What Kipling heard; the death of a great empire, the abuse
Of ignorance by Bible and by sword.

A green lawn, broken by low walls of stone
Dipped to the rivulet, and pacing, I thought next
Of men like Hawkins, Walter Raleigh, Drake,
Ancestral murderers and poets, more perplexed
In memory now by every ulcerous crime.
The world's green age then was a rotting lime
Whose stench became the charnel galleon's text.
The rot remains with us, the men are gone.
But, as dead ash is lifted in a wind,
That fans the blackening ember of the mind,
My eyes burned from the ashen prose of Donne.

Ablaze with rage, I thought
Some slave is rotting in this manorial lake,
And still the coal of my compassion fought:

**Derek Walcott** *449*

That Albion too, was once
A colony like ours, 'Part of the continent, piece of the main'
Nook-shotten, rook o'er blown, deranged
By foaming channels, and the vain expense
Of bitter faction.

                  All in compassion ends
So differently from what the heart arranged:
'as well as if a manor of thy friend's . . .'

# Robert Penn Warren

*Robert Penn Warren, born April 24, 1905, in Todd County,
Kentucky, lives with his second wife, the writer Eleanor
Clark, and their son and daughter in Fairfield, Connecticut.
Currently a member of the Yale faculty, he was educated
at Vanderbilt, California, and Yale and was a Rhodes
scholar at Oxford. He has taught at Vanderbilt, at
Louisiana State, where, with Cleanth Brooks, he edited
the* Southern Review, *and at the University of Minnesota.
The wide public success of his novels, among
them* All the King's Men *and* World Enough and Time,
*has at times obscured the fact that he is one of the most
accomplished of American poets.*

## Bearded oaks

The oaks, how subtle and marine,
Bearded, and all the layered light
Above them swims; and thus the scene,
Recessed, awaits the positive night.

So, waiting, we in the grass now lie
Beneath the languorous tread of light:
The grasses, kelp-like, satisfy
The nameless motions of the air.

Upon the floor of light, and time,
Unmurmuring, of polyp made,

We rest; we are, as light withdraws,
Twin atolls on a shelf of shade.

Ages to our construction went,
Dim architecture, hour by hour:
And violence, forgot now, lent
The present stillness all its power.

The storm of noon above us rolled,
Of light the fury, furious gold,
The long drag troubling us, the depth:
Dark is unrocking, unrippling, still.

Passion and slaughter, ruth, decay
Descend, minutely whispering down,
Silted down swaying streams, to lay
Foundation for our voicelessness.

All our debate is voiceless here,
As all our rage, the rage of stone;
If hope is hopeless, then fearless fear,
And history is thus undone.

Our feet once wrought the hollow street
With echo when the lamps were dead
At windows, once our headlight glare
Disturbed the doe that, leaping, fled.

I do not love you less that now
The caged heart makes iron stroke,
Or less that all that light once gave
The graduate dark should now revoke.

We live in time so little time
And we learn all so painfully,
That we may spare this hour's term
To practice for eternity.

**Robert Penn Warren**  *452*

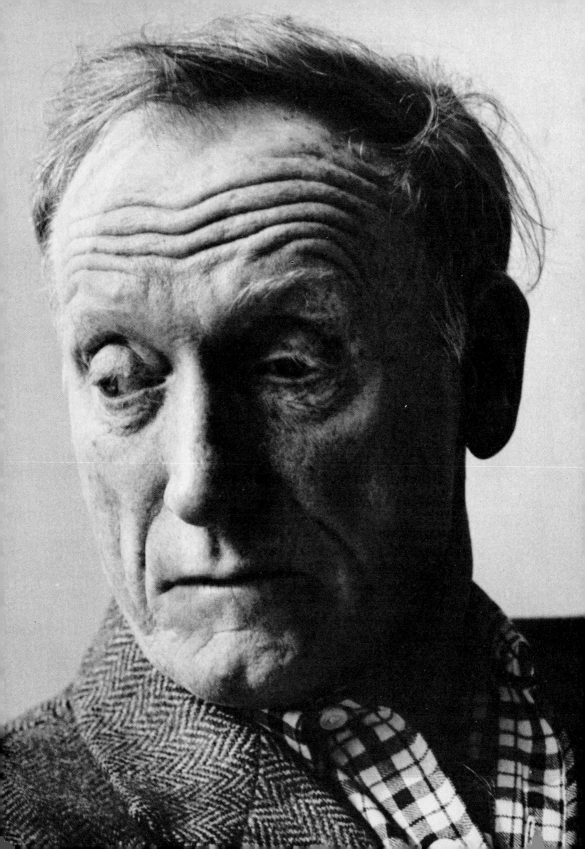

## Pursuit

The hunchback on the corner, with gum and shoelaces,
Has his own wisdom and pleasures, and may not be lured
To divulge them to you, for he has merely endured
Your appeal for his sympathy and your kind purchases;
And wears infirmity but as the general who turns
Apart, in his famous old greatcoat there on the hill
At dusk when the rapture and cannonade are still,
To muse withdrawn from the dead, from his gorgeous subalterns;
Or stares from the thicket of his familiar pain, like a fawn
That meets you a moment, wheels, in imperious innocence is gone.

Go to the clinic. Wait in the outer room
Where like an old possum the snag-nailed hand will hump
On its knee in murderous patience, and the pomp
Of pain swells like the Indies, or a plum.
And there you will stand, as on the Roman hill,
Stunned by each withdrawn gaze and severe shape,
The first barbarian victor stood to gape
At the sacrificial fathers, white-robed, still;
And even the feverish old Jew stares stern with authority
Till you feel like one who has come too late, or improperly clothed, to a
   party.

The doctor will take you now. He is burly and clean;
Listening, like lover or worshiper, bends at your heart;
But cannot make out just what it tries to impart;
So smiles; says you simply need a change of scene.
Of scene, of solace: therefore Florida,
Where Ponce de León clanked among the lilies,
Where white sails skit on blue and cavort like fillies,
And the shoulder gleams in the moonlit corridor.
A change of love: if love is a groping Godward, though blind,
No matter what crevice, cranny, chink, bright in dark, the pale tentacle
   find.
In Florida consider the flamingo
Its color passion but its neck a question;

Consider even that girl the other guests shun
On beach, at bar, in bed, for she may know
The secret you are seeking, after all;
Or the child you humbly sit by, excited and curly,
That screams on the shore at the sea's sunlit hurlyburly,
Till the mother calls its name, toward nightfall.
Till you sit alone: in the dire meridians, off Ireland, in fury
Of spume-tooth and dawnless sea-heave, salt rimes the lookout's devout
    eye.

Till you sit alone—which is the beginning of error—
Behind you the music and lights of the great hotel:
Solution, perhaps, is public, despair personal,
But history held to your breath clouds like a mirror.
There are many states, and towns in them, and faces,
But meanwhile, the little old lady in black, by the wall,
Who admires all the dancers, and tells you how just last fall
Her husband died in Ohio, and damp mists her glasses;
She blinks and croaks, like a toad or a Norn, in the horrible light,
And rattles her crutch, which may put forth a small bloom, perhaps
    white.

---

**Pursuit:** *The "you" in this poem is anyone who seeks some
answer to his nameless sense of guilt, some explanation for
a malady no one can diagnose. He tries the clinic, the past,
and a rest cure in Florida, but nothing works. He suffers and
does not know why. Guilt pursues him as he pursues blindly
some solution to a burden as heavy as original sin.*

# Vernon Watkins

Vernon Watkins, born June 27, 1906, in Maesteg, South
Wales, died in 1967 in Seattle where he was about to
begin a second visit to the University of Washington as
a teacher of poetry. For most of his life he lived near
Swansea with his wife and four children. After studying
modern languages at Magdalene College, Cambridge, he
worked for many years as a clerk in Lloyds Bank.
Through World War II he served in the Royal Air Force,
first as a policeman and then on special duties, eventually
becoming a flight sergeant. He was a close friend and
early poetic mentor to Dylan Thomas, a relationship
documented in Letters to Vernon Watkins, published
in 1957.

## The heron

The cloud-backed heron will not move:
He stares into the stream.
He stands unfaltering while the gulls
And oyster-catchers scream.
He does not hear, he cannot see
The great white horses of the sea,
But fixes eyes on stillness
Below their flying team.

How long will he remain, how long
Have the grey woods been green?
The sky and the reflected sky,
Their glass he has not seen,
But silent as a speck of sand
Interpreting the sea and land,
His fall pulls down the fabric
Of all that windy scene.

Sailing with clouds and woods behind,
Pausing in leisured flight,
He stepped, alighting on a stone,
Dropped from the stars of night.
He stood there unconcerned with day,
Deaf to the tumult of the bay,
Watching a stone in water,
A fish's hidden light.

Sharp rocks drive back the breaking waves,
Confusing sea with air.
Bundles of spray blown mountain-high
Have left the shingle bare.
A shipwrecked anchor wedged by rocks,
Loosed by the thundering equinox,
Divides the herded waters,
The stallion and his mare.

Yet no distraction breaks the watch
Of that time-killing bird.
He stands unmoving on the stone;
Since dawn he has not stirred.
Calamity about him cries,
But he has fixed his golden eyes
On water's crooked tablet,
On light's reflected word.

## The lady with the unicorn

About this lady many fruitful trees.
There the chaste unicorn before her knees
Stares in a glass to purify her sight.
At her right hand a lion sits,
And through the foliage, in and out, there flits
Many a bird; then hounds, with deer in flight:
Light is her element; her tapestry is light.

There is her mediaeval music met.
On the high table-top, with damask set
To charm, between the chaste beast and the strong,
An organ which her fingers play
Rests, and her pretty servant's hands obey
Those pipes with bellows to sustain their song
Attuned to distant stars, making their short life long.

This ended, gathered from some leafy way,
That servant brings her flowers upon a tray.
She lifts them to inhale their magic breath.
Caught in that breath's elusive maze,
She marvels. On a stool a monkey plays
With flowers from wicker trailing, strewn beneath,
A heaven of fragrance breathing through their mask of death.

Next, her right hand upholds that coat-of-arms
Seeming love's guardian against war's alarms,
And with her left she grips the upright horn.
This touch, while birds through branches peer,
Consecrates all the beasts as they appear,
Frisking among dark foliage to adorn
Her fingers that caress the constant unicorn.

A lion rampant grips the upright pole.
Her serving-maid now proffers her a bowl
Of peaches, damsons, almonds, grapes, and sweets.
This lady savours one, and sees

**Vernon Watkins**   *459*

How white of almonds, red of mulberries,
Is each a praise no other tree repeats,
Now strangely on love's tree engrafted while she eats.

The senses leave a chain upon her tongue.
That place is hushed, from which the light is sprung.
Curtains are hung, embroidered with strange art.
The letters 'TO MY SOLE DESIRE'
Crown that pavilion with a band of fire
Whose folds the unicorn and lion part,
Revealing in their midst her love-awakened heart.

O sovereign balm to heal all mortal illness:
Long let him look, and still he will find stillness,
Her one betrothed, who sees her museful face.
This lady, with her flowers and hounds,
Woven in light, in air, in wooded grounds,
Transmits a glory wrought about her grace,
Caught in a sacred bond within the encircling space.

Let him look softly, with some seventh sense
Breaking that circle's hushed magnificence,
And see what universe her love controls,
Moving with hushed, divine intent
Through the five senses to their sacrament
Whose Eden turns between two silent poles,
Creating with pure speed that harmony of souls.

Where is the heart of mathematic space?
Throned on a mystery in that leafy place,
This lady's fingers hold, where distance flies,
The Past and Future like a skein
For her betrothed to wind, and loose again.
Lion and unicorn forbid disguise.
He looks, and she looks forth: there are no other eyes.

**The lady with the unicorn:** *This poem takes its title from the famous set of six tapestries (1509–1513) now in the Cluny Museum in Paris. The first five panels deal with the senses of sight, hearing, smell, touch, and taste, and the sixth is "à mon seul désir."*

# Theodore Weiss

*Theodore Weiss, born December 16, 1916, in Reading,*
*Pennsylvania, is professor of creative arts at Princeton*
*where, with his wife Reneé, he edits and publishes* The
Quarterly Review of Literature. *In 1968 he was made an*
*honorary Doctor of Letters by his alma mater,*
*Muhlenberg College; his teaching career has included*
*positions at the University of North Carolina, Yale,*
*and Bard College.*

## The last day and the first

The stocky woman at the door,
with her young daughter "Linda" looking
down, as she pulls out several copies
of *The Watchtower* from her canvas bag,
in a heavy German accent asks me:
"Have you ever thought that these
may be the last days of the world?"

And to my nodding "Yes, I have,"
she and the delicate, blonde girl
without a further word, turning tail,
sheepishly walk away.
                         And I feel
for them, as for us all, this world
in what may be its last days.

And yet this day itself is full
of unbelief, that or marvelously
convincing ignorance.
                              Its young light
O so tentative, those first steps
as of a beginning dance (snowdrops
have already started up, and crocuses
we heard about last night the teller's
children quickly trampled in play)

make it hard not to believe that we are
teetering on creation's brink all over
again. And I almost thrill with fear
to think of what will soon be asked
of us, of you and me;
                              am I at least
not a little old now (like the world)
to be trembling on the edge
of nakedness, a love, as Stendhal
knew it, "as people love for the first
time at nineteen and in Italy"?

Ah well, until I have to crawl
on hands and knees and then can crawl
no more, so may it every Italian-
returning season be, ever the last
day of this world about to burst
and ever for blossoming the first.

# David Wevill

David Wevill, born 1935 in Japan, was taken to Canada
as a child and grew up in Ottawa. He was educated at
Cambridge, began a teaching career at Mandalay
University, then returned to England where his first
volumes of poetry were published. He later came to the
United States to teach at the University of Texas and is
now on the faculty of the University of British Columbia.

## The birth of a shark

What had become of the young shark?
It was time for the ocean to move on.
Somehow, sheathed in the warm current
He'd lost his youthful bite, and fell
Shuddering among the feelers of kelp
And dragging weeds. His belly touched sand,
The shark ran aground on his shadow.

Shark-shape, he lay there.
But in the world above
Six white legs dangled, thrashing for the fun of it,
Fifty feet above the newborn shadow.

The shark nosed up to spy them out;
He rose slowly, a long grey feather

Slendering up through the dense air of the sea.
His eyes of bolted glass were fixed
On a roundness of sun and whetted flesh,
Glittering like stars above his small brain—

The shark rose gradually. He was half-grown,
About four feet: strength of a man's thigh
Wrapped in emery, his mouth a watery
Ash of brambles. As he rose
His shadow paled and entered the sand,
Dissolved, in the twinkling shoals of driftsand
Which his thrusting tail spawned.

This was the shark's birth in our world.

His grey parents had left him
Mysteriously and rapidly—
How else is a shark born?
They had bequeathed him the odour of blood,
And a sense half of anguish at being
Perpetually the forerunner of blood:
A desire to sleep in the currents fought
Against the strong enchaining links of hunger,
In shoals, or alone,
Cruising the white haze off Africa,
Bucked Gibraltar, rode into the Atlantic—
Diet of squid, pulps, a few sea-perch.

But what fish-sense the shark had
Died with his shadow. This commonplace
Of kicking legs he had never seen:
He was attracted. High above him
The sunsoaked heads were unaware of the shark—
He was something rising under their minds
You could not have told them about: grey thought
Beneath the fortnight's seaside spell—
A jagged effort to get at something painful.

**David Wevill** *467*

He knew the path up was direct:
But the young shark was curious.
He dawdled awhile, circling like a bee
Above stems, cutting this new smell
From the water in shapes of fresh razors.
He wasn't even aware he would strike;
That triggered last thrust was beyond his edgy
Power to choose or predict. This
Was carefully to be savoured first, as later
He'd get it, with expertise, and hit fast.

He knew he was alone.
He knew he could only snap off
A foot or a hand at a time—
And without fuss—for sharks and dogs
Do not like to share.
The taste for killing was not even pleasure to him.
And this was new:
This was not sea-flesh, but a kind
Of smoky scent of suntan oil and salt,
Hot blood and wet cloth. When he struck at it
He only grazed his snout,
And skulked away like a pickpocket—

Swerved, paused, turned on his side,
And cocked a round eye up at the dense
Thrashings of frightened spray his climb touch.

And the thrashing commotion moved
Fast as fire away, on the surface of sun.
The shark lay puzzling
In the calm water ten feet down,
As the top of his eye exploded above
Reef and sand, heading for the shallows.
Here was his time of choice—
Twisting, he thought himself round and round
In a slow circling of doubt,
Powerless to be shark, a spawned insult.

**David Wevill**  *468*

But while he was thinking, the sea ahead of him
Suddenly reddened; and black
Shapes with snouts of blunted knives
Swarmed past him and struck
At the bladder of sunlight, snapping at it.
The shark was blinded—
His vision came to him,
Shred by piece, bone by bone
And fragments of bone. Instinctively
His jaws widened to take these crumbs
Of blood from the bigger, experienced jaws,
Whose aim lay in their twice-his-length
Trust in the body and shadow as one
Mouthful of mastery, speed, and blood—

He learned this, when they came for him;
The young shark found his shadow again.
He learned his place among the weeds.

**David Wevill**   *469*

# Richard Wilbur

*Richard Wilbur, born March 1, 1921, in New York City,*
*lives with his wife and four children in Portland,*
*Connecticut, and in Cummington, Massachusetts. He is a*
*graduate of Amherst College and has taught English*
*literature at Harvard, Wellesley, and Wesleyan University,*
*where he is now professor of English. In World War II*
*he served in the infantry, mainly in Italy, and later spent*
*long periods of residence with his family there and in*
*France, New Mexico, and Texas. He wrote most of the*
*lyrics for the Lillian Hellman-Leonard Bernstein musical*
*Candide. His translations of Molière have been highly*
*praised and widely performed here and in England.*

## Digging for China

"Far enough down is China," somebody said.
"Dig deep enough and you might see the sky
As clear as at the bottom of a well.
Except it would be real—a different sky.
Then you could burrow down until you came
To China! Oh, it's nothing like New Jersey.
There's people, trees, and houses, and all that,
But much, much different. Nothing looks the same."

I went and got the trowel out of the shed
And sweated like a coolie all that morning,

Digging a hole beside the lilac-bush,
Down on my hands and knees. It was a sort
Of praying, I suspect. I watched my hand
Dig deep and darker, and I tried and tried
To dream a place where nothing was the same.
The trowel never did break through to blue.

Before the dream could weary of itself
My eyes were tired of looking into darkness,
My sunbaked head of hanging down a hole.
I stood up in a place I had forgotten,
Blinking and staggering while the earth went round
And showed me silver barns, the fields dozing
In palls of brightness, patens growing and gone
In the tides of leaves, and the whole sky china blue.
Until I got my balance back again
All that I saw was China, China, China.


## Beasts

   Beasts in their major freedom
  Slumber in peace tonight. The gull on his ledge
Dreams in the guts of himself the moon-plucked waves below,
   And the sunfish leans on a stone, slept
    By the lyric water,

   In which the spotless feet
  Of deer make dulcet splashes, and to which
The ripped mouse, safe in the owl's talon, cries
   Concordance. Here there is no such harm
    And no such darkness

   As the selfsame moon observes
  Where, warped in window-glass, it sponsors now
The werewolf's painful change. Turning his head away

On the sweaty bolster, he tries to remember
  The mood of manhood,

  But lies at last, as always,
Letting it happen, the fierce fur soft to his face,
Hearing with sharper ears the wind's exciting minors,
  The leaves' panic, and the degradation
  Of the heavy streams.

  Meantime, at high windows
Far from thicket and pad-fall, suitors of excellence
Sigh and turn from their work to construe again the painful
  Beauty of heaven, the lucid moon
  And the risen hunter,

  Making such dreams for men
As told will break their hearts as always, bringing
Monsters into the city, crows on the public statues,
  Navies fed to the fish in the dark
  Unbridled waters.


## A baroque wall-fountain in the Villa Sciarra

  Under the bronze crown
Too big for the head of the stone cherub whose feet
  A serpent has begun to eat,
Sweet water brims a cockle and braids down

  Past spattered mosses, breaks
On the tipped edge of a second shell, and fills
  The massive third below. It spills
In threads then from the scalloped rim, and makes

  A scrim or summery tent
For a faun-ménage and their familiar goose.

**Richard Wilbur**  *473*

Happy in all that ragged, loose
Collapse of water, its effortless descent

And flatteries of spray,
The stocky god upholds the shell with ease,
Watching, about his shaggy knees,
The goatish innocence of his babes at play;

His fauness all the while
Leans forward, slightly, into a clambering mesh
Of water-lights, her sparkling flesh
In a saecular ecstasy, her blinded smile

Bent on the sand floor
Of the trefoil pool, where ripple-shadows come
And go in swift recticulum,
More addling to the eye than wine, and more

Interminable to thought
Than pleasure's calculus. Yet since this all
Is pleasure, flash, and waterfall,
Must it not be too simple? Are we not

More intricately expressed
In the plain fountains that Maderna set
Before St. Peter's—the main jet
Struggling aloft until it seems at rest

In the act of rising, until
The very wish of water is reversed,
That heaviness borne up to burst
In a clear, high, cavorting head, to fill

With blaze, and then in gauze
Delays, in a gnatlike shimmering, in a fine
Illumined version of itself, decline,
And patter on the stones its own applause?

**Richard Wilbur**   474

If that is what men are
Or should be, if those water-saints display
      The pattern of our areté,
What of these showered fauns in their bizarre,

        Spangled, and plunging house?
They are at rest in fulness of desire
        For what is given, they do not tire
Of the smart of the sun, the pleasant water-douse

        And riddled pool below,
Reproving our disgust and our ennui
        With humble insatiety.
Francis, perhaps, who lay in sister snow

        Before the wealthy gate
Freezing and praising, might have seen in this
        No trifle, but a shade of bliss—
That land of tolerable flowers, that state

        As near and far as grass
Where eyes become the sunlight, and the hand
        Is worthy of water: the dreamt land
Toward which all hungers leap, all pleasures pass.

## Advice to a prophet

When you come, as you soon must, to the streets of our city,
Mad-eyed from stating the obvious,
Not proclaiming our fall but begging us
In God's name to have self-pity,

Spare us all word of the weapons, their force and range,
The long numbers that rocket the mind;

**Richard Wilbur** *475*

Our slow, unreckoning hearts will be left behind,
Unable to fear what is too strange.

Nor shall you scare us with talk of the death of the race.
How should we dream of this place without us?—
The sun mere fire, the leaves untroubled about us,
A stone look on the stone's face?

Speak of the world's own change. Though we cannot conceive
Of an undreamt thing, we know to our cost
How the dreamt cloud crumbles, the vines are blackened by frost,
How the view alters. We could believe,

If you told us so, that the white-tailed deer will slip
Into perfect shade, grown perfectly shy,
The lark avoid the reaches of our eye,
The jack-pine lose its knuckled grip

On the cold ledge, and every torrent burn
As Xanthus once, its gliding trout
Stunned in a twinkling. What should we be without
The dolphin's arc, the dove's return,

These things in which we have seen ourselves and spoken?
Ask us, prophet, how we shall call
Our natures forth when that live tongue is all
Dispelled, that glass obscured or broken

In which we have said the rose of our love and the clean
Horse of our courage, in which beheld
The singing locust of the soul unshelled,
And all we mean or wish to mean.

Ask us, ask us whether with the worldless rose
Our hearts shall fail us; come demanding
Whether there shall be lofty or long standing
When the bronze annals of the oak-tree close.

**Richard Wilbur**   *476*

**A baroque wall-fountain in the Villa Sciarra:** *Spilling language and minute observations from stanza to stanza, this poem imitates an elaborate fountain that spills water in fixed yet constantly varied patterns. A trefoil is a tripartite design. A reticulum is a network. Areté is a Greek word roughly meaning virtue. In Chapter V of the Life of St. Francis, there is mention of Francis's often lying or sleeping in the snow and cold, and, in Chapter VIII of the Little Flowers of St. Francis, the saint tells Friar Leo that perfect joy might come of patiently suffering exclusion by a doorkeeper who ". . . maketh us stay outside hungry and cold all night in the rain and snow."*

**Advice to a prophet:** *The prophet in this poem is a contemporary in whose vision the world is laid waste by a nuclear holocaust. Xanthus is the river, also known as Scamander, which, according to Homer, was scalded by Hephaestus, the fire bringer.*

# William Carlos Williams

*William Carlos Williams, born September 17, 1883, in
Rutherford, New Jersey, died on March 5, 1963, after a
long career as a pediatrician in his native town. He was
educated at the University of Pennsylvania, where he
took his degree in medicine and where he was acquainted
with Ezra Pound and the imagist poet H. D. He published
scores of books which, besides poetry, include his
autobiography, short stories, novels, and plays, some of
which have been given productions here and abroad.
As the leading promoter of a distinctly American idiom
in poetry, he took as protégés many young writers whose
work departs from the English metrical tradition.*

## Pastoral

The little sparrows
hop ingenuously
about the pavement
quarreling
with sharp voices
over those things
that interest them.
But we who are wiser

shut ourselves in
on either hand
and no one knows
whether we think good
or evil.
　　Meanwhile,
the old man who goes about
gathering dog-lime
walks in the gutter
without looking up
and his tread
is more majestic than
that of the Episcopal minister
approaching the pulpit
of a Sunday.
　　These things
astonish me beyond words.


## The lonely street

School is over. It is too hot
to walk at ease. At ease
in light frocks they walk the streets
to while the time away.
They have grown tall. They hold
pink flames in their right hands.
In white from head to foot,
with sidelong, idle look—
in yellow, floating stuff,
black sash and stockings—
touching their avid mouths
with pink sugar on a stick—
like a carnation each holds in her hand—
they mount the lonely street.

## Tract

I will teach you my townspeople
how to perform a funeral—
for you have it over a troop
of artists—
unless one should scour the world—
you have the ground sense necessary.

See! the hearse leads.
I begin with a design for a hearse.
For Christ's sake not black—
nor white either—and not polished!
Let it be weathered—like a farm wagon—
with gilt wheels (this could be
applied fresh at small expense)
or no wheels at all:
a rough dray to drag over the ground.

Knock the glass out!
My God—glass, my townspeople!
For what purpose? Is it for the dead
to look out or for us to see
how well he is housed or to see
the flowers or the lack of them—
or what?
To keep the rain and snow from him?
He will have a heavier rain soon:
pebbles and dirt and what not.

Let there be no glass—
and no upholstery, phew!
and no little brass rollers
and small easy wheels on the bottom—
my townspeople what are you thinking of?

A rough plain hearse then
with gilt wheels and no top at all.
On this the coffin lies

by its own weight.
                        No wreaths please—
especially no hot house flowers.
Some common memento is better,
something he prized and is known by:
his old clothes—a few books perhaps—
God knows what! You realize
how we are about these things
my townspeople—
something will be found—anything
even flowers if he had come to that.
So much for the hearse.

For heaven's sake though see to the driver!
Take off the silk hat! In fact
that's no place at all for him—
up there unceremoniously
dragging our friend out to his own dignity!
Bring him down—bring him down!
Low and inconspicuous! I'd not have him ride
on the wagon at all—damn him—
the undertaker's understrapper!
Let him hold the reins
and walk at the side
and inconspicuously too!

Then briefly as to yourselves:
Walk behind—as they do in France,
seventh class, or if you ride
Hell take curtains! Go with some show
of inconvenience; sit openly—
to the weather as to grief.
Or do you think you can shut grief in?
What—from us? We who have perhaps
nothing to lose? Share with us
share with us—it will be money
in your pockets.
                        Go now
I think you are ready.

**William Carlos Williams**   *482*

## The bull

It is in captivity—
ringed, haltered, chained
to a drag
the bull is godlike

Unlike the cows
he lives alone, nozzles
the sweet grass gingerly
to pass the time away

He kneels, lies down
and stretching out
a foreleg licks himself
about the hoof

then stays
with half-closed eyes,
Olympian commentary on
the bright passage of days.

—The round sun
smooths his lacquer
through
the glossy pinetrees

his substance hard
as ivory or glass—
through which the wind
yet plays—
        milkless
he nods
the hair between his horns
and eyes matted
with hyacinthine curls.

**The lonely street:** *Like his contemporary, the painter Edward Hopper, who is famous for many paintings that illustrate a just-under-the-surface seam of loneliness in American life, Dr. Williams often takes for his subject some small everyday occurrence that evokes pathos, nostalgia, or a sense of isolation. Both poet and painter present these scenes in terms of simple realism, withholding any comment not implicit in the scene itself.*

**Tract:** *Ostensibly a preachment to fellow citizens on the virtues of simplicity in regard to a funeral, this poem, in the light of the author's long crusade for the use of the native rhythms and natural accents of American speech in literature, may also be read as Dr. William's advice to his fellow poets.*

# James Wright

*James Wright, born 1927 in Martin's Ferry, Ohio, teaches
at Hunter College in New York City. Educated at Kenyon
College and the University of Washington, he spent a
year as a Fulbright scholar in Austria before assuming
a teaching career at the University of Minnesota. As in
the case of many other distinguished contemporary poets,
his first book, The Green Wall, was a winner of the
Yale Younger Poets Series.*

## A blessing

Just off the highway to Rochester, Minnesota,
Twilight bounds softly forth on the grass.
And the eyes of those two Indian ponies
Darken with kindness.
They have come gladly out of the willows
To welcome my friend and me.
We step over the barbed wire into the pasture
Where they have been grazing all day, alone.
They ripple tensely, they can hardly contain their happiness
That we have come.
They bow shyly as wet swans. They love each other.
There is no loneliness like theirs.
At home once more,
They begin munching the young tufts of spring in the darkness.
I would like to hold the slenderer one in my arms,

For she has walked over to me
And nuzzled my left hand.
She is black and white,
Her mane falls wild on her forehead,
And the light breeze moves me to caress her long ear
That is delicate as the skin over a girl's wrist.
Suddenly I realize
That if I stepped out of my body I would break
Into blossom.


**Inscription for the tank**

My life was never so precious
To me as now.
I gape unbelieving at those two lines
Of my words, caught and frisked naked.

If they loomed secret and dim
On the wall of the drunk-tank,
Scraped there by a raw fingernail
In the trickling crusts of gray mold,

Surely the plainest thug who read them
Would cluck with the ancient pity.
Men have a right to thank God for their loneliness.
The walls are hysterical with their dank messages.

But the last hophead is gone
With the quick of his name
Bleeding away down a new wall
Blank as his nails.

I wish I had walked outside
To wade in the sea, drowsing and soothed;
I wish I had copied some words from Isaiah,
Kabir, Ansari, oh Whitman, oh anyone, anyone.

**James Wright**  *487*

But I wrote down mine, and now
I must read them forever, even
When the wings in my shoulders cringe up
At the cold's fangs, as now.

Of all my lives, the one most secret to me,
Folded deep in a book never written,
Locked up in a dream of a still place,
I have blurted out.

I have heard weeping in secret
And quick nails broken.
Let the dead pray for their own dead.
What is their pity to me?

---

**Inscription for the tank:** *Each of the figures named in the fifth stanza was a mystic, a prophet, or a poet. Ansari was a Persian who lived in the eleventh century; Kabir an Indian of the fifteenth century.*

# BIBLIOGRAPHY

**Dannie Abse**
*After Every Green Thing* (1949)
*Walking Under Water* (1952)
*Tenants of the House: Poems 1951–1956* (1957)
*Poems: Golders Green* (1962)
*Selected Poems* (1963)
*A Small Desperation* (1968)

**Conrad Aiken**
*Earth Triumphant and Other Tales in Verse* (1914)
*A Jig of Forslin* (1916)
*Turns and Movies, and Other Tales in Verse* (1916)
*The Charnel Rose, Senlin: A Biography, and Other Poems* (1918)
*Priapus and the Pool* (1922)
*The Pilgrimage of Festus* (1923)
*Priapus and the Pool and Other Poems* (1925)
*Senlin: A Biography* (1925)
*Prelude* (1929)
*Selected Poems* (1929)
*John Deth: A Metaphysical Legend and Other Poems* (1930)
*Preludes for Memnon* (1931)
*The Coming Forth by Day of Osiris Jones* (1931)
*Selected Poems* (1933)
*Landscape West of Eden* (1934)
*Time in the Rock* (1936)
*And in the Human Heart* (1940)
*Brownstone Eclogues and Other Poems* (1942)
*The Soldier: A Poem* (1944)
*The Kid* (1947)
*Skylight One: Fifteen Poems* (1949)
*Collected Poems* (1953)
*A Letter from Li Po and Other Poems* (1955)
*Sheepfold Hill: Fifteen Poems* (1958)
*Selected Poems* (1961)
*The Morning Song of Lord Zero* (1963)
*A Seizure of Limericks* (1964)
*Selected Poems* (1964)

**A. R. Ammons**
*Ommateum* (1955)
*Expressions of Sea Level* (1964)
*Tape for the Turn of the Year* (1965)
*Corsons Inlet* (1965)
*Northfield Poems* (1966)
*Selected Poems* (1968)

## John Ashbery

*Turandot and Other Poems* (1953)
*Some Trees* (1956)
*The Poems* (1960)
*The Tennis Court Oath* (1962)
*Rivers and Mountains* (1966)
*Selected Poems* (1967)
*The Double Dream of Spring* (1970)

## W. H. Auden

*Poems* (1930)
*The Orators: An English Study* (1932)
*The Dance of Death* (1933)
*The Witnesses* (1933)
*Poems* (2d ed., 1934)
*The Dog Beneath the Skin; or Where is Francis?* (1935, with Christopher Isherwood)
*Look, Stranger* (1935; published in New York in 1937 as *On This Island*)
*The Ascent of F6: A Tragedy in Two Acts* (1936, with Christopher Isherwood)
*Letters from Iceland* (1937, with Louis MacNeice)
*On the Frontier: A Melodrama in Three Acts* (1938, with Christopher Isherwood)
*Selected Poems* (1938)
*Journey to a War* (1939, with Christopher Isherwood)
*Another Time* (1940)
*Some Poems* (1940)
*The Double Man* (1941; published in London as *New Year Letter*)
*For the Time Being* (1944)
*The Collected Poetry of W. H. Auden* (1945)
*The Age of Anxiety: A Baroque Eclogue* (1947)
*Collected Shorter Poems, 1930–1944* (1950)
*Nones* (1951)
*The Shield of Achilles* (1955)

*Selected Poetry of W. H. Auden* (1958)
*W. H. Auden: A Selection by the Author* (1958)
*Homage to Clio* (1960)
*About the House* (1965)
*Collected Shorter Poems: 1927–1957* (1966)
*Collected Longer Poems* (1968)
*City without Walls* (1969)

## George Barker

*Thirty Preliminary Poems* (1933)
*Poems* (1935)
*Calamiterror* (1937)
*Lament and Triumph* (1940)
*Selected Poems* (1941)
*Sacred and Secular Elegies* (1943)
*Eros in Dogma* (1944)
*Love Poems* (1947)
*News of the World* (1950)
*The True Confession of George Barker* (1950)
*A Vision of Beasts and Gods* (1954)
*Collected Poems, 1930–1955* (1957)
*The View from a Blind I* (1962)
*Collected Poems: 1930–1965* (1964)
*Dreams of a Summer Night* (1966)
*The Golden Chains* (1968)

## Michael Benedikt

*Changes* (1961)
*The Body* (1968)
*Sky* (1970)

## John Berryman

*Poems* (1942)
*The Dispossessed* (1948)
*Homage to Mistress Bradstreet* (1956)
*His Thoughts Made Pockets and the Plane Buckt* (1958)
*77 Dream Songs* (1964)

*Berryman's Sonnets* (1967)
*Short Poems* (1967)
*His Toy, His Dream, His Rest* (1968)
*The Dream Songs* (1969)

**John Betjeman**
*Mount Zion* (1931)
*Continual Dew* (1937)
*Old Lights for New Chancels* (1940)
*New Bats in Old Belfries* (1945)
*Slick but Not Streamlined* (1947)
*Selected Poems* (1948)
*A Few Late Chrysanthemums* (1954)
*Poems in the Porch* (1954)
*Collected Poems* (1958)
*Poems* (1958)
*Altar and Pew* (1959)
*Summoned by Bells* (1960)
*A Ring of Bells* (1962)
*High and Low* (1966)

**Elizabeth Bishop**
*North and South* (1946)
*Poems: North and South, A Cold Spring* (1955)
*Questions of Travel* (1965)
*Selected Poems* (1967)
*The Ballad of the Burglar of Babylon* (1968)
*The Complete Poems* (1969)

**Louise Bogan**
*Body of This Death* (1923)
*Dark Summer* (1929)
*The Sleeping Fury* (1937)
*Poems and New Poems* (1941)
*Collected Poems 1923–1953* (1954)
*The Blue Estuaries: Poems 1923–1968* (1968)

**Philip Booth**
*Letter from a Distant Land* (1957)
*The Islanders* (1961)
*Weathers and Edges* (1966)

**John Malcolm Brinnin**
*The Lincoln Lyrics* (1942)
*The Garden is Political* (1942)
*No Arch, No Triumph* (1945)
*The Sorrows of Cold Stone: Poems 1940–1950* (1951)
*The Selected Poems of John Malcolm Brinnin* (1963)
*Skin Diving in the Virgins* (1970)

**John Ciardi**
*Homeward to America* (1940)
*Other Skies* (1947)
*Live Another Day* (1949)
*From Time to Time* (1951)
*As If: Poems New and Selected* (1955)
*I Marry You: A Sheaf of Love Poems* (1958)
*Thirty-nine Poems* (1959)
*The Reason for the Pelican* (1959)
*In the Stoneworks* (1961)
*In Fact* (1962)
*Person to Person* (1964)
*The Strangest Everything* (1966)

**Lucille Clifton**
*Good Times* (1969)

**Tram Combs**
*Pilgrim's Terrace* (1957)
*Ceremonies in Mind* (1959)
*But Never Mind: Poems etc., 1946–50* (1961)
*St. Thomas* (1965)

**E. E. Cummings**
Tulips and Chimneys (1923)
XLI Poems (1925)
& (1925)
is 5 (1926)
Him (1927; a play)
W (Viva) (1931)
no thanks (1935)
Tom (1935)
One Over Twenty (1936)
Collected Poems (1938)
50 POEMS (1940)
I x I (1944)
Santa Claus: A Morality (1946)
XAIPE: 71 poems (1950)
Poems, 1923–1954 (1954)
95 Poems (1958)
100 Selected Poems (1959)
73 Poems (1963)
Complete Poems (1968)


**Peter Davison**
The Breaking of the Day (1964)
The City and the Island (1966)


**James Dickey**
Into the Stone (1957)
Drowning with Others (1962)
Helmets (1964)
Buckdancer's Choice (1965)
Poems: 1957–1967 (1967)


**Alan Dugan**
Poems (1961)
Poems 2 (1963)
Poems 3 (1967)
Collected Poems (1969)

**Richard Eberhart**
A Bravery of Earth (1930)
Reading the Spirit (1936)
Song and Idea (1940)
Poems: New and Selected (1944)
Burr Oaks (1947)
Rumination (1947)
Brotherhood of Men (1949)
An Herb Basket (1950)
Selected Poems (1951)
Undercliff: Poems, 1946–1953 (1953)
The Oak (1957)
Great Praises (1957)
Collected Poems 1930–1960 (1960)
Collected Verse Plays (1962)
The Quarry (1964)
Selected Poems: 1930–1965 (1965)
Thirty-One Sonnets (1967)
Shifts of Being (1968)


**T. S. Eliot**
Prufrock and Other Observations (1917)
Poems (1919)
The Waste Land (1922)
Poems, 1909–25 (1925)
Poems (1927)
Ash-Wednesday (1930)
Sweeney Agonistes (1932)
The Rock: A Pageant Play (1934)
Murder in the Cathedral (1935)
Collected Poems, 1909–1935 (1936)
Old Possum's Book of Practical Cats (1939)
The Family Reunion: A Play (1939)
East Coker (1940)
Dry Salvages (1941)
Burnt Norton (1941)
Later Poems, 1925–1935 (1941)
Little Gidding (1942)

*Four Quartets* (1943)
*Selected Poems* (1948)
*The Cocktail Party: A Comedy* (1950)
*The Complete Poems and Plays,
1909–1950* (1952)
*Selected Poems* (1954; 1961)
*The Confidential Clerk: A Play* (1954)
*The Elder Statesman* (1959)
*Collected Poems: 1909–1962* (1963)
*Poems Written in Early Youth* (1967)


**D. J. Enright**
*Season Ticket* (1948)
*The Laughing Hyena, and Other Poems*
(1953)
*Bread Rather than Blossoms* (1956)
*Some Men Are Brothers,* (1960)
*Addictions* (1962)
*The Old Adam* (1965)
*Selected Poems* (1968)


**Irving Feldman**
*Works and Days* (1961)
*The Pripet Marshes and Other Poems*
(1965)


**Robert Fitzgerald**
*Poems* (1935)
*A Wreath for the Sea* (1943)
*In the Rose of Time: Poems 1931–1956*
(1956)
*Southmost Twelve* (1962)
*Of Some Country* (1963)


**Arthur Freeman**
*Izmir* (1959)
*Apollonian Poems* (1961)
*Estrangements* (1966)

**Robert Frost**
*A Boy's Will* (1913)
*North of Boston* (1914)
*Mountain Interval* (1916)
*New Hampshire: A Poem* (1923)
*Selected Poems* (1923, 1928, 1934, 1936)
*West-running Brook* (1928)
*Collected Poems* (1930, 1939, 1943)
*A Further Range* (1936)
*A Witness Tree* (1942)
*Come In and Other Poems* (1943)
*A Masque of Reason* (1945)
*Poems* (1946)
*Steeple Bush* (1947)
*A Masque of Mercy* (1947)
*Complete Poems of Robert Frost, 1949*
(1949)
*Selected Poems* (1955)
*You Come Too* (1959)
*In the Clearing* (1962)
*Complete Poems* (1967)


**Jean Garrigue**
*The Ego and the Centaur* (1947)
*The Monument Rose* (1953)
*A Water Walk by Villa d'Este* (1959)
*Country Without Maps* (1964)
*The Animal Hotel* (1966)
*New and Selected Poems* (1967)


**David Gascoyne**
*Roman Balcony and Other Poems* (1932)
*Man's Life Is This Meat* (1936)
*Poems, 1937–1942* (1943)
*A Vagrant and Other Poems* (1950)
*Night Thoughts* (1956)

**Allen Ginsberg**
*Howl and Other Poems* (1956)
*Kaddish and Other Poems: 1958–1960* (1960)
*Empty Mirror: Early Poems* (1961)
*Reality Sandwiches* (1963)
*Planet News: 1961–1967* (1968)
*Ankor-Wat* (1968)
*T.V. Baby Poems* (1968)

**Robert Graves**
*Fairies and Fusiliers* (1917)
*Country Sentiment* (1920)
*The Pier Glass* (1921)
*Welchman's Hose* (1925)
*Poems 1914–1926* (1927)
*Ten Poems* (1930)
*Poems 1926–1930* (1931)
*Poems 1930–1933* (1933)
*Collected Poems* (1938)
*No More Ghosts: Selected Poems* (1940)
*Poems* (1943)
*Poems 1938–1945* (1946)
*Collected Poems 1914–1947* (1948)
*Poems and Satires* (1951)
*Poems, 1953* (1953)
*Collected Poems* (1955)
*Poems: Selected by Himself* (1957)
*Collected Poems, 1959* (1959)
*Food for Centaurs* (1960)
*More Poems, 1961* (1961)
*New Poems: 1962* (1962)
*The More Deserving Cases* (1962)
*Man Does, Woman Is* (1964)
*Collected Poems* (1965)
*Love Respelt* (1966)
*Seventeen Poems Missing from Love Respelt* (1966)

**Thom Gunn**
*Fighting Terms* (1954)
*The Sense of Movement* (1957)
*My Sad Captains* (1961)
*Selected Poems* (1962, with Ted Hughes)
*Positives* (1966)
*Touch* (1968)

**Donald Hall**
*To the Loud Wind, and Other Poems* (1955)
*Exiles and Marriages* (1955)
*The Dark Houses* (1958)
*A Roof of Tiger Lilies* (1964)
*The Alligator Bride* (1969)

**Robert Hayden**
*Heart-Shape in the Dust* (1940)
*A Ballad of Remembrance* (1962)
*Selected Poems* (1966)

**Seamus Heaney**
*Death of a Naturalist* (1966)
*Door into the Dark* (1969)

**John Heath-Stubbs**
*Wounded Thammuz* (1942)
*Beauty and the Beast* (1943)
*The Divided Ways* (1946)
*The Charity of the Stars* (1949)
*The Swarming of the Bees* (1950)
*A Charm Against the Toothache* (1954)
*The Triumph of the Muse* (1958)
*Helen in Egypt and Other Plays* (1958)
*The Blue-Fly in His Head* (1962)
*Selected Poems* (1965)

**Anthony Hecht**
A Summoning of Stones (1954)
The Seven Deadly Sins (1958)
The Hard Hours (1967)


**Daryl Hine**
Five Poems (1954)
The Carnal and the Crane (1957)
The Devil's Picture Book (1960)
Heroics (1961)
The Wooden Horse (1965)
Minutes (1968)


**Daniel G. Hoffman**
An Armada of Thirty Whales (1954)
A Little Geste, and Other Poems (1960)
The City of Satisfactions (1963)
Striking the Stones (1968)


**John Hollander**
A Crackling of Thorns (1958)
Movie-Going and Other Poems (1962)
Various Owls (1963)
Visions from the Ramble (1965)
Types of Shape (1968)


**Richard Howard**
Quantities (1962)
The Damages (1967)


**Barbara Howes**
The Undersea Farmer (1948)
In the Cold Country (1954)
Light and Dark (1959)
Looking Up At Leaves (1966)


**Ted Hughes**
The Hawk in the Rain (1957)
Lupercal (1960)
Selected Poems (1962, with Thom Gunn)
Wodwo (1967)


**David Ignatow**
Poems (1948)
The Gentle Weight Lifter (1955)
Say Pardon (1961)
Figures of the Human (1964)
Rescue the Dead (1968)
Earth Hard (1968)


**Randall Jarrell**
Blood for a Stranger (1942)
Little Friend, Little Friend (1945)
Losses (1948)
The Seven-league Crutches (1951)
Selected Poems (1955)
The Woman at the Washington Zoo:
Poems and Translations (1960)
The Lost World (1965)
Complete Poems (1968)


**Donald Justice**
The Summer Anniversaries (1960)
A Local Storm (1963)
Night Light (1967)


**Bob Kaufman**
Solitudes Crowded with Loneliness
(1965)
Golden Sardine (1967)

**X. J. Kennedy**
Nude Descending a Staircase (1961)
Growing into Love (1969)


**Galway Kinnell**
What a Kingdom It Was (1960)
Flower Herding on Mount Monadnock (1964)
Body Rags (1968)
Poems of Night (1968)


**Thomas Kinsella**
Poems (1956)
Another September (1958)
Moralities (1960)
Poems and Translations (1961)
Downstream (1962)
Wormwood (1966)
Nightwalker and Other Poems (1967)
Poems (1968)


**Stanley Kunitz**
Intellectual Things (1930)
Passport to the War (1944)
Selected Poems, 1928–1958 (1958)


**Philip Larkin**
The North Ship (1945)
Poems (1954)
The Less Deceived (1955)
The Whitsun Weddings (1964)


**Denise Levertov**
The Double Image (1946)
Here and Now (1957)
Overland to the Islands (1958)
With Eyes at the Back of Our Heads (1959)
The Jacob's Ladder (1961)
O Taste and See (1964)
The Sorrow Dance (1966)


**Philip Levine**
On the Edge (1961)
Not This Pig (1968)


**Cecil Day Lewis**
Beechen Vigil and Other Poems (1925)
Bank Holiday (1926)
Country Comets (1928)
Transitional Poem (1929)
From Feathers to Iron (1931)
The Magnetic Mountain (1933)
A Time to Dance and Other Poems (1935)
Collected Poems, 1929–1933 (1935)
Noah and the Waters (1936)
Overtures to Death and Other Poems (1938)
Selected Poems (1940)
Poems (1943)
Word over All (1943)
Collected Poems (1945)
Short Is the Time: Poems 1936–1943 (1945)
Collected Poems, 1929–1936 (1948)
Poems, 1943–1947 (1948)
Selected Poems (1951)
An Italian Visit (1953)
Collected Poems (1954)
Pegasus and Other Poems (1957)
The Gate (1962)
Requiem for the Living (1964)
The Room and Other Poems (1965)

**Robert Lowell**
Land of Unlikeness (1944)
Lord Weary's Castle (1946; with changes, 1947)
Poems, 1938–1949 (1950)
The Mills of the Kavanaughs (1951)
Life Studies (1959)
Imitations (1961)
For the Union Dead (1964)
Selected Poems (1965)
Life Studies (1967)
Near the Ocean (1967)
Notebook 1967–1968 (1969)

**Edward Lucie-Smith**
A Tropical Childhood and Other Poems (1961)
Confessions and Histories (1964)
Towards Silence (1968)

**Archibald MacLeish**
Songs for a Summer's Day: A Sonnet Cycle (1915)
Tower of Ivory (1917)
The Happy Marriage and Other Poems (1924)
The Pot of Earth (1925)
Streets in the Moon (1926)
The Hamlet of A. MacLeish (1928)
New Found Land: Fourteen Poems (1930)
Conquistador (1922)
Poems 1924–1933 (1933)
Frescoes for Mr. Rockefeller's City (1933)
Panic: A Play in Verse (1935)
Public Speech (1936)
The Fall of the City: A Verse Play for Radio (1937)
Air Raid: A Verse Play for Radio (1938)
Land of the Free (1938)
America Was Promises (1939)

Poems (1943)
Actfive and Other Poems (1948)
Collected Poems, 1917–1952 (1952)
Songs for Eve (1954)
J.B. (1958)
Herakles (1967)
The Wild Old Wicked Man and Other Poems (1968)

**Louis MacNeice**
Blind Fireworks (1929)
Poems (1935)
Letters from Iceland (1937, with W. H. Auden)
Poems (1937)
The Earth Compels (1938)
Out of the Picture (1938)
Autumn Journal (1939)
The Last Ditch (1940)
Poems, 1925–1940 (1940)
Selected Poems (1940)
Plant and Phantom (1941)
Springboard: Poems 1941–1944 (1944)
The Dark Tower and Other Radio Scripts (1947)
Holes in the Sky: Poems 1944–1947 (1948)
Collected Poems, 1925–1948 (1949)
Ten Burnt Offerings (1952)
Autumn Sequel: A Rhetorical Poem in XXVI Cantos (1954)
Visitations (1957)
Eighty-five Poems (1959)
Solstices (1961)
Burning Perch (1963)
Selected Poems (1964)
Collected Poems (1967)

**James Merrill**
The Black Swan and Other Poems (1946)

First Poems (1951)
The Country of a Thousand Years of
Peace (1959)
Selected Poems (1961)
Water Street (1962)
Nights and Days (1966)
The Fire Screen (1969)


**W. S. Merwin**
A Mask for Janus (1952)
The Dancing Bears (1954)
Green with Beasts (1956)
The Drunk in the Furnace (1960)
West Wind (1961)
The Moving Target (1963)
The Lice (1967)


**Christopher Middleton**
Poems (1944)
Torse 3: 1949–1961 (1962)
Penguin Modern Poets 4 (1963)
Nonsequences (1965)
Our Flowers and Nice Bones (1969)


**Marianne Moore**
Poems (1921)
Observations (1924)
Selected Poems (1935)
The Pangolin and Other Verse (1936)
What Are Years (1941)
Nevertheless (1944)
Collected Poems (1951)
Like a Bulwark (1956)
O To Be a Dragon (1959)
The Arctic Ox (1964)
Tell Me, Tell Me: Granite, Steel and
Other Topics (1966)
Complete Poems (1967)

**Howard Moss**
The Wound and the Weather (1946)
The Toy Fair (1954)
A Swimmer in the Air (1957)
A Winter Come, a Summer Gone: Poems,
1946–1960 (1960)
Finding Them Lost and Other Poems
(1965)
Second Nature (1968)


**Howard Nemerov**
The Image and the Law (1947)
Guide to the Ruins (1950)
The Salt Garden (1955)
Mirrors and Windows (1958)
New and Selected Poems (1960)
Endor (1962)
The Next Room of the Dream (1962)
New and Selected Poems (1963)
The Blue Swallows (1967)
The Winter Lightning (1968)


**Marge Piercy**
Breaking Camp (1968)
Hard Loving (1969)


**Sylvia Plath**
The Colossus (1960)
Ariel (1965)


**Ezra Pound**
A Lume Spento (1908)
Personae (1909)
Exultations (1909)
Provenca: Poems Selected from Personae,
Exultations, and Canzonieri (1910)

Canzoni (1911)

Ripostes (1912)

Canzoni and Ripostes (1913)

Personae and Exultations (1913)

Cathay: Translations by Ezra Pound (1915)

Lustra (1916)

Lustra with Earlier Poems (1917)

Pavannes and Divagations (1918)

The Fourth Canto (1919)

Quia Pauper Amavi (1919)

Hugh Selwyn Mauberley (1920)

Umbra: The Early Poems (1920)

Poems 1918–1921 (including Three Portraits and Four Cantos) (1921)

A Draft of XVI Cantos (1925)

Personae: The Collected Poems of Ezra Pound (1926)

A Draft of the Cantos 17–27 of Ezra Pound (1928)

Selected Poems (1928)

A Draft of XXX Cantos (1930)

Selected Poems (1933)

Homage to Sextus Propertius (1934)

Eleven New Cantos: XXXI–XLI (1934; English title: A Draft of Cantos XXXI–XLI)

The Fifth Decad of Cantos (1937)

A Selection of Poems (1940)

Cantos LII–LXXI (1940)

The Pisan Cantos (1948)

The Cantos of Ezra Pound (1948)

Selected Poems (1949)

Seventy Cantos (1950)

Personae: Collected Shorter Poems (1950)

Cantos 1–84 (1954)

Section: Rock-drill: 85–95 de los Cantares (1955)

Personae: Collected Poems (1956)

Selected Poems (1956)

Diptych: Rome-London (1958)

Thrones 96–109 de los Cantares (1959)

Love Poems of Ancient Egypt (1962)

The Confucian Odes (1963)

A Lume Spento and Other Early Poems (1965)

Cantos: 1–95 (1965)

Selected Cantos (1967)


**John Crowe Ransom**

Poems about God (1919)

Armageddon (1923)

Chills and Fever: Poems (1924)

Grace after Meat (1924)

Two Gentlemen in Bonds (1927)

Selected Poems (1945)

Selected Poems (1952)

Poems and Essays (1955)

Selected Poems (1963)


**Alastair Reid**

To Lighten My House (1953)

Oddments, Inklings, Omens, Moments (1959)

Fairwater (1957)

Ounce, Dice, Trice (1958)

Passwords: Places, Poems, Preoccupations (1963)


**Theodore Roethke**

Open House (1941)

The Lost Son and Other Poems (1948)

Praise to the End! (1951)

The Waking: Poems 1933–1953 (1953)

Words for the Wind (1958)

I Am! Says the Lamb (1961)

The Far Field (1964)

Collected Poems (1966)

**Muriel Rukeyser**
Theory of Flight (1935)
U. S. 1 (1938)
A Turning Wind (1939)
The Soul and Body of John Brown (1940)
Wake Island (1942)
Beast in View (1944)
The Green Wave (1948)
Elegies (1949)
Orpheus (1949)
Selected Poems (1951)
Body of Waking (1958)
Water Lily Fire: Poems, 1932–1962 (1962)
The Speed of Darkness (1968)

**Delmore Schwartz**
In Dreams Begin Responsibilities (1938)
Shenandoah (1941)
Genesis: Book I (1943)
Vaudeville for a Princess and Other Poems (1950)
Summer Knowledge: New and Selected Poems, 1938–1958 (1959)

**James Scully**
The Marches (1967)

**Anne Sexton**
To Bedlam and Part Way Back (1960)
All My Pretty Ones (1962)
Selected Poems (1964)
Live or Die (1966)
Poems (1968 with Kinsella and Livingston)
Love Poems (1969)

**Karl Shapiro**
Poems (1935)
Person Place and Thing (1942)

V-Letter and Other Poems (1944)
Essay on Rime (1945)
Trial of a Poet and Other Poems (1947)
Poems, 1940–1953 (1953)
Poems of a Jew (1958)
The Bourgeois Poet (1964)
Selected Poems (1968)
White-Haired Lover (1968)

**Jon Silkin**
The Portrait and Other Poems (1950)
The Peaceable Kingdom (1954)
The Two Freedoms (1958)
The Reordering of the Stones (1961)
Nature with Man (1965)
Poems New and Selected (1966)

**Louis Simpson**
The Arrivistes: Poems, 1940–1948 (1949)
"Good News of Death and Other Poems" in Poets of Today II (1955)
A Dream of Governors (1959)
At the End of the Open Road (1963)
Selected Poems (1965)

**L. E. Sissman**
Dying: An Introduction (1967)
Scattered Returns (1969)

**Edith Sitwell**
Clowns' Houses (1918)
The Wooden Pegasus (1920)
Facade (1922)
Bucolic Comedies (1923)
The Sleeping Beauty (1924)
Troy Park (1925)
Elegy on Dead Fashion (1926)

Rustic Elegies (1927)
Five Poems (1928)
Gold Coast Customs (1929)
The Collected Poems of Edith Sitwell (1930)
Selected Poems, with an Essay on Her Own Poetry (1936)
Poems New and Old (1940)
Street Songs (1942)
Green Song and Other Poems (1944)
The Song of the Cold (1945)
The Shadow of Cain (1947)
The Canticle of the Rose: Selected Poems, 1920–1947 (1949)
The Canticle of the Rose: Poems 1917–1949 (1949)
Facade and Other Poems, 1920–1935 (1950)
Poor Men's Music (1950)
Selected Poems (1952)
Gardeners and Astronomers: New Poems (1953)
Collected Poems (1954)
The Outcasts (1962)
Music and Ceremonies (1963)
Selected Poems (1965)

**William J. Smith**
Poems (1947)
Celebration at Dark (1950)
Poems, 1947–1957 (1957)
The Tin Can and Other Poems (1966)

**W. D. Snodgrass**
Heart's Needle (1959)
After Experience (1968)

**Stephen Spender**
Twenty Poems (1930)
Poems (1933)

Vienna (1934)
Trial of a Judge: A Tragedy in Five Acts (1938)
The Still Centre (1939)
Selected Poems (1940)
Ruins and Visions: Poems 1934–1942 (1942)
Poems of Dedication (1946)
Returning to Vienna 1947: Nine Sketches (1947)
The Edge of Being (1949)
Collected Poems, 1928–1953 (1955)
Inscriptions (1958)
Selected Poems (1964)

**George Starbuck**
Bone Thoughts (1960)
White Paper (1966)

**Wallace Stevens**
Harmonium (1923, enlarged ed., 1931)
Ideas of Order (1935)
Owl's Clover (1936)
The Man with the Blue Guitar and Other Poems (1937)
Parts of a World (1942)
Notes toward a Supreme Fiction (1942)
Esthétique du Mal (1945)
Three Academic Pieces (1947)
Transport to Summer (1947)
The Auroras of Autumn (1950)
The Man with the Blue Guitar, including Ideas of Order (1952)
Selected Poems (1953)
Collected Poems (1954)
Opus Posthumous (1957)
Poems: Selected (1959)
Selected Poems (1965)

**Mark Strand**
Sleeping with One Eye Open (1964)
Reasons for Moving (1968)

**May Swenson**
"Another Animal, Poems" in Poets of
Today I (1954)
A Cage of Spines (1958)
To Mix with Time: New and Selected
Poems (1963)
Poems to Solve (1966)
Half Sun, Half Sleep (1967)

**Allen Tate**
The Golden Mean, and Other Poems
(1923, with Ridley Wills)
Mr. Pope and Other Poems (1928)
Ode to the Confederate Dead (1930)
Poems, 1928–1931 (1932)
The Mediterranean and Other Poems
(1936)
Selected Poems (1937)
Sonnets at Christmas (1941)
The Winter Sea (1944)
Poems, 1920–1945: A Selection (1947)
Poems, 1922–1947 (1948)
Poems (1960)

**James Tate**
The Lost Pilot (1967)
Notes of Woe (1968)
The Torches (1968)

**Dylan Thomas**
18 Poems (1934)
Twenty-Five Poems (1936)

The World I Breathe (1939)
The Map of Love: Verse and Prose (1939)
New Poems (1943)
Deaths and Entrances (1946)
Selected Writings of Dylan Thomas (1946)
Twenty-six Poems (1950)
Poems (1950)
In Country Sleep and Other Poems (1951)
Collected Poems 1934–1952 (1952)
Under Milk Wood (1957)
The Early Notebooks (1967)

**Charles Tomlinson**
Relations and Contraries (1951)
The Necklace (1955)
Seeing is Believing (1958)
A Peopled Landscape (1963)
American Scenes and Other Poems
(1966)
The Way of a World (1969)

**Derek Walcott**
In a Green Night: 1948–1960 (1962)
Selected Poems (1964)
The Castaway (1965)
The Gulf (1969)

**Robert Penn Warren**
Thirty-six Poems (1935)
Eleven Poems on the Same Theme (1942)
Selected Poems, 1923–1943 (1944)
Brother to Dragons (1953)
Promises: Poems 1954–1956 (1957)
You, Emperors, and Others: Poems,
1957–1960 (1960)
Selected Poems: 1923–1966 (1966)
Incarnations: Poems 1966–1968 (1968)

**Vernon Watkins**

Ballad of the Mari Lwyd and Other Poems (1941)
The Lamp and the Veil (1945)
The Lady with the Unicorn (1948)
Selected Poems (1948)
The Death Bell: Poems and Ballads (1954)
Cypress and Acacia (1959)
Affinities (1962)
Selected Poems: 1930–1960 (1967)
Fidelities (1968)


**Theodore Weiss**

The Catch (1951)
Outlanders (1960)
Gunsight (1962)
The Medium (1965)
The Last Day and the First (1968)


**David Wevill**

Birth of a Shark (1964)
A Christ of the Ice-Floes (1966)


**Richard Wilbur**

The Beautiful Changes and Other Poems (1947)
Ceremony and Other Poems (1950)
Things of This World (1956)
Poems, 1943–1956 (1957)
Advice to a Prophet (1961)
The Poems of Richard Wilbur (1963)
Walking to Sleep (1969)

**William Carlos Williams**

Poems (1909)
The Tempers (1913)
A Book of Poems: Al Que Quiere! (1917)
Kora in Hell: Improvisations (1920)
Sour Grapes: A Book of Poems (1921)
Spring and All (1923)
Collected Poems, 1921–1931 (1934)
An Early Martyr and Other Poems (1935)
Adam and Eve and the City (1936)
The Complete Collected Poems, 1906–1938 (1938)
The Broken Span (1941)
The Wedge (1944)
Paterson (Book One, 1946; Book Two, 1948; Book Three, 1949; Book Four, 1951; Book Five, 1958)
The Pink Church (1948)
Selected Poems (1949)
William Carlos Williams: Selected Poems (1949)
The Collected Later Poems (1950)
The Collected Earlier Poems (1951)
The Desert Music and Other Poems (1954)
Journey to Love (1955)
Pictures from Brueghel (1962)
Paterson (1963)
Selected Poems (1963)
The Necessary Lie (1965)


**James Wright**

The Green Wall (1957)
Saint Judas (1959)
The Lion's Tail and Eyes (1962)
The Branch Will Not Break (1963)
Shall We Gather at the River (1968)

# INDEX OF TITLES
# AND FIRST LINES